"A true gonzo adventure!" **–Mayor Gonzo Mays,** Official Honorary Mayor of Key West and the Florida Keys

"Changes in latitudes, changes in attitudes …" **–Jimmy Buffett**

"Key West is a city that creates virtue out of vice" **–Reverend Gweko**

"Grinding away, day after day, in the belly of the beast, I finally said 'I'm outta here!' and moved to an island paradise" **–Key West Chris Rehm**

"Something pleasant or exciting that helps you to forget about real life and the boring or unpleasant parts of it" **–the definition of "escapism" in the MacMillan Dictionary**

"… if we value the freedom of mind and soul, if we're partisans of liberty, then it's our plain duty to escape, and to take as many people with us as we can!" **–J.R.R. Tolkien**

D1409205

ABOUT THE AUTHOR

JON BREAKFIELD is the author of four books. These include the Amazon bestseller **KEY WEST**, the sequel (and well thought-out title) **KEY WEST Part II**, the eye-opening **NAKED EUROPE**, and the best-selling crime fiction **DEATH by GLASGOW**. For those with a short attention span, have a squizzy at the endearing and cheeky short story **LIVERPOOL, TEXAS … LONDON, ARKANSAS**.

When not on the lam, he and his wife divide their time between rainy Glasgow, Scotland, and beery Key West, FL.

KEY WEST

Part II

The Seagull...I mean the

Sequel

by

Jon Breakfield

KW
Press

To Popcorn Joe, Chubba, BC and Scaredy Cat

ACKNOWLEDGEMENTS: Special shout out (and free beer for life) to Mayor Gonzo Mays, Mark Terrill at Key Largo Bike and Adventure Tours, Mike Eden at Eden House, Arnaud and Naja Giraud at *Key West the Newspaper (The Blue Paper)*, David Lybrand, the crew at the Bull & Whistle, the gang at Turtle Kraals, the Cork & Stogie, Lloyd's Tropical Bile Tour, Genya Yerkes at the Key West Aquarium, Eric TC Wilson of Falkirk, John Rubin, Chip Bennett, Eleanor T. Beaty, Patti Bright, Tina and Patty, Mindy and Dennis, Steve Caines, James Moore, Kevin Shelper, Rob Mercier, Cam Lang, Mark Buck, and all my FACEBOOK friends (as you amuse and enlighten me)

An enormous shout out to Sheelman for designing the cover

And to Mike Sharkey, let us bring Key West to you

**No snowbirds were harmed during the making of this book

CHAPTER ONE

"You're under arrest!"

I spun around on my bar stool in Captain's Tony's and saw two Immigration Officers handcuffing my wife as she returned from the facilities. This is something that we had feared. I was born in America, but Gabrielle was born in England. We had been living in Key West for the past year and Gabrielle had overstayed her visa by six months.

"Let her go, bumfucks!" I yelled.

I made a grab for my wife, but some Hemingway look-alike was blocking my way as he endeavored to get the phone number from a snowbird who was a commercial for fake tans and breast enhancement. "Leave my wife alone!" I yelled again, and the Hemingway clone gave me a look of *This is your wife?*

"Not Coppertone Dolly, the woman with the natural tan behind her. Get your hands off my bride!" But the Immigration Officers couldn't hear me over the lively Conch Rock coming from Chris Rehm over by the front door.

My wife being arrested aside, I have to tell you right here and now, Chris Rehm rocks! Up until Immigration arrived, the evening had been going along swimmingly.

I fought my way through a gaggle of perspiring bodies as Chris belted out:

WE ALL RIDE BIKES TO GET AROUND TOWN AND ON THE CORNER WE CAN DRINK OUR BREW...

"Hey, youse!" I yelled at the Immigration Officers. "Oh, aye, ahm talkin' tae youse, ye mangy Immigration lot! Take yer polis paws off ma lassie!"

"Jon. Jon," came a soothing voice. "You're having a nightmare ... and you're speaking with a lousy Glaswegian accent."

"Huh?" I cracked an eye open. In the subdued light of our bedroom, I could just make out that Gabrielle was smiling at me in that way wives smile at husbands when they've temporarily fallen off the edge of the world by way of alcohol.

"You always have nightmares when we go to Captain Tony's. Was it the rum?"

"No, ever since we decided to go back home to Scotland, I've been having certifiable dreams."

"What was this one about?"

"About you being arrested."

"But we're leaving ..."

"And it still could happen."

"Well, it won't, so stop worrying."

"Did you see any Immigration Officers at Captain Tony's?"

"No, go to sleep."

"Did we say goodbye to Key West Chris before we left?"

"Yes, we said goodbye to Chris. He was in good spirits, so to speak, some woman tipped him a dollar wrapped around a condom."

"I'm sure he will put that to good use."

"Are you talking about the dollar?"

"Hel-lo-o!"

"Go to sleep."

"Was Popcorn Joe there?"

"Yes, he left early. He has to take Chubba to the vet tomorrow."

"What about Rick Fagan?"

"Yes."

"Gary Cairns?"

"Yes."

"Dan Berger?"

"Yes, he bought you an adult beverage."

"Debbie Williamson?"

"Yes, you kept double-dipping her peanuts."

"How can you double-dip peanuts?"

"You found a way ..."

"What about Todd A. Miller?"

"Yes, why do you keep calling him by his entire name?"

"I do?"

"Yes: 'Hi, Todd A. Miller, what's the haps?' ... 'Say, Todd A. Miller, would you like some more peanuts?'"

"What about Gweko, was he there?"

"No, he was on the air."

"Ginger Keefer?"

"Yes."

"Her mom?"

"Yes."

"Were the pugs there?"

"No, they were back in Galveston. You wanted to Skype them."

"Did I embarrass myself?"

"You wanted to Skype pugs ... what does that tell you?"

"I embarrassed myself BIG TIME?"

"Pretty much the entire evening, and that's not an easy thing to do in Captain Tony's. Now go back to sleep. It's four in the morning. We've only been home for two hours."

"I think I'm going to be sick ..."

* * *

A cold front came through during the night, and I awoke the next morning to crystal clear skies, a temperature of 54 degrees and a life-sucking hangover. I heard footsteps on well-worn linoleum coming from the kitchen and then Gabrielle's voice.

"You're sitting up in bed with your eyes closed?"

"I'm afraid if I open them, they'll bleed."

"We need to go over to our landlord's office and give notice. You know he'd be thrilled to find a reason to not give us our deposit back if we don't give him his thirty-day notice."

"I think I have dengue fever."

"It's called being hung over."

"It's dengue fever. I have a raging headache and my temperature is elevated."

"Dengue fever comes with a rash. Where's the rash?"

"I'm sure there's one here somewhere," I said, lifting the covers.

"C'mon, get up. We need to give our landlord notice."

"There's something else I'd like to give him ..."

"We can't let him get to us this time."

"He always gets to me. He raised our rent because we were late paying it by one day. One day! Said we broke our lease!"

"I remember, but we'll have to endure him if we want our

deposit back."

"But he always talks down to us."

* * *

Gabrielle and I had just over a month before our flight back to Scotland. And there was so much to do. And we weren't looking forward to doing it. No, I take that back, we weren't looking forward to going back, but we now had no choice.

"Does Immigration check our passports when we leave the U.S.?" Gabrielle asked.

"I think both the airline and Immigration check."

"Are you sure?"

"No."

Gabrielle was unusually subdued for a moment. "What if Immigration sees that I've been living here illegally?"

"Perhaps they won't spot it."

"But what if they do?"

I gave this some thought, slapped at a rather fat mosquito, and said: "Can't exactly deport you if we're leaving already, can they?"

CHAPTER TWO

We pedaled our bicycles under a cerulean blue sky down Whitehead Street, past the Green Parrot and over to our landlord's posh offices which were located in Truman Annex. We'd nicknamed our landlord "Mr. Tosser," because he was such a fuckwit. If you don't know what a "tosser" is, go to our new and jaunty Glossary at the back of this very book.

Mr. Tosser was a multi-millionaire who made his money from strip clubs, taking advantage of lesser folk, and cheating equals. Mr. Tosser always demanded that our rent be paid on time, but when there was a problem around our place, such as the toilet backing up, rats behind the walls, or a hurricane-felled palm tree crushing our tin roof, he was slow to respond. No, I take that back, he wasn't slow to respond, he didn't respond at all. Responding, being respectful and polite were not in his DNA. Poison, arrogance and flatulence were in his DNA. In the past, the only thing that had saved us was his secretary, who was sweet and caring and looked after us by calling plumbers and pest control assassins and roofers, behind our landlord's hunched back.

We pulled up in front of the two-story brick building on the far side of the old Marine Hospital, chained our bicycles to a palm tree, paused to watch a gecko scurry along the curb, and went inside. The offices smelt of rancid cigarette smoke. Mr. Tosser's business partner, aka his wife, was a professional chain-smoker and a threat to anyone's lungs who entered the building.

We climbed the stairs to the second floor and announced our arrival to the secretary. The secretary buzzed Mr. Tosser and then rolled her eyes and mumbled something which resembled a statement wrapped around an invective, something like *What an asshole I work for!* She turned a pair of spaniel eyes on us. "He wants to know if you have an appointment."

11

"No, we just wanted to come by and give our notice. We're going back to the U.K."

"I'm truly sorry to hear that," she said, then she relayed the news of our intentions to Mr. Tosser, listened for a moment, then rolled her eyes again. She hung up and turned to us. "He says he needs the notice in writing. Typed up." The secretary then mumbled something which sounded a lot like *pathetic, useless, fucking twat* and exhumed a paper and pen from her desk drawer. "Here. You write it out in longhand. I'll type it up for you, then you both sign it."

We wrote up our notice, the secretary, with flying fingers, quickly typed it up and then we both signed it.

About then, Mr. Tosser stepped out of his office, and it was very obvious that he didn't expect us to still be there. And he was not so very pleased.

"Here's our thirty-day notice," Gabrielle said, making an attempt to hand it over. Mr. Tosser hesitated accepting it, as if he were being served a summons. "Can we expect our deposit back on the day we move out?"

Mr. Tosser looked back and forth between the two of us. "You'll get your deposit back if the place is left as you found it…"

Gabrielle and I almost burst out laughing. We wanted to remind Mr. Tosser that the place had been a rat-infested shithole when we'd moved in and we had spent days cleaning it, done numerous repairs, painted it, landscaped it and had even removed a dead rat the size of a pony from behind the kitchen wall.

Gabrielle was relentless: "We gave you cash as our deposit. Can we expect cash back? We will need cash as we will have to change it back into pounds at the airport."

"If the place is spotless and there's been no damage, it will have to go through bookkeeping. Bookkeeping will have to cut you a check."

"And how long will that take?"

"Hard to say, now if you excuse me, I'm a busy man." And he scarpered.

Gabrielle and I could just see into his office from where we were standing, and we watched as Mr. Tosser sat down at his desk, put his feet up and went back to his computer to what looked suspiciously like a porno site. We could've been mistaken, women in fetish gear could have been from something legitimate, WWE or NASCAR RACING, I'm thinking, and I mean no disrespect.

We thanked the secretary, turned and walked back down the stairs, fuming, as we always did after an encounter of the scum-slum-landlord kind.

"The bookkeeper is his hydra of a wife. We're doomed."

"Let's go see if Al Subarsky is in his 'office,' at Rick's, as he calls it. He's playing for the cruise ship crowd today."

"That's one of the big things I'm going to miss about Key West, live music just about any time of the day or night."

"I've a huge list of things I'm going to miss. Why don't we slide over to B.O.'s after Rick's and get a *con leche*."

"Does B.O. do *con leches*?"

"Who knows? We'll get anything with caffeine in it, then we'll chill and think of various ways to emasculate our landlord."

"You're on."

* * *

The sun was working overtime and the temperature had climbed to fifty-nine degrees. This was the coldest day since we'd first arrived nearly a year earlier.

We didn't know it at the time, but fifty-nine degrees was more than "chilly" for locals (even the scorpions were laying low). In fact, fifty-nine degrees is the equivalent of Siberian winter for Key Westers, and they were pulling sweaters and wooly socks out of old suitcases and armoires. Some were even putting on -- shock horror -- long trousers and northern shoes. You can always spot the true locals after a cold front comes through: they're heavily bundled up and smell of mothballs, while the wannabe Key Westers are reveling in any temperature above freezing, sporting sandals, and have stripped down to tank tops that say JOE'S LONG ISLAND BAR AND GRILL, BAR HARBOR and THE BLACK DOG. I remember Popcorn Joe telling me that really makes them standout as not being from Key West.

"If you want to make it even more obvious that you are not from Cayo Hueso ..." Popcorn Joe had said. "... wear anything that says KEY WEST, or SLOPPY JOE'S, or even that cool T-shirt from BLUE HEAVEN with the chickens on the back. You can wear a T-shirt, sweatshirt or baseball cap that says KEY WEST or BLUE HEAVEN or RICK'S or HOG'S BREATH IS BETTER THAN NO BREATH AT ALL when you are in the Great White North, but you will be pulled over and cited by the fashion police if you do so on the island."

I gave what Popcorn Joe had said some thought, and I would just like to add that this excludes bar staff at the aforementioned bars.

And the dynamic guides at Sloan's GHOST HUNT.

We took the long way to Rick's bar. That means five minutes instead of two. We rode out of Truman Annex by cycling past the guard gate. We waved at Richard, the guard, then exited on Southward, crossed Whitehead and turned left onto Duval. I just love riding a bike down Duval Street on days like this -- early -- it's as if you were in Key West back when it was still a sleepy backwater island (if you don't notice the Starbucks sign). There's little vehicular traffic, the tourons aren't running mopeds up onto sidewalks or crashing them into the sides of cars this early, and it's only professional pissheads and transients about, weaving down the street, puking and taking a leak in public.

Paradise.

We let the sun warm our faces as we passed by the San Carlos (the cradle of Cuba's independence movement), then Jimmy Buffett's Margaritaville (arguably the bosom, if not the cradle, of the Parrot Head movement), Fast Buck Freddie's old domain, and then hesitated a moment at the corner of Fleming and Duval to watch a chicken cluck its way across the road (insert your own joke).

Gabrielle and I watched the chicken. "Do you remember that story John Rubin told us?"

"There've been so many. All good."

"The one about when he was growing up in Manchester, England, and the movie BIRDS was playing at the Odeon?"

"Oh, right, and he smuggled a chicken under his coat and then let it fly down from the balcony during the flappy part of the movie?"

14

"Yes, that story. What do you have in mind?"

"Just thinking of ways to entertain Mr. Tosser."

"We've had success with a snake, why not?"

"It seems a natural transition."

Gabrielle and I both burst out laughing, but I think, just between you and me, she was dead serious.

Now let's carry on down to the corner of Eaton and Duval and if you will be so kind pull your bike over by the curb and stop with us. Look over there to your right. No, not at the passing Budweiser truck, over there at St. Paul's Church. See that glorious tree in front? That's a Royal Poinciana. In the late spring it will be aflame with startling searing reds.

Did you know the land for St. Paul's was donated by the widow of John William Charles Fleming in 1832? The only stipulation was that her husband's remains stay where they were, which seems like a fair enough request. He is still buried on the grounds, but the actual site is unknown, although he gets a mention with the street one-block away being named after him.

What we are gazing at right here is not the original church. The original church was made of coral rock in 1838/39 for $6,550, but the sea reclaimed it when it was totally destroyed by the hurricane of October 11, 1846. A subsequent church was destroyed by the Great Fire of Key West in March of 1886.

For those of you taking notes, the Great Fire of Key West began at two o'clock in the morning on March 30, in a coffee shop next to the San Carlos Hall (now the San Carlos Institute) on the west side of Duval Street, which we just pedaled past. The fire burned to Whitehead Street, where it was stopped at Jackson Square.

The fire company was there in a flash, so to speak, but the *steam* fire engine, which had been in use in Key West for about ten years, had been shipped up to New York for repairs and there was only a small hand-operated engine available to fight the fire. This was an unfortunate turn of events as the fire then jumped Duval Street, raged out of control in the commercial district and savaged the east side of Duval Street all the way down to present day Sloppy Joe's. The fire then jumped back over to the west side -- where Rick's is now -- and leveled: businesses, homes, fences, gardens, palm trees, Royal Poinciana, even outhouses, leaving only cisterns and cooking chimneys standing. It then scorched everything in its path all the way to Stephen Mallory's Pier (now Mallory Square and home to the Sunset Celebration,) burning the pier and its pilings right down to the waterline.

Charles B. Pendleton, Editor-in-Chief of the Key West *Democrat*, eventually the *Equator-Democrat* (and holder of the appealingly user-friendly Key West telephone number "3"), reported at the time: "The terror of that awful sight will never be forgotten by anyone who witnessed the grand but terrible tragedy.

"Fire and wind undid in a few short hours the work of many generations of busy men. Human suffering and hardship was exemplified in the period of woe and desolation that followed. Everyone was dazed and bewildered. Despair was the key note of every voice, and a scene of blackened ruins and ashy waste failed to inspire hope in any heart of reflect a flash from any eye."

The Great Fire of 1886 raged for twelve hours before burning itself out.

Two years later, a moderately sophisticated system of water works was installed, using *saltwater* which is heavier and better adapted than freshwater for extinguishing fires. Good thinking on an island with a limited supply of freshwater. And a limitless supply of saltwater.

Fire would never again destroy the great church.

On October 11, 1909, the church was destroyed by a hurricane.

Are you getting all this down, because we aren't out of the Dade-County-pine woods yet?

In 1991, a major restoration of the church was begun to keep it from falling apart and collapsing, but the concrete used in the construction was mixed with, yes, you've guess it, *saltwater*, which wreaked havoc with the steel reinforced walls and caused it to rust and expand. Duhhh! On account of this error in judgement (and lack of common sense), many of the walls and columns split and ruptured. Work was finally completed in 1993 at a cost of nearly one million dollars, so perhaps drop a buck in the collection box the next time you visit.

And take this bit of history into account when you stop your bikes and regard the magnificent structure as we're now doing, and you won't look at it quite the same ever again.

Get back on your bikes!

Let's rumble!

We're pedaling farther down Duval now. It was tough to slip past the Bull and not make a pit stop, wouldn't you agree? Okay, passing by Shorty's on the right, then the Red Garter Saloon on the left. Durty Harry's and wait! Wait! I think I hear him. Look! There's Al Subarsky playing at Rick's. He's got Big Red with him today. Let's just straddle our bikes for a moment and listen. Good to always counter the bad (dickhead landlord), with the good (Al and Big Red).

Al sings with a golden voice the much requested Jimmy Buffett lyrics:

Mother, mother ocean, I have heard you call
Wanted to sail upon your waters since I was three feet tall
You've seen it all, you've seen it all ...

We listen to Alfonse finish the song, and we can't tear ourselves away, so we stay for the next song:

All my ex's live in Texas
And Texas is the place I'd dearly love to be
But all my ex's live in Texas
And that's why I hang my hat in Tennessee ...

He finishes the George Strait song and we reluctantly turn our bikes around and pedal back up Duval. Cover songs, or fresh originals: Al Subarsky, Sallie Foster, Dani Hoy, Chris Rehm, folk of that ilk, they are one of the reasons people flock to Key West, to listen to their music and perhaps just wish a bit, that they too had the freedom/guts to come down here and make a go of it themselves.

As we approach Caroline Street, I cast my mind back to what Al had told us when he first came to the island: It was mid-October, 1999, he'd crashed on a friend's houseboat in Marathon, then he made his way down to Key West and found a decent room for rent in a compound on Bahama Lane, just off Truman, around the block from the Bare Assets strip club. Gugi and Inga (well-known drag queens) were his neighbors. "Welcome to the neighborhood!"

Not long after arriving, Al was approached by a guitar player named "Freemont John" who had heard him sing at Rick's. Freemont John liked Al's style and asked him to play a gig with him in the Garden of Eden rooftop bar for Fantasy Fest.

Hel-lo-o!

Another eye-opener for Al!

Al settled into the laidback, quirky, bacchanal lifestyle that is Key West, and he and Freemont John continued their acoustic duo every Monday night for about 2 years. One night, just after finishing up their last set (8-12 Midnight), an exquisitely dressed older dame approached the stage and said these memorable words to Al: "I will give you a thousand dollars if you play 'Desperado'." Al had sung "Desperado" often over the years, and he knew this damsel wasn't about to drop a grand on one song, but he said "What the hell!" Perhaps she would at least leave a nice tip. He and Fremont John played. Al sang "Desperado." The grand dame seemed pleased. When it was all over, Al looked over in the direction of the gentlewoman: No one there! No tip! She'd vanished! Classic. Al and Fremont John were packing up when Terrie the bartender came up with a Cheshire-cat smile and informed them that the grand dame had a Black American Express card and she had just left the two of them a tip: $1,000, just as she'd promised. Terrie went on to say that as the queen slipped out the door, she yelled over to Terrie: "Oh, put another $100 on that for YOU!"

By the by, dear Reader, as you all know a tip goes a long way with these talented folk. I'm not talking a $1000 tip, or a dollar wrapped around a condom (although I like that woman's style), I'm just saying let's not forget all the hard work it took for these musicians to get where they are.

Some of you have already seen this:

HIRING A MUSICIAN OR ASKING THEM TO SING AND PERFORM AT YOUR EVENT?

**What you think you're paying for:

Someone to perform some music

**What you are actually paying for:

Someone to perform some music, plus

Equipment and instruments

Hours of rehearsal time

Rehearsal space

Transportation to and from the venue

The amount of money spent on lessons and training to become the musicians that they are

Promotion and website costs

The percentage that goes to income taxes

Telephone and Internet bills spent organizing the performance and rehearsals

Any manager, agent or other booking fees

Insurance

The payment also has to cover: food, housing, utilities, other bills and other living expenses

Or ...

How about this (from Adrienne Coppola):

"To all who moan about the price of musicians: A guy calls the musicians' guild to get a quote on a 6-piece band for a wedding. The rep says "Off the top of my head, about $2000." The guy says "WHAT? FOR MUSIC?" The rep responds "I'll tell you what. Call the plumbers' union & ask for six plumbers to work from 6 to midnight on a Saturday night. Whatever they charge you, we'll work for half."

Nuff said.

* * *

At the corner of Duval and Caroline, we pass by the Bull & Whistle (thirsty!) and the Garden of Eden rooftop bar (scene-of-the crime for Al), and we swing left onto Caroline.

Down by the corner of Caroline and Simonton, right in front of the Cypress House, we stop to read a flyer someone has posted on the telephone pole. It reads: MISSING: WIFE AND DOG -- REWARD FOR DOG.

Look over there to the right, we're passing by the Pineapple Apartments now. There's Chubba lazing in a patch of sun in front of the Efficiency. She must be quite content there, as a gecko is darting right in front of her nose and she's paying him no attention. Knowing Chubba, that little gecko doesn't know how lucky he is.

"Gabrielle! Jon!" Emerging from out back of the Pineapple Apartments is Popcorn Joe.

"Giuseppe!"

"What's the haps?"

"Going to B.O.'s for a coffee. Wanna come?"

"Gotta take Chubba to the vet."

"Okay, we'll catch you at Sunset."

"Later!"

We wave goodbye to Popcorn Joe and Chubba and pedal off.

Look over to the right now. There's the Red Doors Gallery. Wave at Rene. He's the guy with the grey ponytail standing in the open front door talking to Ken Ro. They are admiring a fire engine parked just down the street.

Ken Ro is from paradise north: Belmar Beach. Rene is from French Canada. We don't know it at the time, but over the course of the next few years, Rene will purchase the building just to the left of Pepe's, move his gallery, get sued by Pepe's, sue back, fight with the person who sold him the property for falsifying the deed, dare to fight with Immigration for the right to remain in the US, have a heart attack … and beat them all.

Off to the left is B.O.'s Fishwagon. He might not be open yet, but let's give it a shot, if we can penetrate the venerable domain, we'll treat you to a jolt of caffeine.

Since we had our bikes stolen the previous year, we now use handcuffs to lock them up (and, no, do not go there!), which are much more reliable and the sight frightens away any roving-eye scum as they think only a couple of really twisted motherfuckers would use handcuffs. We chained our bikes to a sign which loudly states PAY TO PARK IN THIS BLOCK (so the city has recourse with attitude). There used to be tons of places to park for free in Key West, but now most have gone.

FYI: If you keep it to yourselves, I will just whisper that there still are a few free spaces over by the courthouse on Southard, you know the spot, just across from the Courthouse Deli, direction Truman Annex.

While Gabrielle checked to see if B.O.'s was open, I ambled over to the newspaper machine, inserted the coins and opened the door. The top newspaper was ruffled and hanging over the ones underneath it. This could only mean one thing: the last patron had purchased a paper, but didn't want to touch the top

20

copy, so he'd snatched the second copy out from underneath it. I've witnessed this over the years. Sunday paper, daily, Key West *Citizen*, *The Miami Herald*, *Solares Hill*, it doesn't seem to matter what or where. Why doesn't anyone want to take that top copy? What do they know that others don't? Anthrax? E. coli? Touched by the same soul with shit hygiene who repeatedly fondles the peanuts in a bar after returning from the toilet? (Please do not include me in here, as I may have had a lapse in decorum with Debbie's peanuts, but I DID WASH my hands after visiting the facilities, thank you very much!).

Or are they afraid the coupons will be missing?

That's probably it, wouldn't you say?

I studied the top newspaper: I wanted to go against the tide. Break the chain of irresponsibility. But then again, I didn't want to be part of the sheep brigade and take the second paper. This was a big dilemma for me and as you can see I'm having a few issues with this.

So I took the bottom copy.

And this set off a domino effect of sorts and destroyed the complete integrity of the stack. I then spent five minutes rebuilding the stack and touching ALL the papers.

We took our copy of the morning Mullet Wrap and slunk over to B.O.'s sign with the mermaid on it, which rightly states GONE FISHIN'. Underneath the mermaid we saw something written that we had never noticed before: "If it looks like fish, and smells like fish, it ain't fresh!" B.O. was born in Key West, he's a conch, and he's a man who knows what he's talking about.

If you happen to pay a visit to a seafood restaurant back in your home town, the menu may well offer CATCH OF THE DAY, but guess what? That bug-eyed creature that's staring back at you wasn't caught "today," or even so very close to "today." But down here in Key West, FL, the end of the world and, might I add, one of the best places in the world to *catch* fish, it's *fresh* indeed and probably was out there in the Gulf flopping around only hours before you sink your famished little teeth into it.

B.O. creates truly local delicacies and you won't find recipes like this anywhere else, scrumptious items such as the Square Grouper Sandwich. I should probably mention that "square grouper" was a term coined back in the 70s when a suddenly giddy fisherman returned to port with a washed-up bale of marijuana. If the fisherman could sell the weed, then he could knock off fishing for a while ... but then if he knocked off fishing for a while, this reduced the chances of finding another square grouper, so life went on. A vicious, albeit sometimes lucrative, square circle.

B.O. is something of a local legend as he started selling his famous sandwiches out of a wagon on Duval Street in the late 1970s. "We were there for close to 20 years," he'll tell you, before a friend of his known as Panama Jack popped for financing for the present day Fish Wagon.

Allegedly.

It's important to note that the late writer and humorist Shel Silverstein was a fan of B.O.'s, and B.O. still racks them up for Jimmy Buffett when Jimmy's in town.

B.O. lives an idyllic life in Key West, as he should, but according to lore, life was not so very laid back for B.O. in the beginning. The police thought he was smuggling drugs -- which he wasn't -- because of the aforementioned "Square Grouper" sandwich.

B.O. had a sense of humor, the Key West police back then, didn't.

But now they do.

Allegedly.

Besides the coveted Square Grouper sandwich, served with beans and rice and green olives and onions, B.O.'s offers a cracked conch sandwich: tiny strips of delicious fried conch stuffed between fresh Cuban bread and shot with Key Lime mayo, Bubbaque!

If you're in the hunt for a fine dining experience, then don't come here to B.O.'s Fish Wagon. If you want to sink your choppers into some of the most original delightful seafood fayre ANYWHERE, with funky, quirky atmosphere like NO WHERE ELSE in the world, then B.O.'s is for you.

There is nothing fancy about B.O.'s, and it is very much a "No Shirt, No Shoes, No Problem!" kind of place. You order wine and you'll get it in a plastic glass. I love it!

One-hundred percent our kind of place.

B.O.'s wasn't really open for business yet, but the man was

there and he waved us in and we took a seat in the back in a splash of sunshine. We ordered two coffees and they came quickly. It doesn't get much better than this, you know, sitting in the sun at B.O.'s, getting your caffeine fix, other than sitting here on a Friday night listening to live music, sipping an adult beverage of choice.

And we were both going to miss it immensely.

I looked over at Gabrielle and she already had her face to the sun. "Doesn't our landlord realize he's a flaming asshole? We've lived in Key West nearly a year and I haven't heard anyone say anything nice about him. Bet he doesn't come to a place like this."

"B.O. would throw him out on his skanky behind for being so full of himself. Plus, B.O. doesn't like people who surround themselves with flunkies who kiss their ass all day long 'cause that's all the loving they need."

I watched a palmetto bug scamper past my foot, then turned my face to the sun and began to think of ways to murder our landlord, but I was coming up empty. I needed inspiration from somewhere, and then I had it: I opened up the Mullet Wrap and turned to the Crime Report.

The Crime Report in the Key West *Citizen* is seriously good reading (and occasionally inspirational). In your newspaper back home, you may read the Sports first, or the Entertainment, or the International News or the Obits (I hope not), but in Key West, it's the Crime Report which most people turn to first thing. It's good to know what your neighbors are up to.

The first story to catch my eye and these are all verbatim and grammatically untouched, by the way:

KEY WEST: A man was arrested on multiple felonies Thursday for allegedly stealing a work truck in April to go on a "crack party" binge in Homestead, according to a Monroe County Sheriff's Office arrest warrant.

This story gave me no inspiration at all, as our landlord clearly looked the type who never got invited anywhere for anything, and certainly not to "Par-tay!" I read on:

Two teens were accused of stealing a marijuana pipe and beating the homeowner to which it belongs on Wednesday, according to a Monroe County Sheriff's Office

arrest report. An 18, and a 17-year-old boy were charged with burglary, battery, petty theft and possession of drug paraphernalia.

Nothing there, either.

A Stock Island woman was arrested Thursday afternoon for firing a gun at two boats. She was reportedly angry that the people on board were snorkeling in her canal for lobster.

Hmmm, our landlord didn't look like the type of person who paid for his lobster either, but this just wasn't offering inspiration.

A 14-year-old Marathon boy was caught burglarizing his neighbor's house Saturday afternoon. He was wearing a mask, a tactical vest and had armed himself by stealing three loaded guns from the home before the homeowner caught him leaving the premises. The boy told Deputy Dennis Coleman he learned how to break in to his neighbor's house on an internet site the night before. He said the web site told him how to do it, and what items he needed to take with him.

Isn't the Internet just wonderful? So much rich and useful information can be found. I read on:

As authorities nationwide warn motorists of the dangers of driving while texting, Florida Keys law enforcement officers add a new caution: Don't try to shave your privates, either.

Florida Highway Patrol troopers say a two-vehicle crash Tuesday at Mile Marker 21 on Cudjoe Key was caused by a 37-year-old woman driver who was shaving her bikini area while her ex-husband took the wheel from the passenger seat.

"She said she was meeting her boyfriend in Key West and wanted to be ready for the visit," Trooper Gary Dunick said. "If I wasn't there, I wouldn't have believed it. About 10 years ago I stopped a guy in the exact same spot ... who had three or four syringes sticking out of his arm. It was just surreal and I thought, 'Nothing will ever beat this.' Well, this takes it."

Dunick added: "It is unbelievable. I'm really starting to

believe this stuff only happens in the Keys."

I re-read this one, then passed on it.

And: **STOCK ISLAND - A 37 year old Stock Island woman was arrested Friday evening for contributing to the delinquency of two teenaged boys.**

Deputy Brian Luth was on patrol just before 9 p.m. when he pulled in to the parking lot of the Tom Thumb store on Maloney Avenue, Stock Island. He saw a woman sitting in a pickup truck. One of the brake lights wasn't working, so he approached the truck. As he approached, he heard two teenage boys inside arguing. One boy said, "My blunt is going to be bigger than yours." The other boy replied, "No, mine is going to be bigger." A blunt is the street name for a cigar which is cut open, the tobacco is removed, and marijuana is inserted inside.

Deputy Luth continued to stand beside the truck and watch as the boys rolled the blunts. After about three minutes, the 37-year-old woman in the driver's seat, Kimberly Todora, turned around and saw him. She exclaimed, "Holy Sh*t, how can I help you, Officer?"

Deputy Evan Calhoun arrived as back up. Todora was arrested and charged with contributing to the delinquency of minors. The two 15-year-old boys said Todora was the one who bought them the cigars. They were given notices to appear in court for possession of marijuana and they were turned over to the custody of their grandparents, who came to the scene to pick them up.

And: **Deputies arrested an 18-month-old's father after they found the man passed out in his mobile home while the toddler was in the yard picking up beer cans and drinking them.**

And: **While he didn't rob it, an unhappy bank customer left quite a deposit. He urinated in a drive-thru bank tube and drove off.**

And: **Two lesbians were arrested for having a knockdown drag out fight in public ... seems they were breaking up and both wanted "the toys."**

I closed the paper and folded it in half. Then opened it all back up again. Did it really say "the toys?" I started to fold the paper again, when I spotted one story I had missed on my cruise through.

KEY WEST -- It was the third blast from the stun gun that persuaded this crack cocaine user to stop kicking and hitting Key West police officers. Robert Campo, 41, of Key West is charged with felony possession of cocaine and felony resisting arrest after allegedly trying to break free from an arresting officer, who used a stun gun on the suspect three times to subdue him.

I looked over at Gabrielle. "How 'bout we go to a flea market and pick up a used stun gun?"

"Does this involve our sleaze landlord or a chicken?"

"Sleaze landlord."

"I'm listening."

"We stun the shit out of him, then do what they did to that groom-to-be back in Glasgow on his bachelor party …"

"Remind me."

"They waited till he passed out, then they stripped all his clothes off and Saran wrapped him to a lamp post in the city center. Everyone on the way to work the next morning saw him hanging there because he was still passed out. Eventually the police came and cut him down, but not till they called the newspaper to get a good photo."

"Do you think we can find a stun gun at a flea market?"

"Well, this is Florida, isn't it? We shouldn't even have to show proof of I.D."

CHAPTER THREE

Later that afternoon, I fired up our dinosaur of a computer we called the "oscilloscope" (on account of the size of the screen), and checked my emails. Over the past year in Key West, I had written a crime thriller entitled "DEATH BY GLASGOW" and had already sent the manuscript out to numerous literary agents and independent publishers. Sadly I had no response from agents or publishers, but I did have three emails in my inbox: something from a Canadian pharmacy, another email offering penal extensions, and one entitled "Local Sluts."

I shut down the oscilloscope, and we headed down to Mallory Square and the Sunset Celebration, or just "Sunset" as it's known. Gabrielle and I had been selling our Sunset Photos, matted and framed, down at Mallory since Spring Break, last year. It had all gone well throughout the summer and autumn, but once winter came and "season" hit, we didn't have the seniority to get a pitch. Not counting performers and musicians and palm readers, there were 50 available places on the pier for crafts people, but there could be 70 or more hopefuls waiting to grab the 50 spots. Winter in Key West was high season and that's when money was to be made, so all the artists and craft folk who lived up north in the heat of the summer always returned for "season."

We went down to Sunset early, dragging our display on a makeshift trolley. By going early we could cut through Truman Annex before they locked the gates to keep out all the people who lived in Bahama Village using it as a shortcut, lest their ethnicity upset the delicate balance of life in a gated community.

When we got to Mallory, our mouths dropped open.

"Look at all the artists and crafts people!"

"Over there! O.J. Dave is Pier Manager tonight. He's of substantial mental health. Let's go ask him if we have a snowball's chance at getting on."

Dave saw us coming. He gave us his usual friendly smile, then shook his head: "Sorry, it's not looking good. All the regulars are back. You might not get on the rest of the season."

We thanked Dave, then muttered "Oh, shit," in unison.

"Not what I wanted to hear."

"What does it really matter? We're going back to Glasgow soon," Gabrielle said.

"Right, but I was hoping we would get some days in, so we wouldn't have to dip into our savings. Dollars don't buy a lot of pounds."

Gabrielle and I took in the magical, colorful, drunken atmosphere that is Mallory Square at sunset. "Look!" Gabrielle pointed.

"What?"

"The back of that guy's T-shirt."

I spun around. An extremely tanned fellow of about forty years was wearing a black T-shirt with white lettering. It read: **RULES FOR DATING MY DAUGHTER**, then it listed the ten rules underneath it. I quickly grabbed a pen and wrote them down for you:

1) Get a job.
2) Understand I don't like you.
3) I'm everywhere.
4) You hurt her, I hurt you.
5) Be home 30 minutes early.
6) Get a lawyer.
7) If you lie, I will find out.
8) She's my princess, not your conquest.
9) Whatever you do to her, I will do to you.
10) I don't mind going back to jail.

I looked at Gabrielle: "His daughter won't get a date till she's forty."

"My father could have authored that ... although having said that he liked you because you drank whiskey with him and sang loudly when I played the piano." Gabrielle pointed: "Look, there's Popcorn Joe!"

We schlepped our trolley/display over to Popcorn Joe. He was flapping a paper bag in the air and already doing a business.

28

We waited until he finished filling five bags of popcorn for a family from the U.K. The family walked off and we all watched them go. Their faces and fronts of their legs looked like fried lobsters, their backs looked peely-wally white and nearly blue, not unlike a walking Union Jack flag.

"They need to be put on a spit and rotated every fifteen minutes," Popcorn Joe mused.

"Sunblock would help, as well," Gabrielle said.

"Perhaps a little Coppertone, Sea & Ski, or Bullfrog SPF 50," I said.

We turned to Popcorn Joe and he said: "There is no stronger sunscreen than sitting in a bar ..."

We couldn't refute what Popcorn Joe had just said. Soon a line formed to purchase popcorn, so we bid him farewell."

"See you at the Bull after sunset, Giuseppe?"

"See you there. Grab a table by the front window. I just might have a surprise for you."

Gabrielle and I wondered what the surprise could possibly be. We hoped it would be good as we were a bit down with the *financial slap in the face* that we would make no money tonight, that coupled with going back home. Tails between our legs, we dragged our trolley laden with unsold wares back off in the direction of Whitehead.

"Perhaps we should take our display home and then go somewhere and discuss a game plan?"

"What do you have in mind?"

"For a game plan?"

"No, a place to go."

"I do my best thinking at the, ah, Bull."

"Do you mean your best *drinking*?"

"Well, for sure that. Whaddaya say?"

"Thought you were hung-over."

"Won't be if we go."

"I would say your logic is flawed, but in your case I know it's not."

"We have to go, we said we'd meet Popcorn Joe. Plus, he has a surprise."

"Why do I feel like I'm being manipulated?"

"So are we going?"

"We'll be five hours early."

"So are we going?"

"Have I ever denied you anything?"

* * *

Through the magic of literature, Gabrielle and I are now ensconced in one of the large open front windows at the Bull. We're looking out on Duval watching the world go by -- and possibly a few individuals from further afield. I need to report to you that it's ten in the evening and the temperature has somehow managed to climb to an exceedingly agreeable 74 degrees.

Not bad for January.

Not bad for the dead of winter.

Or when the day started out as chilly as it had.

One of the many glorious attractions of Key West.

Since we are sitting here people watching -- and purposely avoiding discussing a game plan -- I'm making notes. If you wish, you can look over my shoulder and see what I'm scribbling down. First of all, I would like to paint a picture for those of you who are not au fait with the rituals of winter in Key West. As I overheard a bartender say once: "The winter is high season, and high season spawns a curious breed of creature."

Grab a pen and pencil. You may want to make notes, as well:

1) THE FAMILY WITH YOUNG CHILDREN. The *family with young children* come on vacation only to realize that there isn't so very much for kids to do after one lap on the Conch Tour Train, Dominique and his Circus Cats ("What a show! What a show!"), a trip to the Key West Aquarium, a few repeat visits to Key Lime Pie Factory at 412 Greene Street, or after a couple of bags of popcorn from Popcorn Joe at the sometimes eye-opener of "sunset" down at Mallory Square. The kids don't go to clothing-optional bars. The kids don't drink like fish. And the kids don't smoke weed -- yet.

2) THE SLIPPERY DICKS. These are normal, respectful people, and can be of any age. They are from up north somewhere ("up north" can mean anywhere north of West Palm Beach, but usually refers to anywhere that gets snow ... which could mean anywhere north of West Palm Beach). Like their namesake, the *slippery dick fish*, they are shy and reserved. Because they are shy and reserved back home, they have come to partake of things that they would never be caught dead doing back home, like sipping a mojito, wearing a thong, not wearing socks, and even gay sex. "I kissed a girl and I liked it ..."

The *Slippery Dicks* respectfully embrace the quirky, funky island, and are on the endangered species list. They are fun to sit next to at the bar, because they listen, enraptured, with bug-eyes and open mouths to all your stories, and they buy you lots of beer.

I turn to Gabrielle and I show her what I've written.

"What's your next category going to be?"

"I'm thinking *Snowbirds*."

I scribble **3) SNOWBIRDS** on my notepad, making it bold like that, but then am not so sure what to write. I realize someone is staring over my shoulder, so I turn, and no, it's not you, but it is Gary Ek. Gary Whitney Ek is known affectionately as the Soundman From Hell or Reverend Gweko W. Phlocker. *Soundman From Hell* when he's on the air on his Pirate Radio X 104.9 and *Reverend Gweko* when he's performing marriages. He is the original man for all seasons, or perhaps that should be MAN FOR ALL REASONS.

Gweko picks up my notepad, peruses it, and immediately knows what I'm doing.

"Do you mind if I chime in?"

"Chime away. I'll write it down."

"*Snowbirds* are seasonal, insufferable schmucks who come for most of winter ..."

"Wait! Do you think I should write that down?"

"Hel-lo-o?"

"Okay, keep going. Don't pull any punches."

"Do I strike you as the kinda guy who pulls punches?"

"Not in the least ..."

"Many *Snowbirds* drive down in gas guzzlers, so they can drive around an island that is only one-and-a-half miles wide when they should be riding a bicycle. They know who they are. They will have out-of-state license plates, but the tags will make some longing reference to Key West. The male *Snowbirds* put their hair in a ponytail, even though it is not quite an inch long.

31

The women folk have scary cleavage ..."

"Did you just say 'scary cleavage'?"

The good reverend gave me a look. "Yes, write it down! The scary cleavage will make you never want to have sex again. May they burn in hell! There's that, plus they parade down Duval wearing too much makeup and too much jewelry. They will have a drink in one hand and a Botox syringe in the other. Despite the Botox syringe they will sport bingo wings. Both male and female of the *Snowbird* species will have purchased their bathing suits in the Great White North. They live in timeshares or posh condos or up-market resort hotels -- and they let you know it. They frequent Blue Heaven and Pepe's and Louie's Backyard and Sloppy's and frighten the locals with their mating calls. They smoke Cuban cigars even though they don't smoke back up in the Great White North. And even though they aren't authentic Cuban cigars. *That* they will *not* let you know. In short, they are a right pain in the tuchas."

Gweko has finished, and Gabrielle and I are nearly breathless. "Do you think perhaps if I put all that in my next book, I'll offend anyone?"

"Fuck 'em, put in a disclaimer."

So I write: Perhaps I've offended a small niche of *Snowbirds* who really aren't like this at all. If that is the case, you may move into the **SLIPPERY DICKS** category or, if more appropriate, into the coveted (with a waiting list to get in, mind you) **I WOULD KILL TO LIVE IN KEY WEST ILK** category, which I will address shortly.

And I turn to Gweko: "Does that work for you?"

"Absolutely," Gweko says. "Just add that they have to stop flashing the bling, and stop trying to impress. Less is more!"

I thank Gweko for his take, and he says: "Gotta bolt. I'm on the air in an hour."

Gweko takes his leave ... but he certainly has left me with inspiration. I give some thought to what I should write, then I feel someone else looking over my shoulder (and, no, it's still not you). It's Captain Jerry. You may remember that Captain Jerry or "Geraldo" as we called him was homeless, and the self-proclaimed "Wizard of Key West." Geraldo was university educated, but had little respect for the work ethic and as an alternative had chosen a career of alcohol abuse. He could often be found sneaking up to tourists on Duval and asking for thirty-seven cents. Remember? It was his creative way of panhandling and the thirty-seven-cent approach was cleverly successful. Captain Jerry dutifully scanned my notes, then said: "Write down "SNOWFLAKES."

"Snowflakes?" I say, I've never even heard of them.

"Write it down."

So I write **4) SNOWFLAKES** bold like that, and Captain Jerry goes on to say: "Snowflakes aspire to be snowbirds. Need I say more? They are transient Snowbirds, which means they are transient *transients*. Snowflakes don't have enough migratory seniority in the department to fall into the *Snowbird* category, nor have they developed that enervating and annoying habit of spewing how wonderful they are to everyone. Don't get me wrong, they believe they are."

Captain Jerry suddenly stops.

"Is that it?" I ask.

"Gotta go. Got a date at Rick's with a beer. *Ciao!*"

Truly inspired, I write down:

5) WANNABE CONCHS, and suddenly Gweko is back, hovering there looking over my shoulder again.

"Thought you had to be on the air?"

"Shitloads of time," he says. "I'm enjoying this ..."

Gweko takes the pen from my hand, and he writes: *Wannabe Conchs* have been living in Key West for a week already. They found jobs in the service industry on account of turning up for the interview sober. They were fresh-faced and personable when they arrived, but now they have copped an attitude and are haughty and condescending to the *Slippery Dicks* ...

"Good stuff!" I say.

"Don't interrupt me. I'm on a roll here ..."

And he writes: *Wannabe Conchs* have attitude because they live on Bone Island and the *Slippery Dicks* don't (even though the *Slippery Dicks* have been coming for years). They get three hours of sleep a night and are developing a credit-card scam they can put to use at their place of employment, so they can finance their newly acquired drug habit. They will return to the Great White North sooner than later. They will go back with a great tan, a

33

common STD and less common sense than they arrived with.

Gweko splits, turns and gives me a smile and a cheeky, devilish middle digit.

Nobody puts Baby in a corner.

And no one will ever accuse the Reverend Gweko W. Phlocker of being dull.

He should clone himself.

Or open his own sperm bank. Would be one of the first men of the cloth to do so. Officially.

I look quickly around to make sure no one is there. I would love to write some of this book myself. So I write:

6) THE TOURON (tourist/moron). The *Touron* is a remora subset of the above aforementioned categories, excluding the *Slippery Dicks*. *Tourons* do not know how to behave on holiday. They dress inappropriately, are loud and demanding, can't adjust to the island lifestyle, talk about possessions a lot, don't know how to tip and, if they are from the U.K., want Heinz beans and ketchup with all entrées. The *Tourons* make locals run for cover with their hands flailing in the air. The *Touron* will never be on the endangered species list.

On a roll myself, I now write (as I promised you I would):

7) The: **I WOULD KILL TO LIVE IN KEY WEST ILK**. The *IWKTLIKWI* are really good people. These folk would move in a heartbeat if they weren't anchored back home by career, family, friends, mortgages, 32 acres, cute animals (that counts as family) … or simply a lifestyle that is safe and pleasing and fulfilling. They are happy, successful and content (and give really good seminars). They are respectful and live life to the fullest and appreciate and enjoy every second when they get the chance to come to Key West, which is often. They, too, frequent Pepe's, Blue Heaven and Louie's Backyard and tip the balance in their favor away from the *Snowbirds*. They do not soil the bed they sleep in. The world is a better place because of the *IWKTLIKWI*, and they will always be welcome.

They can be found on Facebook.

* * *

****FYI**: If you were born in Key West, you are a *Conch* (like B.O.). If you *weren't* born in Key West, but have lived here for seven or more years, you are a *Freshwater Conch* (like Popcorn

Joe). That's the rule, but nobody goes much by the rules in Key West. In reality, it's more like: If you are an arrogant, uptight, schmuck, you will never be a local. If you are a respectful, decent, laid-back sort (with dubious credentials and skeletons in your closet), you are well on your way to becoming accepted.

I looked over at Gabrielle and she was staring back at me.

"What?"

"So should we discuss a game plan?"

"That's what we came for ..."

Gabrielle gave me one of her amused looks.

"Okay, okay, that's the excuse I used to get us here. Let me just nip upstairs to the toilets. There's something I'm dying to know."

"Too much information."

"Ha, ha."

I knocked back my shot of tequila, chased it with a slug of my Corona and headed through a pulsing swarm of pissheads to the toilets. I started to climb the steps, but was frozen in place by a torrent of revelers coming down. Me, the lone salmon trying to get up river. I wasn't heading to the toilets for the reason you may think, I was on my way to make use of the breathalyzer which was located right across from the bog. As it should be.

There was a queue. For the breathalyzer, not the loo. I looked at the price it cost to check your alcohol level. It was two dollars. For that price I could go back downstairs and invest in another beer. Somebody shouted: "You're up!"

I always do as I'm told, so I flipped in quarters I was meant to use for the laundry and breathed out heartily. I waited, then checked the gauge when a light flashed on. A few folk behind me applauded. A deeply tanned surfer type enthused, "Dude!"

Not wanting to go down the interior stairs in a conga line, I took the outside stairs back to the street level and encountered a creature of indeterminate sex aiming for the Garden of Eden rooftop bar where clothing was optional. You may remember that Gabrielle and I were accidental tourists in this venue upon arrival on the island nearly a year ago (with panicked, albeit thrilling results).

I entered the Bull by the back door on Caroline Street and

re-commandeered my seat.

Gabrielle held both palms up. "And?"

"I'm clinically drunk in just about every country in the world," I slurred.

"Even Russia?"

"I fear so."

"Kazakhstan?"

"Probably."

"Poland?"

"No, not Poland! You can't include the professionals with the amateurs."

"Too right."

I put a dollar tip on the edge of our table, and we watched as Max the black Labrador sniffed it once, then plucked it off and took it to the bar.

Gabrielle and I turned our attention to Sallie up on the stage. If you've never seen Sallie perform, drop everything it is you're doing and rush over to the Bull. Sallie's a hoot! She knows every song ever written, she gladly takes requests and she shreds a very mean guitar. When she used to play down at the Quay, she didn't restrain herself to playing on the stage inside the restaurant and we would often see her lying out in the middle of Duval, flat on her back, ripping on her electric guitar and belting out your favorite oldies but moldies.

Sallie was now singing "Sweet Home Alabama." She had four Go-Go Girls up on stage behind her and folk showing lots of tanned skin -- and others showing lots of sunburned lobster skin -- were holding drinks, glistening with perspiration and dancing just in front of her. Tanned-skin folk with lobster-back folk usually translated to a tourist/local encounter. Visitors had found deep, long-lasting love -- at least until tomorrow morning when they were sober.

With the music and the balmy night and the glistening bodies and the Sodomy and Gomorrah -- I mean Sodom and Gomorrah feel of it all -- it was all far-flung and magical.

And the Bull & Whistle on Duval Street, Key West, Florida, seemed *the* place to be on the planet tonight.

Most nights, actually.

Gabrielle pointed to a bloke walking past our window, the

type of guy who spends 50 weeks a year in a three-piece business suit in an ivory tower rife with the norovirus. From the front, his legs were stone-white. From the back, he was part of the lobster brigade, sunburned beyond melanin belief or hope. And he was not so very steady on his scotch eggs. We watched him stumble along. The back of his black T-shirt had white letters, and at first I thought he was Black T-Shirt Guy from earlier, but this T-shirt didn't have rules about dating someone's daughter, it simply stated: **MENACE TO SOBRIETY**.

Then another individual pierced our line of sight.

"Check it out!" Gabrielle said.

Coming toward us in a wobbly fashion was the poster child for inebriates. He, too, sported a new and jaunty T-shirt. It read: **I CAME, I SAW, I PUKED**.

"A touron-litigator from the Great White North," someone mumbled in our ears. We turned to see Shark Man balancing on his bicycle, holding onto the windowsill with one hand.

Gabrielle noticed that Shark Man was wearing a new necklace made of shark teeth. "Is that new?"

"It *is* new. Came from a bull shark."

"What happened to the old one?"

"The old bull shark?"

"No, the old necklace."

"Lost it swimming out by the reef."

We knew that Shark Man would have some toothy tale about how he wrestled the bull shark into submission and individually extracted each tooth himself while the bull shark protested vociferously, but he didn't, rather: "I got it from the Key West Web Store. You can get anything on there."

Gabrielle and I laughed.

Shark Man pointed to a buxom goddess walking toward us. The goddess sported a tight top with these words on it: **YOU WERE BETTER LOOKING ON FACEBOOK**.

Shark Man gave us a smile (all teeth) and pedaled on down Duval in the direction of a group of co-eds.

"The shark is circling," Gabrielle said.

"Sharks never sleep," I said. Perhaps not one-hundred percent ichthyologically accurate, but you get my drift.

Gabrielle suddenly changed the subject. "Can't believe

we've been here almost a year already."

"I know, I was just thinking about that."

"Can't believe we only came for a week."

"Can't believe we're going back home to Glasgow."

I sipped my Corona. Gabrielle lapped at her Merlot. Neither of us spoke for the longest time, then Gabrielle pointed at a tall fellow with prematurely graying hair. His T-shirt read: **NOTHING SCARES ME … I HAVE A DAUGHTER**

"Wonder if that's what gave him the gray hair?"

We laughed, then Gabrielle nodded at one of the pink taxis as it motored by. It had a bumper sticker which read: **DRIVER CARRIES NO CASH … HE'S MARRIED**.

We laughed again, then became suddenly sullen. We would miss the quirky sense of humor which flourishes in Key West.

That, and about a million other things.

Eventually, Gabrielle turned to me and did like Dawn French does, when she makes like she's coughing into her hands, but then says something critically important: "Maybe we shouldn't go back …"

"What? What? What did you say?"

"Just clearing my throat."

"No, no, you said something."

"Okay … who says we have to go back?"

"You're not serious, are you?"

"Nothing wrong with thinking about it."

"But we've told everybody that we're coming home, and we've given our notice at Villa Alberto."

"And?"

"There will be hell to pay if we don't go back."

"There was hell to pay last year when we didn't go back. We have experience with 'hell to pay'. We could make it a yearly event," Gabrielle drove home her sentiments.

I looked deep into Gabrielle's eyes and those eyes twinkled back … as they always did.

"What if we stay and you're arrested?"

"Is that what the nightmare and subsequent screams were about?"

"I screamed?"

"Repeatedly."

"I'm worried."

"I'm not running guns or smuggling Cubans into Florida, you know. I just overstayed my visa."

"By *six* months."

"It can't be that big of a deal."

"Does Krome mean anything to you?"

"I'm not that bothered."

'If you are nabbed, you will be frog-marched off to the Key West jail, not so lovingly referred to as the Stock Island Hilton. The accommodation will not impress and they don't offer the 3-ply quilted TP. Then you will be unceremoniously processed, cavity searched by someone who refuses to wear the latex gloves, and taken in a prisoner bus – like that one in the *CON AIR* movie with Nicolas Cage – up to the poorly air-conditioned Krome Detention Center, which is located in a Burmese python infested swampy suburb of Miami, might I add."

"Krome Detention Center?"

"The one and only. The overcrowded one where syphilitic staff offer release in exchange for sexual favors."

"Okay, you've got my attention."

"Because you're from Glasgow, you will be considered a flight risk. You won't be able to post an Immigration Bond. You will be thrown in a holding cell with Haitians, Mexicans, Guatemalans, Chinese and El Salvadorans. By the time I would be able to take the Greyhound Bus up there or locate Popcorn Joe or O.J. Dave ... or Dan Berger to give me a ride on the back of his black Harley Road King, you will be fluent in pidgin."

"Perhaps we should look into getting me legal. We could contact an immigration attorney?"

"No, most are scum and double-bill for sitting on the kludgie while making a phone call."

"True. What then? Can't exactly go up to the next Immigration Officer we see and ask how the whole thing works."

"You're married to me, so that must mean something."

Gabrielle gave me a look.

"You think that will *hurt* your chances?"

"I didn't say anything."

"But you were thinking it ..."

Neither of us spoke for a long time again, then I muttered. "You being illegal makes me nervous. Think we'd just better stick to our plan of going back home."

I looked at Gabrielle and she was unusually subdued. So I tried to cheer her up.

"Want to go up to the Garden of Eden and check it out?"

Gabrielle gave me a bad-dog look. "We haven't been there since our first day on the island nearly a year ago. Don't think I'm quite ready for a repeat visit."

Gabrielle flipped open her cell to check the time. "Let's have one for the yellow-brick, then we'd better get up to Cowboy Bills and pick up Mr. Leroy. He'll be finishing his shift soon."

I waved over to the cocktail waitress, but she was caught in a scrum of Parrot Heads on the other side, so I fought my way up to the bar and ordered a Merlot for Gabrielle and another Corona for me. With a smaller lime this time, so I could suck some of the beer out. What? What did you say? I'm not supposed to penetrate the bottle opening and leave it stuck in there? I watched the barmaid in action. She was like Air Traffic Control. She was taking orders and making change and chatting away to about 30 people all at the same time. And she was sober. I had never seen anyone working the bar in the Bull sober before. It was quite something to behold.

I paid for the drinks, thanked ATC and headed back to my seat. But someone had taken it. It was Popcorn Joe. And he was with some adorable blonde.

"Giuseppe!" I yelled. "Seventy-five!"

"We can't use that expression anymore," Popcorn Joe said somberly. "Folk in Stanley, Idaho, keep kicking the bucket and now the population is down to just 63."

"Good to know," Gabrielle said.

Popcorn Joe gestured to the young blonde. "This is Becky."

We introduced ourselves to Becky, then I asked: Brewski?"

"Why the hell not-ski," Popcorn Joe said.

"Absolute-ski," Becky said, smiling.

Right off, Gabrielle and I liked Becky. She had a smile that would thaw a glacier.

I went up to the bar and ordered Joe and Becky a beer-ski

and returned.

"Did you hear what the Soundman From Hell was talking about on the radio tonight?"

"Dengue fever?"

"No, that was two weeks ago."

"Genetically modified mosquitoes?"

"That was last week?"

"What then?"

"Something washed up out at Smathers Beach?" Popcorn Joe said.

"Let me guess," Gabrielle said. "Last year it was a bale of pot?"

"Smaller than that," Becky said.

"A kilo of coke?"

"Larger than that," Popcorn Joe said.

"We give in," Gabrielle and I intoned like children (or inebriated adults) do.

"A head."

"A head!"

"No ... body?"

"Nope, just the head."

"Christ, I think that has just sobered me up, and I was pretty much drunk everywhere."

"Except Poland," Gabrielle reminded me.

Popcorn Joe and Becky lapped at their beers, then we all turned our attention to a woman who was strolling by just outside our window.

"She looks like Nancy Pelosi," Popcorn Joe whispered.

"Looks like, but it's not," Gabrielle added. "This woman has to fly commercially."

Popcorn Joe continued: "They haven't been able to identify the head yet, for obvious reasons—"

"No fingerprints?" I said.

Popcorn Joe gave me a look. "You are quick aren't you?"

"Nothing gets by me."

"NO! That's not the reason."

"What then?"

"No teeth." Joe knocked back his beer.

"And there was just the one eye, Becky said. "Remember

41

the scene in *JAWS*... Ben Gardner?"

Gabrielle and I let this bit of beachy news settle in, then turned our attention back to Sallie. She was now kicking ass up on the stage with "A Horse with No Name."

But all I could think about was a dude with no head.

CHAPTER FOUR

By the time we left the Bull it was starting to get late, but you would never know that by walking down Duval Street. Unless the parade of drunks gave you a clue. Wait! There just might be a parade of drunks in the middle of the day, as well.

As we passed St. Paul's, across the street on the left, we heard a blood-curdling scream coming from the area of the graveyard behind the church.

Gabrielle gave me a look.

Then we heard another scream.

Then laughter.

"That would be David Sloan doing his Ghost Hunt."

"Like a ghost tour?"

"His is much more than that. He's taken the ghost *tour* to the next level—"

We heard another scream.

"See what I mean? Key West is usually considered just about the most haunted city in all of America. David was inspired when he went on a ghost tour in Edinburgh—"

"Scotland?"

"Oh, aye lassie, is there any other? Then he quit his job, moved to Key West and started the original ghost tour in 1996. He sold it six years later to pursue paranormal research."

"So, he's the real deal?"

"All that, plus some. He's evolved. He's got first-hand experience with Santeria and Voodoo and demonic possession and ghost communication. Even cleansing haunted locations."

"Holy crap."

"Took the words right out of my mouth. It's believed Key West's limestone foundation anchors spirits of the departed to the island. He uses more sophisticated gadgetry than you see on all those TV shows, very state-of-the-art. He has one gadget, a laser temperature gun that actually measures immediate temperature drops."

"Sounds like the type of guy you want on your side when supernatural trouble erupts?"

"Indeed. He's an author, as well, written about a million books about ghosts and Key West. Much to be gleaned and learned from that man."

"If only he could make a killer Key lime pie ..."

I gave Gabrielle a look. "You winding me up?"

"I do read, you know ..."

Just before we reached La Concha, Gabrielle motioned with her head. Coming toward us with a smile as wide as a slice of watermelon was Joke Man. We had been spotted! *This* Joke Man, by the by, is not to be confused with the "Dirty Joke Man" who now resides in the Stock Island Hilton for beating the living shit out of his live-aboard girlfriend. Anyway, *this* Joke Man, as was his wont, had his face painted like the Joker in Batman, and he was wearing his familiar sandwich boards, which, factoring the downturn of the economy into the equation proclaimed: "Jokes 25 cents ... I got cheaper ones but they're not as funny."

I looked over at Gabrielle and she was already pulling twenty-five cents out of her pocket. She handed over the quarter and the Joke Man's smile became wider, if that was physically possible.

Then he became very serious: "Mama mole and papa mole and baby mole were tunneling under a bakery. Mama mole says: "I smell cinnamon." Papa mole says: "I smell marzipan." Then they both turn back to baby mole and ask him what he smells. "I smell molasses!"

The Joke Man laughed heartily at his own joke. He was always his best audience.

Gabrielle leaned toward me. "Don't get it." Then we laughed heartily just like the Joke Man. No, we DIDN'T get it, but we didn't want him to get a complex and give up show business. He was one of earth's unusual creatures, but he was at least endeavoring to make a living. He wasn't panhandling, or selling heroin, or an immigration attorney, and for that we respected him.

We hurried up the street, past Margaritaville, and saw more of the usual suspects: The python wrangler, Iguana Man, two scantily clad babes in the cockatoo trade and "Feather."

Feather was a bearded transient (aren't they all? No, really, aren't they all?) who collected feathers from some of the grander birds of prey which call the Florida Keys home: ospreys, bald eagles, great horned owls, kites, Eurasian kestrels, peregrine falcons and turkey vultures. Feather displayed his feathers in a well-worn fedora.

"Isn't it past Feather's bedtime?" Gabrielle wondered out loud.

"Never seen him out this late. Perhaps he's on his way home?"

"On his way *bush*," Gabrielle corrected me.

You see, Feather didn't live in a house, or an apartment, or a trailer, or on a boat, or even in the back of an abandoned car. Feather resided in the bushes out in front of the Porter House, and he usually tucked himself in while the little arts-and-crafts businesses in the Porter Place garden were still open. And while folk were still sitting out on The Porch. Many transients repaired late and rose early, but it just wasn't something that Feather could adapt to. He needed his sleep. He went to bush early and often slept in. And this caused unbridled chaos for the keen-eyed tourists, you see, it wasn't unusual for an eager buyer to be standing in the open-air Gallery Uno selecting a print or oil painting of the Hemingway House from Alberto and be frozen in mid-purchase by the sight of a body, wearing a hat with feathers in it, lying in the bushes nearby, snoring.

At least, it wasn't just a head.

Most of the artists and other entrepreneurs in the "garden" endured Feather because all his daylight hours were spent with a broom in his hands, sweeping Duval Street from the corner of Caroline all along in front of the garden.

Feather loved Key West and it just killed him when people littered. But he'd found a way to slake his frustration: he took it out on the litter. It was not uncommon to see him giving a good tongue lashing to a rogue candy wrapper or cigarette butt some irresponsible schmuck had discarded. Perhaps a bit lacking in the mental health department, but the world a better place because of his dedication to litter control.

"What do they do with the homeless in Key West when

they die?" Gabrielle wondered out loud.

"They have an annual memorial service at the cemetery ..."

"How do you know that?"

"I do read, you know."

"Ha, ha. Learn something new about you every day."

"See ..."

"But the homeless don't just hang on and wait until the annual memorial service and then call it a day. So what happens to their bodies when they keel over?"

"I know that answer: they're cremated."

"Who pays?"

"The county."

"You are the proverbial fountain of knowledge. Then what?"

"The ashes are placed in vaults at the Key West Cemetery."

"Wonder how many there are each year ..."

"There were 53 last year, that included two infants."

"Homeless!"

"Well, no, only fourteen were homeless, the others didn't have anyone come forward to collect the bodies or, if there was family, there was no money to pay for the burial."

"Crikey."

"It runs about $900 for each individual. The county comes out and collects the body and searches for next of kin. If no one comes forward or there's no funds to pay for a proper burial, they take care of it all."

We let this unsavory tidbit sink in.

"The previous year there were 71 bodies."

"No one should have to die alone or be buried alone."

"Amen."

We carried on up Duval, weaving through devoted participants of the Duval Crawl, and followed a rather corpulent woman (and I mean that in the nicest way), who had a drink in each hand and was sporting a T-shirt which read:

**IF I EVER GO MISSING
I WANT MY PICTURE ON A 40 oz. BEER CAN
RATHER THAN A MILK CARTON,
BECAUSE I WANT FUN PEOPLE TO FIND ME**

Nothing wrong with this logic is what I was thinking, when I

46

looked up and we were standing in front of Cowboy Bills (which used to be the Mobster Lobster). Cowboy Bills is not your standard restaurant. Much of it is set in the open-air, which is appealing on an island where the average January temperature is right around 75 degrees. More importantly, the back door to the kitchen opened just beyond the end of the tropical lane where we lived.

We enter through the front door of the southernmost honky tonk in the US of A and wave at one of the Beer Tub bartenders. She smiles and waves back. Sitting nearby is a former bartender who worked here when this place was the Mobster Lobster. I will call him "Mitch" because that's his name. Mitch waves, as well, and smiles shyly back. He always wears T-shirts with great sayings that we had never seen before (see what I mean about T-shirts?). Tonight's read, on the front: **BODY OF BAYWATCH**. And on the back: "Can you please turn around, Mitch?" **FACE OF CRIMEWATCH**.

For those of you who were here with us in the last book, you may remember that Mitch had moved to Key West with his wife of five years. Shortly after arriving in the Keys, his wife fell in love and ran off with another -- woman. This dignity-busting, masculinity-destroying, scrotum-shriveling chain of events had given Mitch a serious dose of neuroses and, on account of that, he was now fitting into Key West as if he had grown up here.

We weren't at Cowboy Bill's tonight to listen to music, or for the biker-babe sexy bull riding (check the webcam!), or for the line dancing, or to eat rare steak, or drink cheap well drinks (as we had already killed off enough brain cells back at the real Bull), or watch future doctors in the form of University of Miami Med Students try some pole dancing, so Gabrielle and I slipped into the kitchen and greeted the cooks. The cooks in Cowboy Bills have to be the most docile, pleasant, of a sunny-disposition cooks on the planet. At least the ones who haven't been sacked for being grumpy and aggressive to the bar staff, waiters, waitresses and Cuban bussers.

A cook with a shaven head, impressive tattoos on his neck, and biceps to die for, looked up at us from his cheeky dish of repatriated steak as we came in: "Okie, dokie, Mr. Leroy, your mom and pops are here to take you home now."

47

One of the cooks offered us a joint, but we just picked up Mr. Leroy instead.

"How did he do, tonight?" Gabrielle asked.

"He worked the tables real well," came a crooked, albeit warm smile.

"Has he eaten?"

"Non-stop."

"Thanks for looking after him …"

"Pleasure, ma'am. Y'all walk carefully now."

Gabrielle and I said our goodbyes and stepped into Aronovitz Lane out behind the restaurant and let Mr. Leroy back down onto the ground.

"Wonder why Mr. Leroy comes home to sleep with us?"

"Because he adopted us and we've become family."

Aronovitz Lane was more of an alley, and it ran from Whitehead Street by the Green Parrot, past the Pig Man's house for about eighty yards, then it hung a right just past the man-with-one-leg's shack and spilled out on to Angela.

It took us twenty seconds to get home. This was about as long a commute as Mr. Leroy could tolerate. He wasn't designed for a big city.

Or a small city.

Only an island.

A small one.

As we entered the back gate at Villa Alberto, I cast my mind back to when we first met Mr. Leroy. We had just moved out of the attic at Popcorn Joe's and were thrilled to have our own little home, even though it had formerly been a WWII military barracks. To celebrate our good fortune of having moved out of an attic apartment that we couldn't stand upright in, into a military barracks about as wide as the submarine in the movie *Das Boat*, Gabrielle and I had celebrated by splashing out and going to dinner at a restaurant on Duval called, yes, you are so clever, Cowboy Bills.

And it was here that we found Mr. Leroy.

Or should I say, he found us.

Mr. Leroy was a black alley cat with a white moustache and white spats, and he worked the dinner crowd. As the dining area was more of a jungle than the type of restaurant that most of us grew up patronizing, no one seemed to mind that it had a resident cat. Resident cat in Key West meant no resident rats.

The restaurant's location had been an attractive consideration. We could consume alcohol and not have to use our bikes to convey back home. You can pretty much stagger around Key West with an open container in your hand, but you'd better not ride a bike. Folk get arrested in Key West for riding a bike, tipsy.

We opened the back door to Villa Alberto and stepped into the kitchen. In the summer we usually stepped into a furnace as the heat never seemed to be able to escape the island with the heat index somewhere between OMG and WTF, but in winter, Villa Alberto was like living in a 15th century castle. I'm talking about the cold, not the opulent, historical décor. We didn't have any heating. Many places in Key West don't have any means of heating.

Gabrielle and I slipped through the kitchen which led to the bathroom which led to our bedroom and Mr. Leroy was already feigning sleep in the middle of our bed.

"How did he get past us?" Gabrielle asked. "Does he have has his own key?"

"Want to sleep in the hammock tonight?"

"THAT is a great idea. We'll leave the back door open in case Mr. Leroy wants to come out and join us."

I pulled the hammock out of a closet in the living room and strung it between two palm trees out back in our leafy garden. In the summer we spent most nights in the hammock as it was just too stuffy inside Villa Alberto. Tonight was mild, a bit humid even for January and the stars hung large and bright in the sky. A perfect night for the hammock. Sleeping in a hammock, at least until the Key West roosters wake you, was a glorious experience and it almost felt as if you were on a permanent holiday.

Gabrielle and I climbed up in the hammock and we said our goodnights. Coming from Snake's house next door, we could hear the radio. The Soundman From Hell was talking to Sheri Pogue about the washed-up head. The conversation got a bit rude, something about "giving or getting good head." At least that's how I remember it.

Then the Soundman From Hell did the weather and played

a short blast of Paul Anka's "Put Your Head On My Shoulder."

Hilarious.

Soon after, we felt a small furry lump as Mr. Leroy settled down in between us.

"Jon?"

Snore.

"Are you asleep?" Whispered now.

Snore.

"Are you really asleep?"

"No, just messing with you."

"I want to take Mr. Leroy back with us to Glasgow."

CHAPTER FIVE

I had twisted, certifiable dreams (read: disturbing-in-need-of-psychological-counseling nightmares) *again*, but these weren't about Gabrielle being frog-marched off to the hoosegow, they were about staying in Key West, asking our piss-poor buffoon/landlord if we could stay in Villa Alberto even though we had already given our notice and him saying "Forget it!"

Then the storyline got worse, with exceedingly few cliffhangers at the end of each chapter. It was about swinging him about by the testicles, and murdering him (Death by Chicken), and *his* head washing up on the beach on the south side of the island.

When I awoke in the morning, reality set in and it was obvious we'd have to go back to Scotland, but we really needed that deposit. The deposit was six-hundred dollars and with the exchange rate being awful with the Scottish pound (yes, not the *British* pound) and the fees we would have to pay, we would only end up with about three-hundred pounds sterling. Not tons of dosh, but we would need every last penny to get set up all over again, and now I was agonizing over if we would get it back.

And what were we going to do for jobs back in Scotland? Couldn't exactly sell Sunset Photographs (as the sun has been known to play a bit hard to get), or work in a clothing-optional guest house, or do Jet-ski tours on the river Clyde through the Glasgow city center.

But we needed to go back. Immigration was coming down harder and harder on illegals. Just before Christmas, when everyone was at their least defensive enjoying the holiday -- spirits -- Immigration had made one of their famous sweeps along Duval scaring the living shit out of half of the patrons at Cowboy Bill's, Sloppy's, the Hog's Breath, Rick's, the Bull and Fat Tuesday.

And one at La Te Da.

To make matters worse, Immigration was not only arresting the Poles and Czechs and Germans and Hungarians, they were now going after the many illegal Britons.

Just before dawn, while Gabrielle and Mr. Leroy were still asleep, I slipped out of the hammock (try slipping out of a hammock sometime without waking up your spouse -- or cat). I went into our kitchen and made coffee using Bustelo Cuban coffee (*"El sabor que no se detiene"*). I used a French press and I'm fairly sure you can be arrested in some countries for doing that: making Cuban coffee with a French press.

I went into our office. Our office never saw the light of day. It was a room that had the same amount of light, whether it be night or day. I fired up the oscilloscope and quickly checked my emails. I had two: one was from a literary agent in London who said my crime thriller was "too gritty," the other was from a literary agent in New York who said my book "wasn't gritty enough."

I blew out my cheeks, then Googled "DENGUE FEVER," as I needed something to lighten my mood. This is what I found out: Dengue fever is a mosquito-borne, infectious tropical disease transmitted NOT by all mosquitoes, rather *specific* species of mosquito.

And, are you ready, dengue has recently re-established itself in Key West for the first time since 1934. It's not a strain that someone brought back in their carry-on luggage from the Caribbean or Central America, it's a strain that's evolved its own genetic fingerprint and is unique to Key West. What this means is that when there was an outbreak in 2010, it wasn't contracted abroad, but right here in Florida.

Now, before you panic and change your holiday plans, might I just point out that the Monroe County Health Department says there has not been a confirmed case of dengue in Key West since November 2010, and we know they're telling us the truth, so no worries there.

In case you're wondering what it would be like to contract dengue, check out these symptoms: flu-like fever (mild to high), rash, severe headache, pain behind the eyes, muscle and joint pain. The joint pain can be so severe and debilitating that dengue has been given the name "break-bone fever" because it feels like your bones are splitting. Nausea, vomiting, and loss of appetite are also common. In the more severe form, sometimes called dengue hemorrhagic fever (DHF), blood vessels start to leak and cause bleeding from the nose, mouth, and gums. Without prompt treatment, the blood vessels can collapse, causing shock (dengue shock syndrome) and ultimately death. There is no vaccine for dengue (although one is being presently tested) and there is no cure. You contract it, and you may not die, but you are in such extreme misery, you wish you would.

In 2009, a 34-year-old woman from Rochester, New York, caught dengue while vacationing in Key West (up until then, she had been having a lovely holiday). Including the Rochester woman, there were 28 cases of dengue reported in Key West by the end of 2009. Then in 2010, there were 63 locally-acquired cases in Key West, one in Broward County, and one in Miami-Dade County.

The CDC reports that about 5 percent of the Key West community has been exposed to dengue, but they only tested 240 residents. Hmmm, talking to 240 out of 25,000 and publishing results, what do you think? Fair? Unfair? Crying wolf?

As I've mentioned, this shouldn't put you off paying a visit to Cayo Hueso, but you might want to give Puerto Rico a miss. As I write this, Puerto Rico reported over 5,000 cases just in 2012.

FYI: The word "dengue" is a Spanish attempt at the Swahili phrase *ki denga pepo* which describes a cramp-like seizure.

It is only the female mosquitoes that bite, and no they are not dining on us, rather they need the "blood meal" to nurture their larvae.

The only way to control the disease, is to control the mosquito: *Aedes aegypti*. And perhaps his cousin: the Asian tiger mosquito, *Aedes albopictus*. Just as there's beer and then there's *beer*, there are mosquitoes and *mosquitoes*. There are 45 species of mosquitoes in Key West, (75 species in Florida) but only those two are bent on giving you dengue fever. Unlike the mosquitoes you grew up with in the Great White North, the mosquitoes that carry the dengue virus do most of their biting during the day, but may on occasion bite early in the evening. This could put an

53

itchy damper on Happy Hour, but then there's always DEET.

So, what can we do about this?

We can spray the shit out of them, but this is having less and less of an effect as they become resistant to pesticides.

We can unleash thousands of genetically modified *male* mosquitoes. These sterile males will only mate with females of the *same species*, so those other 43 "good" mosquito species won't be directly affected. For a multitude of reasons, many of them valid, a percentage of Key West residents are not thrilled with this plan of action until further research is done.

We can ensure there is no standing water in and around our homes like old cisterns, birdbaths, untreated pools, plant pots, backed-up drainpipes, gutters, a pet's water bowl (change frequently, at least once a week, the dog or cat would like it done *daily*, BTW) and even old tires. A container even as small as a beer cap is enough for a female mozzie to lay down her eggs.

We can slap on a bit more bug spray (with DEET or Picaridin) when we sit at an outdoor bar where mosquitoes just love to dive bomb the legs from beneath the barstools.

We can avoid wearing dark clothing. Mosquitoes do use eyesight to take a peek at us and they are attracted to black, red, blue, this means they are attracted to colors "contrary to nature."

We can avoid drinking beer. WTF?!? Thought I might get that response from you. Sadly, the little losers find us more appealing when we drink beer (most alcohol, really), because our skin chemistry changes.

Mosquitoes are also attracted to movement, *larger* people, lactic acid from our sweat glands, uric acid and, get ready, cholesterol on our skin. Yes, you heard right. They are also attracted to the carbon dioxide we emit and can sniff us from up 163 feet away.

And ... are you ready again? They just love *pregnant* women. About TWICE as much. Pregnant women exhale more CO2 ... and their abdomens have a warmer temperature. Mosquitoes are attracted to heat.

Mosquitoes like Type O blood twice as much as Type A.

And mosquitoes like our feet a bunch, but they love our hands about TEN times even more than our feet.

Only about one in ten of us is deemed juicy enough for a

mosquito to give us even a second glance, and it's mostly only the non-dangerous "black salt marsh" mosquito that bites everyone down here in Key West, so as I said, I don't want to put any of you off paying a visit to the end of the world.

Mosquitoes have been around for 170 million years, so they aren't going anywhere any time soon.

The bottom line here is this, there's a lot we can do ourselves while decisions are being made that we will either agree with or disagree with.

And remember, you have a much greater chance of falling off a bar stool or succumbing to alcohol poisoning than contracting dengue in Key West.

So come on down!

I checked my immediate area for mosquitoes then took a sip of my coffee and blew out my cheeks again. Now I was in the right frame of mind for my next area of research, so I Googled: "APPLYING FOR U.S. CITIZENSHIP."

The first thing I read froze me in my Google tracks. It essentially stated that you may not apply for residency *in* the U.S. unless you are *outside* of the country. And this was bad news. We certainly couldn't afford to *leave* the country just so we could apply to *stay*. And what if they didn't let us back in? And what were we supposed to do with all our *stuff* in Key West?

And what about Mr. Leroy?

I went back to the computer and Googled BRINGING A CAT INTO THE UNITED KINGDOM. The first thing that came up was about QUARANTINE: "Fearing the importation of rabies and other animal diseases, Britain has some of the strictest importation laws in the world. Virtually all mammals, apart from horses and farm livestock, are subjected to a six-month quarantine period in an approved kennel." Hmmm, I didn't like the looks of this. Then it got worse: the cost of an approved kennel was in the region of two-hundred pounds a month. Two-hundred pounds a month for six months. We wouldn't be able to afford that.

I went into the kitchen, sipped my coffee and peeked out the back window. Gabrielle and Mr. Leroy were still curled up in the hammock. How was I going to break the news to Gabrielle that we couldn't take Mr. Leroy back with us? No, the money wasn't the reason, although that would set us back, the six-months' quarantine was the reason. How many years do cats live? How old was Mr. Leroy? I didn't know for sure, but one thing I did know was that six months out of a cat's life was asking too much.

I took another sip of my coffee. If you ever want motivation in the morning, pour yourself a cup of Cuban ambition. I returned to the oscilloscope and Googled like crazy. After about ten minutes, I unearthed a recent innovation called the PET TRAVEL SCHEME. With this new scheme, you could bring your dog, cat, rabbit or "rodent" into the U.K. That's what it said: *rodent*. Who takes a rodent with them on holiday? Who needs to? If you go on a cruise ship, they provide them.

Can you imagine passing through customs? "Anything to declare?"

"Well, I do have this pet … his name is Ben."

I delved deeper into the rules and regulations governing the Pet Travel Scheme: We would have to get a chip implanted into Mr. Leroy and get him a little Pet Passport, which would detail vaccinations and other veterinary palaver. But there were a few catches, Mr. Leroy would only be able to travel on specified air, rail and sea routes. A *cat*amaran, I'm thinking.

And not all countries were signatory to this scheme. I quickly searched the list of countries, and there it was, the USA, but it stated rather clearly USA (mainland). Oh, oh, nobody who lived in Key West considered the island part of the mainland, in fact when they traveled up to Miami, they said they were "going up to the mainland" or "going up to America."

"Morning …"

I turned and saw my cheery better-half standing in the doorway of our office. She had Mr. Leroy in her arms.

"Y'know, I've decided that I really don't mind returning to Scotland, now that we've decided to take Mr. Leroy back with us…"

CHAPTER SIX

"We hear you're going back to Glasgow ..."

Gabrielle and I were watching the Cat Man's show. We didn't have enough seniority to secure one of the fifty spots on the pier, so another night of not making any money.

Dominique's cats were prancing over the backs of three enchanted children who had been picked out of the crowd and pressed into show business. So as not to interrupt the Cat Man's act, we led Don and Shirley over to the water's edge.

"How did you hear that?" Gabrielle asked.

"Popcorn Joe. He hears all, knows all."

We all sat on the edge of the dock and let our feet dangle down toward the water. It was a warm evening for January with the temperatures still in the upper seventies. None of us spoke as the sun slipped from the sky, then squatted on the horizon for a moment before disappearing over the backside of the earth. Everyone around us applauded and we could hear somebody blowing a conch shell from neighboring Mallory.

I glanced over at Gabrielle and she was smiling one of her great smiles. We had been so happy here in Key West. It had been different than any other place we had ever been to. Shame we had to go.

Gabrielle motioned with her eyes down toward the water. I gave her a questioning look. Then I realized she wasn't motioning down at the water, she was motioning at Don's feet. He had the tannest feet we had ever seen.

Don was intuitive and he picked up on what we were doing. "Haven't worn socks in 23 years. Don't even have a sock drawer."

Something to our right breached our attention. It was Fish Man. He was chumming the waters with popcorn, preparing for his last show of the evening.

"Didn't know he had been released," Don said.

"Released?"

"He was thrown in jail for trying to untie a cruise ship *again.*"

Everyone turned toward me.

"What? Everyone makes mistakes."

We looked back at Fish Man for a moment. He had an uncanny way of being entertaining and frightening all at the same time. Presently he was getting in the face of a group of beer swilling snowbirds. Presumably they had taken offense to being told to "Fuck off and go back up north!"

Don turned toward us. "Want to go over to Turtle Kraals and drink until we run out of money?"

Gabrielle and I laughed. Don had a wicked sense of humor and rapier wit.

"I'm not joking," he said.

"Whose money are we going to be using?" Gabrielle asked.

"Ours," Shirley said.

"Yes, ours," Don added. "There's something I want to ask you two …"

"Let's fly," Shirley coaxed, "or we'll be late for the turtle races."

"And the alcohol luge run," Don added.

"The what?"

"The alcohol luge run. They have a block of ice with a miniature luge run etched out of it. The bartender pours an amount at the top of the block of ice, which is on an angle, and then you sit, mouth open, at the bottom…"

"They do this sort of thing?" Gabrielle asked.

"Onward," Don said. "It's time to educate."

A fight was breaking out on the pier between two drunks as we wended our way through the crafts folk, past Buschi and Claudia and Joanne and Larry. We waved at Popcorn Joe who was scooping fresh popcorn into the maw of the bag for Adrienne Coppola. Adrienne had Popcorn Joe in stitches.

"Must be trying out one of her jokes."

"Does she write them herself?"

"Don't know, but if she doesn't, she's got a very fresh source. I've never heard any of them. What was that one she had

58

about a charity?"

"Oh, you mean the one where she said she was holding a fundraiser for people who couldn't reach orgasm and anyone who couldn't come should let her know?"

Laughing, we slipped past the Statue Man and bowling Ball Frank balancing a shopping cart on his face and Dale the Sword Swallower and the escape artist who had yet again gone blue in the face.

We curled around O.J. Dave and his juice cart, and O.J. gave us a smile, then we cut down Wall Street, Front Street, stopped for a moment near the Conch Seafood Farm to listen to Dani Hoy singing "DRUNK ON MALLORY SQUARE" (with Cheryl on the steelpan), then we turned right on Simonton, left on Green and slipped into the lane at Lazy Way. It was a glorious night to be strolling and the streets were heaving with colorful folk in various stages of undress and deteriorating levels of sobriety. Halfway down Lazy Way we overtook the legendary Barry Cuda, who was pushing his pianimal over to B.O.'s Fishwagon. Barry was chatting animatedly with Ken Ro making some reference to how Key West had a "piano path" and how pushing a piano through the streets in Key West was much like skiing downhill. I can't remember Barry Cuda's exact words, but they were something like "It's kind of like skiing. Just a controlled fall. I'm falling forward right now."

We left Barry and Ken to their devices, and I turned to Don: "So what do you want to talk about?"

"We'd better order drinks first, before this place gets slammed. Turtle racing's a big draw."

We entered Turtle Kraals, found seats at the bar and looked around.

Isn't Turtle Kraals one of the most unique venues you've ever been to? Turtle *Kraals* takes its name from the Dutch African word for *corral*. Once upon a time, the building was used as a turtle cannery. Green turtles were in abundant supply back then and were a delicacy. The green turtles were caught just off Key West and then brought to the neighboring dock and kept alive in "kraals" until it was time to go to the cannery.

Believe it or not, the turtle industry somehow flourished in Key West until the early 1970s, which means many of you reading this right now were coming to Key West when this industry was still alive. Sadly, the green turtle is now on the endangered species list and fights for survival. If you get a chance the next time you are here, check out the many great photos of green turtles throughout the restaurant.

As Turtle Kraals mentions: "Green turtles are rare and beautiful creatures to see, and if you're lucky enough, you just might spot one in the waters off Key West. Thanks to conservation measures, wildlife rescue and hatchling programs, the green turtle population has substantially increased."

A bartender with an independent eye, who looked like he stepped out of the movie "Escape From New York" approached and undressed Gabrielle and Shirley with his eyes.

"Evenin', folks, what can I do you for?"

"Alcohol," Don quickly responded.

"I got you covered," the bartender replied, tongue flicking, and then he disappeared.

"How does he know what we want?"

"Even I'm wondering that," Shirley said.

"He's clairvoyant," Don said.

"Carnivorous, I'm thinking," Gabrielle said.

The bartender returned with four beers and four shots. "Bottoms up," he chirped, and I don't think he was referring to the drinks.

"What's this?" Shirley asked. "Beer?"

"Yours is coming, that's for Jon."

Might I just interrupt this chapter for a moment and take you aside? It seems that ever since I wrote the first KEY WEST book, everyone seems to think I'm a pisshead, but in reality, I'm just like you. No, I didn't just call you a pisshead, what I mean to say is, I enjoy the odd beer or glass of wine when I go out and, in reality, I'm a cheap drunk. You're not buying this, are you?
**AUTHOR'S SOTTO VOCE NOTE: In defense of beer, I must admit that I've done some really stupid things while sober.

I looked back over at the four beers and the four shots and they were gone. "What happened to the beers and depth charges?"

"That wasn't for us. Here it comes."

Eyeing Gabrielle and Shirley, Mr. Independent Eye placed

two glasses of Merlot on the transom in front of them, then a Michelob in front of me and some lethal looking tropical concoction in front of Don. "This is something new I whipped up, Don, why don't you test drive that!"

"Think I just might drink it right off the showroom floor."

The bartender slipped off to help three college co-eds who looked as if they were trying to get a leg up on Spring Break by coming down to Key West three months early.

Don made a toast ... of sorts: "Hurry up and drink before he takes them back. Down the hatch and up yours!"

Shirley took a sip of her wine. "Lay claim."

"So, what do you want to talk to us about?"

"Ah, there's enough time to talk about that later. Drink up. Want another?"

I looked at my Mich. I'd only taken one slurp.

"Hey, bartender!" Don yelled good naturedly. "What d'ya think Jon is a fucking camel? Get him another Mich!"

Turtle Kraals—a great place to have a drink or three and it's a great place to have dinner. They serve gloriously refreshing appetizers with fetching names, such as: Bucket of Bones (spareribs), Deep Dish Nachos (a skillet of refried beans and melted cheese served with a splat of sour cream, *pico gallo* and black olives), Flash Fried Calamari (parmesan dusted, served with tangy Key lime aioli), Peel and Eat Shrimp (shrimp that we get to, well, peel and eat). And there are *mucho* entrées on offer, as well, such as: Dolphin Picatta (char-grilled dolphin with lemon caper sauce, served with rice and sautéed vegetables ... **BTW**: this is not Flipper, this is Mahi Mahi, (Flipper is our friend, we do NOT eat our friends), Best of the Bay (shrimp, Florida lobster, grilled scallops, served with steam vegetables and grilled corn).

And dessert: Key Lime Pie (orgasmic).

Besides the mouth-watering bill of fayre, the place is dark and moody and backwater and end-of-the-world, and it really is our kind of place.

Don ordered a Bucket of Bones, presumably so holding a glass would be an exercise in dexterity.

"How's your new house?" Gabrielle asked.

"It's great," Shirley said. "We're starting to get some

61

lucrative illegal rentals and Captain Jerry has been keeping a low profile.

FYI: Captain Jerry lived in the crawl space at Don and Shirley's. He kept trim by not wasting good beer money on things like food.

Don and Shirley's two-story conch house, which they built themselves, had been a lesson in jumping through narrow, sometimes flaming, hoops. After scouring the Old Town, they had found a swatch of land (no easy trick) on Sawyer Lane, just behind Pepe's. Don had had to go in front of a worryingly somber city council and present his case on why he should be allowed to build in a part of the Old Town where few permits were being granted. In an attempt to impress, Don had worn a suit jacket and tie. Rumor had it he won over the city on account of his mellifluous vocal delivery and the fact he had worn -- along with the suit jacket and tie -- Bermuda shorts.

Don and Shirley built their great conch house and even built the beds, using a Key West picket fence design for the headboards. Cool.

Well ... (this said while slurring), it was about three or four drinks -- and another bucket of wings -- later when Don whispered out the side of his mouth: "Soooo, we were thinking ... since you're going back to Glasgow ... Shirley and I were thinking that ... perhaps you could give us some clues about ... doing sunset photography.

"You're thinking about doing sunset photography on the pier?" Gabrielle asked.

"Thinking about it," Shirley said.

Well, why not, Don and Shirley were great people and like many people who had fallen in love with Key West, they were simply trying to improve their lot.

So we told them everything we knew: where to get the film developed so you would get a good deal ... where to throw all away all the terrible sunsets photos that they would take before they captured that one special shot. We even told them about our secret spot where we had captured our big seller "Blue Lagoon."

"You got THAT sunset THERE?" Don said.

"Only took us about a month of retina-burning frustration

to capture it."

Don was uncharacteristically subdued for a moment, then: "I could find pieces of driftwood and make the frames."

Gabrielle and I gave each other a look. THAT was a brilliant idea. They were already being wildly creative, plus Don was a master carpenter. If he could build a conch house, he could certainly build a picture frame.

Well, this particular early evening, became a late evening, and Turtle Kraals got wall-to-wall people and it was humid and sticky with heady smells and we laughed so much our ears bled and we really wondered what we were doing going back to Glasgow.

CHAPTER SEVEN

Gweko posted this on Facebook this morning:

How to wash a cat:

1. Put both lids of the toilet up and add 1/8 cup of pet shampoo to the water in the bowl.
2. Pick up the cat and soothe him while you carry him towards the bathroom.
3. In one smooth movement, put the cat in the toilet and close the lid. You may need to stand on the lid.
4. The cat will self agitate and make ample suds. Never mind the noises that come from the toilet, the cat is actually enjoying this.
5. Flush the toilet three or four times. This provides a "power-wash and rinse."
6. Have someone open the front door of your home. Be sure that there are no women or small children between the bathroom and the front door.
7. Stand behind the toilet as far as you can, and quickly lift the lid.
8. The cat will rocket out of the toilet, streak through the bathroom, and run outside where he will dry himself off. Both the commode and the cat will be sparkling clean.

Sincerely,

The Dog

    I read through the posting again.

    Bad dog!

    Poor little cat.

    I looked over at Mr. Leroy. Mr. Leroy looked back at me.

    It was time to take him to the vet.

    We found an empty cardboard box, made some air holes and gently lifted Mr. Leroy up and placed him in the box. If cats can have subtext, then Mr. Leroy did. The look on his mustachioed face read: "If you even think about closing the lid on this box, I will rip your face off!"

Cats love to play with cardboard boxes. They dive into them, scoot sideways in them, turn them upside down and get caught inside … and that's all in good fun. And I've never seen it piss them off. But when you need to take a cat to the vet, it's a different story. They sense the box is there for nefarious purposes. They sense they are on their way somewhere, where someone in a white coat will be sticking, poking and prodding them in orifices they do not wish to be stuck, poked and prodded.

Gabrielle placed a little kitty treat in the bottom of the box and I quickly closed the lid. That would work! It was the same as the "self-agitating cat" or not unlike throwing a lit match into a five-gallon can of gasoline. Like a volcano exploding, a tiny kitty fist shot through the top of the box, followed by the face of the snarling hissing cat from hell. Gabrielle and I both jumped back, startled that our little adorable Mr. Leroy had just become a toothy gremlin like the one that got chucked in the microwave in the movie and didn't take it lightly.

Now, Mr. Leroy had just his head sticking out of the box with a collar of cardboard. He looked like one of those fat ladies who would get into an old-fashioned weight-loss steam box with just the head protruding.

"He doesn't like to be closed up in a box," I said.

"You have a knack for stating the obvious," Gabrielle said. "I'll just carry him in my arms."

"But we were going to take the bus out to the vet's. They won't let you on if he's not in a box."

Gabrielle and I gave this some thought.

"There's only one thing to do when trouble erupts in paradise," Gabrielle said.

"Call Popcorn Joe!" we both said at the same time.

Popcorn Joe had just returned from rollerblading around the island and he was always happy to help. Plus he had three cats and he knew the ins and outs of dealing with incensed felines.

Joe pulled up in his old red van and saw us standing there holding Mr. Leroy.

"What a little angel," Joe said, stroking the top of Mr. Leroy's head. Mr. Leroy purred. "Glad you called me and didn't try to take him out there on the bus. That would have been *cat*astrophic!"

Laughing, we climbed in the truck. Popcorn Joe driving, Gabrielle and Mr. Leroy riding shotgun, me sitting between the seats on an overturned milk crate.

"This won't take long," Joe said.

And do you know what? Popcorn Joe was right, the second he cranked the engine over, the cat from hell returned. Mr. Leroy exploded out of Gabrielle's arms, scratching her, rocketed around the van at hyper-warp speed like those motorcycles used to race around a cage at a seaside fair, and then he peed on a mattress that was in the back.

"He doesn't like to travel," Popcorn Joe duly noted.

* * *

Popcorn Joe knew a good vet. They had been friends for years, so the vet made a special house call. And Mr. Leroy was as good as gold. He was on his own turf, in the comfort of his own home, with the bed or the hammock just a short leap away.

The vet started by injecting a microchip in the scruff of Mr. Leroy's neck. Mr. Leroy opened his mouth in a little silent cry, but refrained from mauling the vet. Then the vet gave him a thorough physical and various injections, and filled out a bunch of forms.

"This will be his Pet Passport," the vet said. The vet had an accent like Victor Laszlo in *CASABLANCA*. "When you get back to U.K., these are five rules to remember: Number One, set up room that's quiet, away from anything that may stress cat like noise or dogs or children. Put food, water and kitty litter box in there. Throw in some toys. Take cat bed, or towel that cat sleeps on and knows—"

Gabrielle interrupted. "He doesn't have a cat bed or towel. He sleeps on the bed with us. If it's cold, he creeps under the covers or gets around my neck ..."

The vet stared dumbly at us for a moment, then turned back to his notes: "Number Two, once settled in new house, allow cat to explore new environment. Let cat get used to sniffing new home."

"I do pretty much do the same thing," I said.

The vet regarded me for a moment. "Sense of humor is different over there?"

I just smiled back.

"Number Three, do not let cat outdoors unsupervised for few weeks or cat may try to return to last house—" The vet stopped and looked over at Mr. Leroy. Mr. Leroy was sitting there listening with rapt attention to everything the vet said.

"When time comes for going out, take some of cat's bedding ... or in your case the kitty litter, and spread around outside, near garden, around backyard, just make sure you put it out there. If he gets lost, he will smell the litter and know it is his—"

"But then he wouldn't be lost ... I mean ... if he could smell the litter ..." Gabrielle said.

The vet forged on: "Other cats in neighborhood will know this is now his turf as well."

"Or Mr. Leroy will rip their whiskers out one by one," Gabrielle said.

"Number Four, when cat is ready to go out, you can either place cat on cat leash and harness. Then walk with cat to area where you sprinkled litter and let cat smell it. This way cat will know tiny, damp Victorian apartment without garden -- we have sense of humor, as well -- is new home. Make sure cat stays in house for at least week so it can get comfortable.

"Having said that, still keep eye on cat."

Gabrielle and I thanked the vet for his treatise without the use of many definite articles. Then we thanked Popcorn Joe. After the two of them left, Gabrielle and I looked around.

"But cat, I mean, Mr. Leroy still doesn't like to travel. If he can't handle a box, he won't be able to handle a portable kennel. If he can't survive two minutes in the car, how will he ever manage a flight to Miami, change of planes, a flight to London, change of planes, a flight to Glasgow, clear Customs and Immigration, and a half-an-hour taxi ride home?"

"Where's Mr. Leroy?"

We looked outside. We looked in all the places he liked to hang out: the hammock, the shade beneath the larger palm tree, under the plumeria bush. Finally we found him in the middle of our bed, sound asleep.

"Poor little beggar," Gabrielle sighed, "It's been a rough day for him."

"I have a headache," I said. "I need a coffee."

"How about with cinnamon?"

"Or marzipan."

"Or molasses."

Gabrielle and I looked at each other and burst out laughing. We had just got the Joke Man's Joke: "I smell mole asses!"

CHAPTER EIGHT

This just in:

The head that had washed up on the beach on the south side of the island was at first thought to belong to a little-known porn actor murdered in Miami Beach the previous week. But when local authorities were informed that the fledgling porn actor had bleached-white hair and the, ah, beached head was clearly that of a brunette, all communiqués were revised.

Reports now pointed to the head belonging to a Cuban "rafter." Five Cubans had died at sea during an attempt to escape from the Communist island in a poorly constructed vessel made of foam blocks and inner tubes, while another 18 who had been jammed into the same "boat" were rescued by the Cuban army and nearby oil workers. The boat capsized in treacherous seas, killing four Cubans. It was theorized that the fifth Cuban nearly made it to Key West, hanging on to the stern of the capsized boat. In an attempt to right the boat and climb back onboard, the rafter was decapitated by a motor which unfortunately sputtered back to life.

No one knows where the now headless corpse will wash up.

The incident has not been off-putting for the thousands of snowbirds who are free to travel where they wish, when they wish, and have come down to Key West to capture a winter tan and take advantage of all the freedoms most Cuban rafters could only dream about.

The other 18 Cubans who were rescued -- the youngest being three and the eldest being 80 -- were taken back to Cuba to hospitals in Havana and Matanzas. The rafters had slipped away from the northern province of Artemisa and had been fighting currents in the Florida Straits for three days. A joint effort by the Revolutionary Armed Forces and the Interior Forces were in the process of conducting an aerial search along the northern coast for possible survivors or bodies. But rumor had it they weren't looking so very hard.

These brave Cubans who did not die at sea, will probably now die in a Cuban prison for seeking something that we all take for granted.

There was a time that an average of six Cubans a day died trying to escape the island. Plus 30 Cubans have been killed in the past year while attempting to seek asylum at the Guantanamo Naval base -- either shot by Cuban soldiers or killed by landmines -- while a record 831 Cubans have made it safely to the base.

FYI: United States Naval Station Guantánamo Bay, which is -- as you know -- often called Gitmo or GTMO or G-Bay, is located on Cuba's southeast coast (facing Haiti and Jamaica), on the shore of exceedingly picturesque Guantánamo Bay. The naval base is huge: 45-square miles of land and bay that was originally leased for use as a coaling/fueling station following the Cuban-American treaty of 1903. The base is the oldest existing Navy Base outside of U.S. territory, and the only one in a country with which the United States does not have diplomatic relations.

As you know, the Cuban government is not so very thrilled to have a U.S. presence there. They claim the lease is invalid under international law as Cuba was not a sovereign nation at the time of the signing. The U.S. counters with this being a moot point because Cuba ratified the lease post-revolution, and with full sovereignty, when it cashed one rent check.

As you also are aware, since 2002, when the Bush administration established it, the U.S. government has used Guantanamo Bay as a detention center for detainees in its never-ending war on terror. This allows the guv'mint to maintain a controversial detainment and interrogation base that would be deemed illegal if it were located on the U.S. mainland.

The naval base at Guantánamo is strictly off-limits to Cubans and foreign tourists, but you can get a great view of the entire base from the surrounding hills at Mirandar de Maknes.

WHAT NOBODY WILL TELL YOU: On 6 February, 2014, "Skinny Puppy," the band that paved the way for Marilyn Manson, sent a bill to the devilish tune of $666,000 to the

Pentagon after learning that its music was being used as a *form of torture* during interrogations at Guantanamo Bay. "We sent them an invoice for our musical services considering they had gone ahead and used our music without our knowledge and used it as an actual weapon against somebody," Cevin Key, one of the band's founding members explained in an interview with *CTV News*. "I wouldn't want to be subjected to any overly loud music for six to 12 hours at a time without a break," he continued, adding that the band members were "offended" that their music was being used to "inflict damage."

They learned about the interrogation tactics from a former Guantanamo Bay guard.

The former guard is a fan.

CHAPTER NINE

Gabrielle and I decided to ride our bikes out to where the head was found, and the sun was bright and warm, so we pedaled out to Higgs Beach.

Higgs Memorial Beach is a favorite hangout for locals. Probably because it has all the nostalgic charm of a laid-back Key West setting. If you wish to partake of it, there's "Yoga on the Beach" on Saturdays, concrete picnic tables with nifty paintings on the supports which hold up the little roofs, beach chairs and umbrellas, volleyball courts, grills for cooking out, a bicycle path, a restaurant *right* on the beach for slaking thirst and hunger, FREE tennis courts (imagine that!) and a sunning pier.

We spotted Dani Hoy and Chris Rehm walking the whippets along the water's edge. Reverend Gweko readying to perform a marriage ceremony, his second that week. The Bongo D Band playing, setting a steelpan, Trinidadian mood. We also saw a few elderly Cuban gentlemen playing dominoes under one of the beach huts. A transient using one of the picnic tables as his "office." Two other transients occupying two other picnic tables, using them as places of repose.

"There!" Gabrielle pointed.

Over near the AIDS Memorial by the White Street Pier, a forensic tent was set up. Is this where they found the head?

I spied a cop I knew from when I had been arrested the previous January, so we parked our bikes and leaned them against a palm tree. Gabrielle stayed with the bikes so they wouldn't get nicked by some of the cheery and chatty dirt-bags who slept on or near the beach and showered at the communal showers.

And so she wouldn't be bringing attention to herself from the police, even though Immigration was our real concern and the two departments weren't big on sharing information.

I greeted the cop, knowing he wouldn't remember me.

"Untied any cruise ships lately?"

"Very funny, but no, I've gone straight. I've turned my life around."

"You're here about the head, right?"

"No! Well, yes …"

"For the love of God, you're worse than a bunch of rubber-neckers on the highway."

"I'm writing my second crime novel."

"What's that supposed to mean?"

"It means that I need to be around gore and the police to see if I can pick up any inspiration."

"Let me guess: Your book will be filled with gratuitous sex and violence …"

"Well … yes. It's set in Key West and Glasgow."

"Glasgow, Kentucky?"

"No, Glasgow, Scotland. So is this where you found the head?"

"No, that was over by Smathers Beach."

"Then what do you have here?"

"Headless corpse. Wanna take a peek?"

"You serious?"

"No, I'm not serious, buttfuck. We're the police. We're supposed to protect the corpse and honor the dead."

"You shittin' me?"

"Yeah, amigo, I'm just jerking your chain."

"So, you think this headless corpse belongs to the head?"

"Well, let me turn the question around and ask you, Columbo. We found a head yesterday and a headless corpse today. Do you think there's a connection? Do you think we should try to match DNA? Perhaps try to screw the head back on and see if it fits? Any other questions?"

The cop just stood there for a long time, looking at me with a look of *Life's too short to deal with wastrels like you*. Having just said that, wastrel would not have been in his vocabulary of 300 words.

I felt a bit of a schmuck and didn't know what to say, so I just sort of blurted out: "Is there really a Glasgow in Kentucky?"

And then I headed back over to our bicycles to meet up

with Gabrielle.

"Did he recognize you?"

"Unfortunately."

Gabrielle motioned with her head to someone approaching. I turned to see the smiley face of Key West's renowned photographer Sheelman. Sheelman gave us a friendly wave and headed off in the direction of the pier, schlepping his photographic gear with him.

Gabrielle turned to me: "He's on assignment."

"Have you seen his work?"

"It's awesome, isn't? He has the eye of a tiger."

"He roams the island, really capturing the pulse of Key West. He's got this one shot of a storm coming in. You can almost feel the temperature and wind change."

We watched Sheelman stop to adjust his shoulder bag.

"What do you think," Gabrielle said. "Is he going to shoot the wedding or the crime scene?"

"I'm thinking head shots ..."

"So that leaves out the crime scene ..."

CHAPTER TEN

Gabrielle and I biked back over to Duval.

As we pedaled along, I hit a pothole and the wisdom tooth on the upper-right side exploded with pain. I had been here before with the little blighter. It had been terrorizing me off and on for the past ten years. Every time I went to the dentist -- which was too often as far as I was concerned -- he told me that I had to have it extracted.

"It will only get worse," he had said. "You don't want to wait until you're older," he had said. "It's impacted and it will wait until it's a holiday and all the dentist offices are closed, and all the dentists are out on their yachts that you've paid for -- and then it will strike like a viper on crystal meth." Perhaps not his exact words, but that's how I interpreted it.

"So, when can you remove it," I had asked.

"Oh, I won't touch that little bugger. Your Viva Las Vegas nerve, which is attached to the fringe-benefit synapses of the scrotum and general sense of well-being, runs right alongside the hair canal. If that nerve is severed, the right side of your face and lips will be frozen for the rest of your life."

"What about my scrotum?"

"Pardon me?"

"Is that likely to happen?"

"Is what likely to happen?"

"That my face will be frozen ..."

"Absolutely! It happened to my son. I wished I had advised him to never have the procedure."

So here I am now, riding my bike down Duval Street, over four-thousand miles from my family dentist (even more if there's heavy traffic on the Kingston Bridge in the Glasgow city centre and I have to go through Govan).

"Gabrielle, pull your bike over."

75

Gabrielle pulled her bike over in front of the old Fast Buck Freddie's and gave me a look.

"Is there a holiday coming up?"

"Yes. I think it's three days long. Everything will be closed except the bars, strip clubs, T-shirt shops and Conch Tour Train and Old Town Trolley."

"So, everything will be open ..."

"What are you trying to say?"

"What about dentists' offices?"

"Closed."

"Let's go visit Sheelman."

"Why?"

"He's got great teeth."

"What are you talking about?"

"Let's just go ..."

"He's busy."

"Popcorn Joe?"

"He's out on his boat with Becky."

"Alberto, then."

"What for?"

"Wanna ask him if he knows anyone."

"Alberto knows a lot of people ..."

"I mean a good dentist."

"Is it acting up again?"

"Killing me."

"But the nerve."

"I know."

We pedaled down to the "garden" and saw Alberto sitting at his easel painting "Mallory Square" during the Sunset Celebration.

"*Ciao, bello!*" Gabrielle yelled.

"*Ciao, bella!*" Alberto yelled back to Gabrielle.

We pulled our bikes up the few steps and leaned them against the banyan tree that governed the garden.

"Did you hear about head?" Alberto asked.

"We were just out there. It looks like a scene out of *CSI: Miami*, except without everyone wearing sunglasses on the cloudy days and suits in 90-degree heat. Say, you don't happen to know a good dentist, do you?"

Alberto gave me a funny look, then: "Oh, yes, I heard the head was found without any teeth."

"No, that's not what I meant, for me, not for the, uh, head."

"Oh, yes, I do know a dentist. Don't know how good he is."

I didn't like the sound of this, but then my tooth began to throb, big time.

"What's his name?"

"I write it down for you. He not listed anywhere."

CHAPTER ELEVEN

Key West might be the most unequivocally arresting place to live on the planet.

It's romantic. It's bacchanal. It's free-spirited. It's cultured. It's decadent. It's the end of the world. It's only 90 miles to Cuba (in actuality 94 statute miles). And it has a sense of danger and naughtiness. It's an island that is so funky and quirky and eccentric and eclectic that nothing ever surprises you.

Yet it always finds a way to do so.

An eyeball has washed up on the beach. No, not his. This is a gigantic eyeball the size of a softball, and it's clearly not human.

Even Marty Feldman would have been impressed.

Eyewitnesses (excuse the choice of words) speculate that it may have come from a whale or a giant squid or that squid-of-a-waitress down at that Cuban restaurant run by Mexicans who always gives you the eye when you don't leave a sizeable gratuity. You know the one.

Please, stay tuned ...

I went online to see if I could find out any arresting info, but found nothing but two emails from literary agents. One agent said my crime thriller *DEATH BY GLASGOW* was too gory, the other said I overused "close third person." I didn't even know what that meant, so I decided to do a rewrite and make it even gorier.

CHAPTER TWELVE

The dentist.

Popcorn Joe gave me a ride out to the New Town to a strip mall where the dentist was located. It was located next to a strip *club*. Is this why it's called a strip mall? In this case it was, I fear.

I'm sitting in the dentist's chair now. The dentist's chair is not where I like to spend a lot of time. I can honestly say that I can look back at all my visits to the dentist and the only fond memory I have is jumping up from the chair and running out the front door like the little boy in *HOME ALONE*, hands flailing the air, mouth open in stark terror.

Alberto's dentist doesn't speak English as a first language, or possibly a second, and I'm looking at that as a good thing. When he theatrically motions to the dental hygienist, his adoring wife, Cruzilla, and whispers something sinister like "Bring the jaws of life," it's in another language, an eastern European tongue, and I just don't get it. But I am wondering what curious sequence of events transpired for them to end up in Key West, FL, end of the line, last stop, no connection to Clarksville.

The dentist has now taken enough X-rays to match my roentgen count with that of those who used to live in the Fukushima province of Japan. I'm thinking of sticking a 40 watt bulb up my backside when I get home, *if* I get home, to see if I can illuminate it. The bulb, not my backside.

Now the dentist is probing with what I fear is the same instrument I saw used the last time I was at the proctologist's. Or was it the Home & Garden Show? It's an instrument that resembles a cross between a hoe and a javelin.

Only smaller.

And more pointy.

"Zee visdom teeth, she needs removing," he tells me.

"Ziss, I mean *this*, I'm already knowing," I respond.

He smiles at me, then says something in his foreign tongue to his wife/assistant which sounds suspiciously like "wanker."

Then he says: "The Viva Las Vegas nerve runs very close to the tooth, but I can extract it and not damage the nerve."

As he speaks, he gestures with the hoe/javelin and I realize he has sausages for fingers. I wonder how in the hell they will ever fit in there, let alone extract the tooth without severing the offending nerve and breaking my jaw into thousands of pieces.

The dentist has a trillion-watt light illuminating my mouth. It's so strong, it's probably illuminating my testicles, as well. The assistant/wife/co-conspirator adjusts the light (which has a dead moth in it), but fails to take into account my eyeballs and I'm being blinded. I would close my eyes, but I'm afraid what they would do if I weren't paying strict attention.

Perhaps my eyeballs would end up on the beach. Or my *huevos rancheros*.

The scrotum-shrinking dental assistant/wife/harpie has seen the error of her ways and has adjusted the light, but now I have a winter tan and diminished visual acuity.

The shrew/harridan/*Frau* has also provided me with a tinted shield to cover my eyes.

Now they are both slapping on rubber gloves like they do at the, yes, proctologist's and this makes my blood run cold, yet, oddly, elevates my BP.

"Vould you like the needle, gas, or conscious sedation?"

"Sorry?"

"The needle, the gas or the conscious sedation?"

Just so you know, dear Reader, I'm a bit of a student of history when it comes to pain and terror, and the term "needle" conjures up the second grade and that first injection with the accompanying: "This won't hurt." Then…the term "gas" conjures up Birkenau, and…"conscious sedation" conjures up nothing as I don't have a clue what that means (could it have something to do with "close third person?").

"Door number three," I say.

"Am sorry?" the dentist says.

"I'll go for the *conscious* sedation," I'm quick to answer. There's no way I want to be "out" around these two.

"Okie, dokie," the wife/inquisitor says. "Take off shirt."

"Am sorry?" I say.

"Take off shirt, schmuck."

"Did you just call me a schmuck?"

"Not *schmuck*, schmock. Take off shirt, schmock." She's holding up one of those robes we wear when we want to look foolish in hospitals with our fundament hanging out.

"Just to remove a tooth?"

"Take off shirt," she commands.

Now, I don't know about you, but I take my shirt off at the beach when I'm paddle boarding, at the swimming pool, on an outdoor asphalt basketball court when the heat index climbs to over one hundred. Occasionally -- although it's becoming less and less *occasional* -- even when I shower at the gym ... but it doesn't feel so socially correct at a dentist's office. I have always been the kind of person who checks his dignity at the door to a doctor's or dentist's office, but this taking off of the shirt just doesn't seem so prudent.

"Is there a screen I can go behind?"

The wife/sex therapist sighs heavily, as Eastern Europeans do when it comes to taking clothes off in public with Westerners.

"Take off shirt. I leave room."

She exits and I am the fastest human on earth to rip off a shirt and throw on a *schmock*. But then like a speeding bullet she's back and that's when I realize the dentist has never left the surgery. He's over in the corner giving a *syringe* the obligatory squirt in the air.

WTF?

They both smile at me the way a lawyer does after you've signed on the bottom line of a contract filled with so much freaking legalese, that even Ruth Bader Ginsberg would struggle through it.

Then the dentist presses a red button next to the dental chair that is as big as the red button on *THE VOICE*, and a young man enters who resembles Andy Warhol, but with less color in his cheeks. Andy wheels in a "crash cart" with all sorts of nasty digital readouts and tubes and wires ... and something which resembles shock/horror defibrillation paddles. I want to quip that I'm not up for a jaunty game of Ping-Pong like Michael

Bublé right now, but I've suddenly lost my sense of humor.

Such as it is.

"Who's he?" I ask Cruzilla, in a shaky voice.

"He's the paramedic ..."

"Paramedic?"

"*Ja.*"

"What's he needed for?"

"In case we need to kick start your heart."

On that, the dentist squirts the *needle* into the air again and some of it lands on my now naked arm. I'm afraid the "liquid" is going to burn through my arm, and then through the floor, like the blood from the creature burned through the spaceship in the movie *ALIEN*."

"Thought I wasn't going to get a *needle?*"

"Little prick," he says.

"Did you just call me a *little prick?*" I say. But he's not listening, he has his blood-letting agenda to attend to.

"I just want to numb area around molar so you will have less discomfort after."

This is what he's says, but what he really means is: *I just want to deaden the fuck out of the right side of your face, so that you won't know I've severed the Coochie Coochie Viva Las Vegas nerve until you are long gone from here and I'm back home, sipping wodka, counting my money.*

Then as my face freezes like Dan Berger's driveway did this past winter, and before I can protest, Andy jumps me and slips a *needle* into a vein in my bare arm so professionally I don't even realize I've been penetrated. With childlike wonder/horror, I follow the offending *needle* to a tube and then to one of those "drips" which is hanging from something resembling a hat rack that looks suspiciously like a cross between a hoe and a javelin.

Andy's cheeks flush with heliotrope and he coos gently to me: "Count backwards from one hundred ..."

I do as I'm told. "One hundred ... ninety ni—" And I'm out cold.

****AUTHOR'S KINKY NOTE**: Cast your mind back to the most aberrated, twisted, sexual dream that you've ever had. You know the one, the one where you hear an imploring voice wail: "No! No! Not in the face!" Do you remember that? Well, thanks to the conscious-freaking-sedation, I'm now having it in

HD color with cum-surround, I mean sensurround.

* * *

The dental assistant/wife/exterminator is gently prodding my shoulder now.

"Leave me alone," I hear my disembodied voice command, "I've just hit out of a sand trap on only my third attempt ..."

And then, that's when I realize it's all over. I look up at the dentist's angelic face and he's holding a tooth in his gloved hand like the one Richard Dreyfus found sticking in the gaping hole in the bottom of Ben Gardner's boat in the movie *JAWS*. And, yes, I realize I've made reference to Ben Gardner *twice* in this book, but we live on an island and a toothy presence is just out there and never very far from anything, especially if you know Shark Man.

"Is it safe?" I now say like Dustin Hoffman did to Sir Laurence Olivier in *MARATHON MAN*.

The dentist looks at me in an avuncular sort of a way, then says: "Let's just go take another X-ray." Barely able to stand, and not at all un-drugged, I'm led to something which looks an awful lot like one of those tanning booths you stand up in, not that I need the tanning booth what with the blast of the dental light earlier in the visit. As I exit the surgery, stage right, I look out the window and Andy the Paramedic is out there -- smoking! Has he just had sex?

"Can I see the tapes?"

"Oh, you mean the X-rays," the dentist says. "Sure, happy to show you, then he steps behind a lead shield and SNAP! my sperm counts drops to about 63 -- same as the population of Stanley, Idaho.

The dentist and I are now studying the X-ray. I take that back: The dentist is studying the X-rays, I'm trying to focus my eyes and perhaps drooling just a bit out of the frozen side of my mouth.

"You see here," the dentist says, "there's the Viva Las Vegas nerve which is attached to your shriveled scrotum. It's still intact. The nerve AND the shriveled scrotum. See, and you thought I had sausages for fingers..." Well, that's not what he said, but in my "conscious sedation" dotage, I *thought* that's what he'd said. In actuality, he'd said "You see here, there's the Chitty-Chitty-

Bang-Bang Viva Las Vegas nerve. It's still intact. Now you may pay. Cash only. We don't accept insurance. And no checks. Cash. *Now.* We have a flight to catch."

"You have symmetrical sideburns," I said, then vowed never again to have the "conscious sedation."

* * *

What the dentist failed to tell me was that I would be ushered out of the dentist office in a wheelchair. By Andy. This, in order to get me out on the pavement, where I could stand up and pass out on someone else's liability policy. I was still so drugged out and loopy, I almost keeled over when I stood up from the wheelchair. I wished I had brought Gabrielle along as co-pilot.

Popcorn Joe was up in Marathon, so I wended my way through the parking lot and stood at the bus stop with a shit-eating grin. Others waiting kept well clear of me. Including Ken Ro. It was hot and I needed to go someplace dark and lie down. Plus there was the wad of cotton the size of grandma's yarn ball jammed in my mouth to stem the flow of blood. I asked someone how long until the next bus came, but when I spoke, the cotton/yarn ball conspired against articulation and elocution. The Conch Loop bus arrived. Conch Loop ... loopy passenger. I ended up staying on the bus past my stop and only alighted after two loops around the island.

On his way back from Marathon, Popcorn Joe saw me wandering the streets of Old Town and he kindly gave me a lift back to Villa Alberto.

To make a long boring story, a short boring story, the area of the incision healed quickly, miraculously there was no nerve damage and life is good.

I have since found out that the dentist and Cruzilla were from Kazakhstan, and had first come to America to work a summer at Lego Land up in Orlando at Disney World. They had flown Aeroflot from Moscow into New York's JFK, then naively/stupidly taken the Greyhound all the way to Orlando -- 1200 miles and about a thousand hours. That was the first and last time they did that. Plus, they were so frightened by all the weirdoes at the downtown Orlando Greyhound station, they vowed to never come back to America ever.

But that all changed after Dental (proctology) School. Upon

graduation, they longed for the freedom/ability to hide out in the open that America offers. Orlando was out of the question, and they had heard about the numerous conmen working in Miami in the medical profession, so South Florida it was. Upon arriving in Miami, they found that no one spoke English, so they decided to give Key West a try. Key West afforded ample opportunity for a new practice as there was such a turnover of residents, and ample opportunity to over-prescribe prescription drugs, so they had settled on Cayo Hueso.

CHAPTER THIRTEEN

I awoke in the middle of the night.

This is what I do now. No, it wasn't about my dentist. And it wasn't a nightmare about Immigration cuffing my bride, and it wasn't about our landlord's testicles (which would have been genuinely acceptable in one of my twisted dreams), this was about the wind. I could hear it in the palm trees and I could hear something scraping our tin roof every time there was a strong gust. I shivered. It conjured up memories/nightmares of the hurricane, something we didn't need reminding of. We never wanted to revisit that experience. If a hurricane ever threatened Key West again, we had decided to evacuate. Not hang around for the hurricane parties and the shit-your-knickers adrenalin rush. And the life in a Petri dish after effect where there is no electricity for a week and mold runs rampant and is free-range.

I shivered again, then realized it was cold. So that was it: another cold front was marching through. I tried to snuggle up to Gabrielle, but Mr. Leroy had beaten me to it, so I snuggled up to Mr. Leroy. Was he ever the lucky one, sandwiched between Mr. and Mrs. Bookends.

Are you ready for this? When we awoke at seven o'clock, it was 44 chilly degrees Fahrenheit. Let me repeat that lest you feel you had too much to drink last night and your eyes are playing up: 44 degrees. The lowest temperature ever recorded in Key West was 41 degrees on January 12th, 1886, and again on January 13th, in 1981.

We weren't that far off.

I padded to the kitchen on ice-cold lino and made two Cuban coffees, watched a line of ants ascend from the floor and up to the sink, then made sure Mr. Leroy had enough water in his bowl. I took the steaming elixir back to Gabrielle who was sitting up in bed. Mr. Leroy was still a lump under the covers.

"You won't believe what I'm thinking," Gabrielle said. "Remember last summer during hurricane season when we had that awful storm with torrential rain right up until it was time to go down to sunset and try to sell our photos?"

"Yea-ah …"

"Do you remember that we figured none of the crafts people or artists would turn up on the pier, but we went anyway?"

"Yea-ah …"

"We did really well, because even though there weren't a lot of tourists, we were the only show in town and they threw their money at us."

"And you're telling me this because?"

"How many vendors do you think will show down at Sunset when the temperature's in the forties?"

"I get what you're saying: a whole bunch won't show 'cause it will be too cold for everyone except the tourists from the Great White North."

"Right, they will come down to Mallory in shorts and sandals …"

"And we will get on the pier!"

* * *

Later that afternoon, about three hours before sunset, Gabrielle and I loaded up our make-shift, shit "trolley" with our photo display.

We had constructed a display by purchasing four "grids," both two-feet wide and six feet high. Then we took fishing line and wove it through the grid, so that we could slip matted photos behind the fishing line. Are you following me here? For the framed sunset photos, we simply hung then from "s" hooks. In order to get this all down to "Sunset," we placed the matted and framed photos in a huge plastic storage bucket, pancaked the grids together and then used bungee cords to secure it all to a two-wheel dolly, a poor-person's version of what the UPS man uses to deliver a shitload of boxes to the neighboring business while illegally parked out in front of *your* establishment.

As we skulked down the street dragging this contraption, it looked as if we were stealing someone's bedsprings. Someone with bad taste in bedsprings. It hadn't dawned on us yet to do what many of the other vendors do: These clever folk built little trailers which were attached to the backs of their bicycles, so they could look cool riding down to Sunset. These nifty mobile devices would open like gull wings and they were ideal for hanging T-shirts or displaying jewelry or concealing an unmentionable product that needed to be concealed till after the sun went down.

Duval Street was always too crazed a thoroughfare and chocka with tourists to drag our display down to Mallory that way, so we chose to go through Truman Annex again. As we passed by the gatehouse at the entrance to Truman Annex, we waved at the gate guard, Richard, who always looked so dapper in his Bahamian whites. Richard opened the door to the gate house and greeted us with his infectious smile, but we just stared back.

"What?" he said.

"What are *those?*" Gabrielle asked, pointing to his legs.

"We call them trousers. Freezing my you-know-what off."

"Never seen you in long trousers before," Gabrielle said.

"I wore them last summer."

"I don't remember it being cold last summer?"

"It wasn't. I wore them to a fancy-dress party. I went as a drunken Italian cruise ship captain …" Richard thought back to that special evening: "I wasn't the only one there dressed like that."

We bid Richard farewell and hauled our bedsprings down along behind the Little White House. When we got to the gate at Front Street at end of Truman Annex, the gate was locked.

"What's the gate doing locked so early?"

"It's probably frozen. Try it again."

"It's not *that* cold."

I fiddled with the lock. Then I kicked the shit out of the lock. Then we turned around and schlepped our bedsprings all the way back.

"Hi, Richard."

Richard gave us a look. "Don't tell me the gate's locked?"

"You got it."

"*Jesus Cristo,* that's not our doing. It happened a few months ago. Someone is putting their own lock on that gate, then they are coming late at night, using their own key and breaking into all the expensive homes down on that end of the Annex. Thanks for telling me. I'll get maintenance to cut it off. Go back that way, if you want, it'll be gone when you get there."

We bid Richard farewell for the second time in fifteen minutes and aimed for the offending gate. As we approached we heard the sound of a hacksaw at work, and by the time we got to the gate, it was open and we just cruised on through. Very efficient and not at all banana republic work ethic here!

Richard was the type of guy you wanted on your side when life went pear-shaped.

We came out of Truman Annex not far from the Audubon House and into a blowy northeast wind. When we arrived at Mallory Square, our eyes grew stalks: We were the only ones there.

I gave Gabrielle a look: "Are you kidding me?"

"We're early. Let's just wait and the vendors will start to make an appearance."

We waited. O.J. Dave eventually rumbled up, pulling his colorful orange juice cart. Dave was sporting a heavy coat and scarf.

"That's one," I said. "That leaves forty-nine spaces."

"No," Gabrielle corrected me, "O.J. Dave counts as food. He doesn't count as one of the fifty places."

Then Louie and Ginger pulled up, hauling their grill and falafel maker. *Nobody rolls them fatter than I do!*

"That's one," I said.

Gabrielle gave me a look. "Where were you when I just said O.J. Dave is *food?* Louie and Ginger are *food*, as well. We're still the only vendors here."

We watched as Popcorn Joe arrived, pushing his PRETTY GOOD POPCORN cart. He gave us a friendly wave.

"One!" I said.

Gabrielle gave me a withering look.

"I'm just messing with you. I should have said 63."

"Ha, ha."

Then Will Soto arrived and began setting up paraphernalia for his tightrope-act on Will's Hill. Ever the quintessential trouper, Soto was there to put on a show, inclement weather or not. Modest crowds or not. Will Soto, in many ways, *was* Sunset Celebration.

Soto first came to Key West in 1966 when he was in the Navy and the destroyer he was stationed on smoked into port. He made his 2nd visit to Key West 10 years later and was enamored with the island's funky charm, the "glorious disrepair" of the houses and the colorful folk who were drawn to Mallory to watch the setting sun. At the time he didn't know it, but he was coming home to a magical island he had only briefly visited once before.

"Sunset" back then was an eclectic gathering of locals, hippies, fishermen, artists selling trinkets, hippies, a few musicians (bongo drums and guitarists) and really anybody else who was lured by the far-flung, laidback appeal of it all. And did I mention hippies?

Wine and rum were passed around, a few folk did the limbo, perhaps -- shock horror -- someone lit up a joint. Or sold some weed. There was a palpable magic in the air, or perhaps that was the cannabis.

Will Soto, Marylyn the Cookie Lady, Richard Bertocci, Featherman Louie, Love 22, Sister, and a host of others were drawn to Mallory each night and soon realized that the coveted tradition of celebrating the setting sun needed to be preserved, so in 1984 they formed the Key West Cultural Preservation Society, a not-for-profit corporation. The Cultural Preservation Society drafted guidelines for those who would perform or flog wares down on the pier, then they negotiated a lease with the City of Key West with the understanding that "CPS" would manage "Sunset" and maintain and ensure its artistic integrity.

So catch Will Soto's act the next time you are at Sunset and remember why he's up there on the tightrope and remember all that he has done, not only for Mallory Square, but for Key West, as well. Then go buy some popcorn from Popcorn Joe and some refreshing juice from O.J. Dave. They, too, are pillars of the pier.

Key West is a cultural, colorful jewel like no other place in this great world of ours and it is what it is, thanks in part, to the free spirits, creatives, eccentrics and renegades who fell in love with this enchanting island and strove to make it what it is today.

We heard a scream of laughter and applause. Will Soto was

leading a group of ten tourists, both male and female. They were standing on the edge of the pier, mooning the passing Sunset Cruise.

Will Soto, the face of "Sunset" (and sometimes the moon) and an ambassador to the city of Key West.

And that's one of the many reasons we love it here so much.

And why we don't want to leave.

We waited until it was time to draw our keys out of the bucket. Other vendors arrived, but not many, and we got on the pier, business was brisk, but not as brisk as the wind coming in off the Gulf.

Gabrielle took me aside and mentioned: "You do realize, that this freeze-your-bahookie-off day in Key West, is a veritable scorcher in Glasgow during the summer?"

And the statement bit into me almost as much as the biting wind.

* * *

After Sunset, we schlepped our display back home, then went for a walk on Duval. With the temperature in the forties, many shops, restaurants and bars had their windows closed. After having walked down Duval all year long with doors open (even when the A/C is blasting) it was strange to walk down Duval with many windows and doors shut tight. The music was muffled, bar smells were muted and the open-window intimacy that is one of the signatures of Key West's high street was missing.

Over the course of the next few days, temperatures remained uncharacteristically low for this time of the year, and cold weather and sweaters just didn't seem to go with palm trees and banyan trees and Royal Poinciana and bird of paradise. Or with Jet-ski tours, even though the ocean was still a glorious and very user-friendly 72 degrees.

Lloyd, who does "Lloyd's Tropical Bike Tour," only had five guests. He's so popular, it usually looks as if he's leading the Tour de France. Twelve beach cruisers with fat tires, wide seats and little flags atop a twanging aerial follow him through the unknown, secret tropical lanes as Lloyd slays you with his sense of humor and gives one of the island's best narrations, talking about Key West's glorious flora (30 different varieties of fruit trees), eclectic fauna and rich history. You even get to sample coconuts and mangoes and star fruit and, if lucky, Key limes.

* * *

Speaking of history (I don't know where else to put it in, so I'm putting it in here), did you know that in 1763, Great Britain grabbed control of Key West and shipped out all the Spaniards and Native Americans living on the island? They were resettled, often kicking and screaming, in Havana. When Key West once again came under Spanish control round about 1783, the repatriation of those who had been uprooted was ineffective at best.

Not much was going on in Key West back then. Fishermen from Cuba would stop off, fish the reef, fish the flats, drink a few bottles of rum, light up a stogie, and then head back to La Habana.

Even though the newly independent nation of the US of A was just up there … and Spain, in the form of Cuba, just down there, neither nation exercised de facto control over those living on Bone Island back then. By the way, *de facto* control means, sort of: "in practice, but not necessarily ordained by law."

I had to look it up.

In 1815, the Spanish governor of Cuba at the time, deeded Key West to an officer in the Spanish Navy, who was posted in St. Augustine.

In 1821, Key West along with the entire state of Florida, was transferred to the US of A. The Spanish naval officer was so keen to sell Key West, he sold it twice: first for a sailboat worth $575, and then to John Simonton over a *con leche* in a Havana café.

Okay, put down the mojito and see if you can follow: The owner of the sailboat immediately sold Key West to General John Geddes, the former governor of South Carolina. Geddes tried (in vain, I might add) to nab the rights before Simonton did, but Simonton had influential friends in Washington and they were able to clear title.

And here's why some of the streets in Key West have the names they do: John Simonton had a friend by the name of John Whitehead, and Whitehead had encouraged Simonton to buy because of Key West's "strategic location." Whitehead had been stranded in Key West after a nasty shipwreck (aren't they all?) and he'd been impressed by the deep-water harbor. Back then Key West was thought of as the "Gibraltar of the West" due to its position on the 90-mile-wide shipping lane (the Straits of Florida), between the Atlantic and the Gulf of Mexico.

So there you go, give that some thought the next time you are riding your bike around the island.

Or taking Lloyd's tour.

CHAPTER FOURTEEN

Popcorn Joe has taken me to the gym.

He's rollerbladed and I've followed on my bicycle. I had difficulty keeping up with him. The man can motor! Then I temporarily lost him. Then found him just in the nick of time.

The gym is located on the edge of the Old Town and it's rough and beaten up and tired, but frightfully hot despite the lower temperatures of the past few days. What will it be like in the heat of summer?

Inside, I'm startled by a dust ball as it rolls by. It's big enough to frighten small animals and could pass as tumbleweed. It enjoys its own shadow.

Popcorn Joe is bench pressing "his weight" with ease. I am bench pressing only the bar. Now Popcorn Joes is doing curls with 50 pounds in each hand. I'm using bright-pink rubber dumbbells that weigh 2 pounds each and are meant to be reserved for the ladies' Legs, Buns and Tums Class.

Twenty minutes later, Popcorn Joe is doing pull-ups on a horizontal bar while holding a 30 pound weight between his ankles. So as not to be a piker, I find a piece of equipment that allows me to do pull-ups while *kneeling* on a platform. The contraption is counter-balanced and I've used too much weight to counter balance, and on my first pull-up I almost take flight.

To impress Popcorn Joe, I go over to the leg-press machine, but two endomorphic steroid abusers are well-juiced and they frighten me away with their acne, so I spend the next ten minutes looking at myself in the mirror, because that's what all the guys with really great muscles are doing.

The women are looking in the mirror at their bums.

As is one gay caballero.

Perhaps I don't fit in a gym such as this one, as I don't have a pierced nipple ring and the plunging tank top. But then neither does Popcorn Joe.

But he does have the muscles.

And the bulge.

And really good calves.

Not knowing what to do, I spot an available bicycle over in a neighboring room filled with women and climb up on one (I'm talking about the bikes, not the women). When I hear an over-caffeinated voice bark "Hill!" I realize I have unknowingly penetrated the Spinning Class. I'm too embarrassed to leave, but there's no way I can stay, what with the hill. Eventually, I run out of stream and, during a much needed water break, clandestinely de-bike and go back to the mirrors, where the same guys who were there before are still there.

I want to see if I can bench press more than just the bar, but when I go over to the bench-press apparatus, it's loaded with about a thousand pounds as the last gorilla using it has failed to replace the weights on the rack. I would gladly replace them:

1) If I could, and

2) If I wasn't afraid of the hernia.

After our workout, Popcorn Joe showers, but I don't as I haven't worked up a sweat standing in front of the mirrors. Even though I have not perspired, I will still need to wash my workout gear when I get home as no one wipes down the benches and seats after using them and I now smell as if I had a really killer workout.

I peruse the items on sale in the lobby. There are energy drinks, which have enough caffeine in them to kill a horse, vats of muscle-building powder that costs a fortune and health bars that are so riddled with sugar, if you ate just one, you would be wired like the national grid.

After the gym, Popcorn Joe and I meet Gabrielle for a *con leche* at the "Garden" and we watch Alberto painting something we have never seen before: Alberto is painting "names" using tropical icons such as flamingoes and dolphins and lighthouses and palm trees. The names end up being about 8-10 inches high and 30-inches wide.

They are gloriously beautiful.

Alberto looks over at Gabrielle who's mesmerized by the colorful art. "I'm just learning how to do this, Gabrielle, perhaps you could learn with me?"

"But we're going back to Scotland."

"Perhaps you should stay ..." says Popcorn Joe.

CHAPTER FIFTEEN

I have to report to you today that the wind is out of the north at 18 knots.

And there is a light chop in the toilet bowl.

The gusts of wind shake the house like a dog shaking water off, and the house, which is built on a few cracked cinder blocks and stubby stilts, vibrates.

Try using the facilities when there is a light chop in the bowl. Trust me, you don't tarry. This is not the time to read a good book.

Or a bad book.

Get in.

Get on.

Get out.

When there's a tropical storm ... or, and I will just whisper this next bit: *a hurricane*, it can be like riding one of those mechanical bulls like they had at Armadillo World Headquarters in Austin ... or Old Town in Kissimmee ... or now Cowboy Bills in Key West, FL, not quite the USA.

In a particularly menacing thunderstorm, I was actually thrown off, the commode, not the ride at Cowboy Bills. Sure the tequila I had consumed at the Bull earlier in the evening could have been factored into the equation, but there you go, whatever the source of the spinning motion, I ended up on the floor ... nearly face-to-face with Mr. Leroy who had hurried in to give me a look of *What the fuck?*

Gabrielle knew better and didn't budge from the couch/futon where she was reading the latest James W. Hall crime thriller. Although I did hear muffled laughter.

Laughter aside, the entire misadventure has brought back the unwanted, unsought horror of what it was like last year during hurricane season, so if there is a bright side to going back

97

to Scotland, this would be it.

Later that evening, I tuned in the Soundman From Hell on 104.9 the X, Key West. He was telling an enraptured listening audience that the Florida Fish and Wildlife Conservation Commission were now reporting that the softball-sized eye that had washed up on the beach came from a swordfish. Joan Herrera, curator of collections at the FWC's Fish and Wildlife Research Institute in St. Petersburg, said: "Experts on site and remotely have viewed and analyzed the eye, and based on its color, size and structure, along with the presence of bone around it, we believe the eye came from a swordfish. Based on straight-line cuts visible around the eye, we believe it was removed by a fisherman and discarded."

The Soundman From Hell, finished the news update, then added his *dos centavos*: "Why in the hell slaughter one of the Florida Keys' great game fish? What's wrong with people! It beggars belief."

Then he played "The Beach" by KW Chris:

... IT'S A SUNNYY DAY
AND I'M ON MY WAY
AND I LOVE
TO FEEL THE HEAT ...

And that made me feel a little bit better.

Until I remembered what we had to do the next day.

CHAPTER SIXTEEN

Have you ever slept really well, then awoken to sunshine and birdsong, and the good night's rest and the sunshine and the birdsong have put you in a really great mood? Then the voice of doom chimes down from above and your great start to the day went right in the *pissoir*? That's what just happened to us this morning: We just remembered we have to buy our flight tickets for our trip back home to Glasgow.

And this sucks the joy from our lives down here at the end of the world.

There's a travel agency in the Old Town. It's only a few blocks away, but we are going to convey by bike and take a circuitous route, so we can remember all the enchanting things about this quirky island that made us fall in love with it in the first place. We go out in the backyard to fetch our bikes and I find mine with a flat tire. Have you ever tried to fix a flat bicycle tire all by yourself? The rear tire? I turn the bike upside down and balance it on its seat and handlebars. Then Gabrielle brings me out all our tools, which amounts to a flathead screwdriver, a Phillips screwdriver, a crescent wrench and something which resembles an impressive sexual adjunct.

Mr. Leroy comes out to supervise.

I study the mechanism of it all. If I unbolt that bolt there, then it will affect the length of the chain there. If the length of the chain is altered, then the chain will wait until we are on the other side of the island one day, when there is a storm coming up from Cuba loaded with lightning, and then the chain will slip off its track or whatever the heck it is that chains slip off of when you are the farthest point from home. It will not only slip off, it will get caught in that little rut between the little sprocket thingies, and the center of the wheel, where chains get caught. It will get so jammed in there, three steroid abusers from the gym wouldn't be able to disengage it.

"What are you going to do first?" Gabrielle asks, picking Mr. Leroy up in her arms.

"Turn the bike back right-side up."

"What?"

"This is not happening."

I turn the bike right-side up. "We're going to have to take it up to the bike shop. You ride your bike over there, I'll walk this one over.

The Bike Shop Key West is located at 1110 Truman Avenue. It's the oldest bike shop in Key West. This is where you want to take your ailing conch cruiser when trouble looms in the form of a very flat rear tire.

Gabrielle beat me to the Bike Shop and alerted them to my plight. I knew I had to leave my bike and come back another day, but they must have seen the weepy, pained look in my eyes and they told me they could fix it right then and there. And they didn't laugh when they saw what a clunker I was riding.

While the technicians (for that's what they are) in the service department worked their magic, Gabrielle and I drooled over all the new bikes. There was a brand new, Retro-style conch cruiser-looking bike, called a Trek Cruiser, where "old-school simplicity meets up with modern design touches for relaxed, good times." This is a bike to die for and would have ended up on our Christmas list if we were staying and didn't have to go back to the U.K.

"Check it out," Gabrielle said. "They rent bikes here, as well. Good to know when friends come."

"But we're not staying ..."

Gabrielle looked at me with sad eyes. "Forgot."

I read the sign regarding rentals. They offered "Beach Cruisers" and "wide soft seats." That, plus "no advertising on the bikes."

"Look at these bikes. They're hot!"

Gabrielle gave me a look. "I don't mean it that way. Not like most of the bikes painted black on this island."

"They're cool?"

"Yes, cool, not hot, that's what I meant."

Well, it was only a short time later and my bike had been

fitted with a new rear tire, greased, wiped off, and I was ready to go. We paid, thanked the team for taking us right then and there, and with a frisson of excitement clashing with the thought of leaving, we took a little tour around the Old Town. We rode down Truman, then turned left on Duval and cruised past the Cork & Stogie, a fine watering hole, might I add. As we pedaled by, someone gave us a wave. It was Chris Rehm! Chris was chatting in an animated fashion with Tom Corcoran. I looked over at Gabrielle and I knew what she was thinking: *That was something else we would miss about Key West, there were always luminaries hanging about, willing to chat over a beer or a con leche, or a shaker of salt.*

* * *

****AUTHOR'S HOLY SHIT! NOTE**: Chris would later tell me that he had been sitting in the Cork & Stogie for a bit, supping a beer and chatting to the interesting gentleman next to him, when he felt he should make an introduction. That's when Chris found out he was chatting to famed crime writer Tom Corcoran. "I love his books!" Chris said.

Small world.

Neat world.

Down here at the end of the … world.

We waved to KW Chris, saluted Tom, then tooled on down to United, hung a left, turned left again when we reached Watson, then cruised up to Frances, pedaled gently uphill (barely) and cut behind the Key West cemetery. We carried all the way to Fleming, then turned left and pulled our bikes up to a stop in front of the Eden House. Have you ever seen the Eden House? Have you ever stayed here? This is the place to stay if you're coming down for a holiday. They are just far enough removed from Duval to get a good-night's sleep, yet just close enough to go by foot so you can stay up all night and forgo the sleep.

"Why have we stopped here?" Gabrielle asked.

"I've always liked the look of this place. It's the oldest hotel in Key West and it just has that charm that we won't find back home in Glasgow. Have you ever read Mike Eden's blog?"

"Cool?"

"The coolest."

I must have been admiring the Eden House and the

surrounding area for quite some time, when Gabrielle broke me out of my dreamy state.

"Are you questioning our decision to go back?"

"Always," I said. "C'mon, want to show you something ..."

We pedaled off down Fleming, then I led Gabrielle left on Margaret and we cruised back up to Passover Lane.

"The cemetery?"

"It's loaded with history. There are over 100,000 people buried here."

"Along with a few pets ..."

"Indeed."

We rode in through the main entrance to the cemetery. If you think there are colorful characters walking Duval, out at Higgs Beach, or down at Mallory Square of an evening, check out some of the true originals resting here in peace. Although, having said that, these locals are the only ones who don't party at night.

Or do they?

As you would have learned from my first book, the original cemetery was located down on the southern side of the island, near Whitehead Point, but had to be relocated after the hurricane of 1846 disinterred bodies and scattered them in the neighboring forest, leaving many of them hanging in trees. There is now a dedicated African Memorial Cemetery near Whitehead Point to honor the slaves who died during sea voyages to America and were buried here prior to the Civil War.

To avoid the storm surge and dome of water that accompanies a hurricane, the "new" cemetery now rests at the foot of Solaris Hill, the highest part of the island at a towering, nose-bleeding 18 feet.

"Hey, do you hear that?" Gabrielle said.

"What *is* that?"

Gabrielle and I looked around. We heard music and it was not coming from a distant bar or pumping out of a neighboring conch house.

What was going on?

We listened. Could that be a piano?

We pedaled deeper into the cemetery and came upon, are you ready? None other than Barry Cuda sitting at his pianimo, tickling the keys as only he can, singing the bluesy "Saint James Infirmary." Standing nearby, videoing, was Gary W. Ek of Southernmost Media.

And Barry Cuda sang:

I WENT DOWN TO THE KEY WEST CEMETERY
DOWN OLD TOWN BY THE MALLORY SQUARE
SEVEN GHOSTS AS USUAL
AND A FEW ROOSTERS ALSO WERE THERE
I WENT UP SEE MY BABY
MISS MARGARET'S HER NAME
SHE WAS STRETCHED OUT ON A COOL
TOMBSTONE
SINGING THE SAME OL' SAME
I WENT DOWN TO THE GREEN PARROT
SAW MY BUDDIES THERE
THEY WERE SERVING DRINKS AS USUAL
AND ALL MY GOOD BUDDY BARFLIES WERE HERE

This was an improv tribute to a beloved one departed: Margaret Fryer. It gave us goose bumps and was eerily poetic and just, and we felt somehow blessed to have been witness to it. Only in Key West would someone of the ilk of Barry Cuda be requested to push his piano through the streets of the Old Town and up gently sloping Solares Hill to pay homage.

It was a scene we would never forget.

Barry carried on singing the rest of the song. Out of respect, we silently slipped away and pedaled our bikes off and soon came upon the plot of one General Abraham Lincoln Sawyer, a forty-inch "little person" whose dying wish was to be interred in a man-sized tomb. Fair request, say I. Then we walked our bikes over to the greyish marble monument which marks William Curry's place of rest. On the other side of Curry's tomb is an obelisk which has toppled over. If you look closely you can see the name "Ellen Mallory" etched right down there. Ellen Mallory was the mother of Stephen Mallory, the U.S. Senator and Secretary of the Confederate Navy. Once again, think about these surnames ... when you are down at Mallory Square or staying at the Curry Mansion on Caroline Street (just down from the Bull and on the way to the Pineapple apartments).

Okay, back on your bikes! *Vamos!* Pedal up 4th Avenue, then hang a right on Violet. See just over there where that iguana is sleeping in a patch of sun? That's where Sloppy Joe Russell now lays his head. If you peek behind the crypt, you will see the hand painted words: "eternal flame."

Let's bike over to Seventh Avenue now, to the black archway labeled: "B'nai Zion." This is the entrance to the Jewish Cemetery. See over there, just to the left? That's the large white crypt with "I TOLD YOU I WAS SICK," which I told you about in book *numero uno*.

"What's all that?" Gabrielle said.

Next to the crypt were a bunch of black plastic cups.

"Those are "ovitraps.""

"What?"

"Egg traps. They're laced with poison to kill female mosquitoes and their eggs. Lots of standing water in the cemetery after a rain."

Okay, moving out already, stay close as we're pedaling across the cemetery, past another iguana sunning itself, and back to Angela Street. Do you see it? Yes, that's it, the raised marble casket. Here lies a modest in stature Cuban woman whose grandfather penned the national anthem of Cuba. I just love these little bits of history. Presumably, you do, as well, as you are still here with us and not over at Rick's listening to Al Subarsky … although we will do that later.

If you will be so kind and now have a squizzy off to your left, yes over there, see that rather large brick plot with the pink granite gravestones? They bear the remains of three Yorkshire terriers and a pet deer named "Elfina."

Told you there were pets.

Turn and look to your right. The right, I said, see that somewhat private area over in the corner? That's the Catholic Cemetery.

Okay, now we are going to leave you to your own devices, but we will meet you at Rick's later.

* * *

After our tour around the cemetery, we were in a decidedly somber mood … perfect time to pay a visit to the travel agency.

The travel agent was a woman from NYC who was just pulling up to the south tower when the first plane hit. Her husband had been at work in Brooklyn and tried to get into the city to see if she was okay. He said he would have swum the East River if he had to, he was that distraught. The events obviously took an emotional toll and the couple decided to relocate just a few weeks later. Any loud noises: a popping balloon, a firecracker, even a slamming door were simply too much for the poor woman, so they relocated as far away as they could and tried to start a new life.

You only live once.

The woman asked to see our passports. When she thumbed through Gabrielle's, she stopped, studied it and we could tell that she was aware that Gabrielle had overstayed her visa.

"Are you planning on returning to Key West sometime in the near future?"

"Yes ..."

"As I'm sure you are aware, things have tightened up after 9/11. Have you thought about paying a visit to Havana on your way home?"

I looked over at Gabrielle, then we both looked back at this dear, switched-on lady.

"I can get you a great fare, Havana to London Gatwick."

"How do we get to Havana?" Gabrielle asked.

"Do you know anybody who has a boat?"

We knew what this lady was saying to us. Fly commercially, the traditional way out of Key West or Miami or points north, and you just might be pulled over by Immigration. They may check your passport and spot that you have overstayed your visa or they might not check it. Why risk it if you're planning to come back one day.

We were about to go, when I stopped and said one word to the travel agent: "Canada?"

"Not in January with tans like that."

CHAPTER SEVENTEEN

Gabrielle and I pedaled back to Villa Alberto a bit out of sorts.

My wife is the most "up" person I know, but she seemed uncharacteristically subdued. I made us both a Cuban coffee and then we went out in the backyard and worked in the garden, even though it was something we rarely did. Oh, sure we went out in the backyard from time to time to *fight* with the jungle out there, but rarely to just putter.

I looked around at the floral boscage that our backyard had become. I cast my mind back to the hurricane that ripped down the surrounding fence, the palm tree that crushed part of our tin roof, the countless yards of gravel we had laid down to give our dump a semblance of "presence" and of Villa Alberto.

Plus, there were the 25 coconuts that we had inadvertently "planted" by simply using them to form a border around the backyard. No one told us that they would take root and become hearty little palm trees, shooting up faster than expected. In a matter of years, our backyard would be an inaccessible palm tree forest.

Gabrielle was watering the plumeria tree, when I heard a knock at the front door. I entered Villa Alberto by way of the back door and did the submarine thing by passing through our many "hatches" and connecting rooms to get to the front door. I opened it, but no one was there. Strange. I closed the door and headed back through the warren that was our former military barracks.

I heard a knock at the front door again.

I opened the front door again, but there was still no one there. Popcorn Joe messing with us? John Rubin secretly flown in from Manchester messing with us? Ken Ro, who seems to materialize out of thin air? I started to close the door, then heard the knock again, but it wasn't anyone knocking on our door, it

106

was someone pounding a sign just out front and to the right. The sign said FOR RENT, and the person doing the pounding was Mr. Tosser.

After Mr. Tosser split, I went out to the backyard and told Gabrielle about what the tosser was up to.

"Nutter!" Gabrielle said. Then, she had a brainstorm: "Wait a minute, how long have I overstayed my visa by?"

"Six months."

"How many days, exactly?"

Gabrielle sat there by the plumeria tree for a moment, watching a gecko scurry after an ant, counting days on the fingers of both hands.

Then Gabrielle shouted out: "162 days! I've overstayed by only 162 days ..."

"And?"

"I think if I've overstayed less than 180 days, they won't skin me and hang me from a yardarm. Let's go Google it."

We hurried inside and fired up the oscilloscope and Googled the hell out of all things *Immigration,* and here's what we found out -- paraphrased: It essentially stated that if you were under the 180 days it was like being pulled over by the police after drinking just two cans of 3.2 beer, perhaps still not prudent to drive, but not a reason to throw you into the slammer ... BUT if you overstayed your visa by MORE than 180 days, then you might as well have drunk an entire bottle of JD, chased with a six pack of Land Shark Lager.

Gabrielle was energized by the results, but I wasn't really getting it.

"What does it all mean?" I asked.

"It means, we have 18 days to come up with a solution. Let's ring Popcorn Joe and have him meet us at the Bull. He always has great ideas."

Gabrielle and I walked out of Aronovitz lane and passed the FOR RENT sign that Mr. Tosser had erected in front of Villa Alberto. When we reached the mouth of the lane at Whitehead Street, we froze, Mr. Tosser had erected a larger FOR RENT sign here, as well.

We walked by the Green Parrot on the corner of Whitehead and Southard. The Bongo D Band was playing Bob Marley's

"One Love." The locals' haunt was heaving. Outside bicycles were parked awaiting their owners. It would be a long wait.

And it was a glorious scene.

We ambled over to Duval. *Amble* is what you do in Cayo Hueso. This is not the place for the "airport walk," or the "big city walk of stress." We amble and the only change of pace comes when you do the Duval Crawl ... or the Whitehead Wobble.

Or try to find your way home afterwards.

We entered the Bull from the Caroline Street entrance and took a seat right there at the bar, so we could keep an eye on the front door and look out for Popcorn Joe.

"Hey, check it out!" Gabrielle said. "Chris Rehm just walked in behind us with his all his gear. He doesn't usually play the Bull."

"This is the second place we've seen him at today. The man's making the rounds!"

Chris put his stuff down on the stage and started fiddling with the sound system. About now, he spotted us sitting at the bar and gave us a big smile. I gave Chris a *What's up?* look. He mouthed these words: *My first gig here! Just got called in!*

Well, were we ever the lucky ones, we hadn't expected the Bull *and* Key West Chris. We watched Chris setting up. Soon his fiddling with the sound system turned into Apollo 13 desperation. He looked over at us and rolled his eyes.

"Oh, oh," Gabrielle said. "Something's up."

Chris fought a while longer, then finally figured the *new*, meaning *different*, sound system out.

"Technology!" Gabrielle said. "Nothing like a burst of adrenaline before your first set of your first gig in a new venue."

I glanced at my watch. It was just before the top of the hour. Whatever had happened, Chris had defused an explosive situation and got it all squared away before the pivotal top of the hour.

Chris played and sang. We ordered a Michelob and Shiraz from Debbie the bartender. While she was getting our drinks, she had one eye on Chris up on stage. Something was still not right. After two songs, Debbie motioned Chris off the stage and we could just make out what she was saying: "It sounds really distorted, Chris, what's going on?"

A few patrons got up and left.

My heart sank for Chris. All he wanted to do was give a good show, play his music, make a good first-time impression and, for some reason, it was going in the toilet.

"He must be dying inside," Gabrielle said.

"But he'll never let it show. He's the quintessential pro."

Chris is a trouper and he went right back up on stage, made a few adjustment and began to play again. But the distortion was worse. Chris came back off stage and the bar-back said to him these words, which would have been immediately emblazoned on his soul: "If you can't fix it, then just stop playing. That sound will drive people out of here."

A couple more patrons got up and left.

Apollo 13 was passing around the backside of the moon and it was going to be a dark day for all involved.

Chris approached us and beads of sweat were beginning to pop out on his forehead. This, from a man, who lives for the heat and the tropics.

"I'm substituting for my good friend Dora Gholson. I brought my Rainsong carbon fiber guitar. I didn't have any monitors, so the sound I was hearing was actually in front of me and I really couldn't hear it all that well. I'm going to run out to the van. Shit, they're never going to ask me back!"

Gabrielle and I watched as Chris hurried back in with a load of new gear and began changing the cords to his guitar, then the mic cable, then the mic, itself. He was a man clutching for straws and the tide was sweeping him farther and farther from land.

Finally relieved, Chris did another song. I looked over at the bar-back and he had the look you get on your face when you step in dog shit. He mouthed to Chris: "No difference. Same thing!"

The bar was slowly emptying.

Gabrielle and I were feeling for Chris.

Chris stopped playing and came over to the bar-back. "The only thing I can think of is that it must be the Rainsong guitar."

"So what are you going do?"

Chris has always been able to think on his feet. "I'm going to run home and get my other guitar."

OMG.

Ten minutes later, Chris appeared at the side door. As he passed by, he had a big smile on his face and he said these soothing words: "An Ibanez Special Woods series that is absolutely stunning and sounds fantastic to boot!"

"How can he have a sense of humor at a time like this?" Gabrielle whispered.

On that, Chris jumped up on stage, plugged in, began to warble and we were all relieved to see the bar-back give him the thumbs up.

It could have been altogether a different digit.

I looked at my watch. Chris had played exactly 10 minutes out of the last hour. He gave us a Murphy's Law look, but played and sang valiantly on. As you know, these venues in Key West pride themselves on having some of the best, colorful musicians anywhere. If there's no music coming out of the open front door and windows, there no business going in.

Chris had essentially started an hour late and left 50 minutes of *dead air time*.

An inauspicious start at the Bull.

To make up for it, Chris didn't take a break for the next three hours.

And the place started to fill back up. Folk were being drawn in off of Duval to listen to Chris' music.

Chris soldiered on until the bitter end. The crowd was happy. The bar-back was happy. Debbie the barkeep was happy. But Chris was not. He knew that they were all nice people working there, but he knew he would never be invited back again. Ever. It's a small town. Word gets out.

First impressions mean everything.

At the end of his gig, Chris began picking up the tons of cords and cables he had hauled in, his Rainsong carbon fiber guitar, his Ibanez Special Woods guitar, his gig bags, and he was just about to exit with his tail between his legs when Debbie approached him on stage. Debbie had her back to us, so we couldn't hear what she was saying. And Chris' body language screamed out: *Oh, here we go ... I'm about to be eviscerated!*

"What do you think she's saying to Chris?" I asked Gabrielle.

"Telling him to never set foot in the Bull again?"

"Really wasn't his fault ... Just technical hiccups."

"But the buck stops at the entertainer in these venues ... Here he comes!"

Debbie the bartender returned to the bar and a subdued Chris slipped by us, like, well, bulls exploding out of the pen, we followed Chris outside, expecting the worse.

"What'd she say?"

Chris blew out his cheeks then burst into one of his trademark smiles. "She said: 'That was fantastic! You're exactly what we need here. So often we have other players filling in and you can't hear yourself talk. With you, we have the option to talk or listen. Your music was perfect as well. We have to get you back here!'"

"Holy shit," Gabrielle said.

"Holy shit," I said.

Chris went on: "I apologized for the earlier incidents and she just waved it off. She said: 'Things like that happen, don't worry about it. The important thing is that you were exactly what we need here.'"

Life in Key West, FL, not quite the USA, end of the world, last stop, was good.

Absolutely grand.

And after what Key West Chris went through, perhaps our problems were not insurmountable either.

* * *

Gabrielle and I went back inside and re-commandeered our seats.

I ordered another Michelob and Gabrielle switched to a Merlot. The drinks arrived and we just sipped our beverages and stared out the open windows out onto Duval. The air smelled of salt and was warm and appealing. We saw Shark Man ride his bike by, then Don and Shirley *ambled* passed and gave us a wave, then Rick and Fran Fagan, then Dale and Yvonne Logsdon from Greenock, Scotland. If you're looking for someone in Key West, just sit in a bar on Duval and there's a good chance that person will walk by -- perhaps even stop in for a pop.

Up on stage, Sallie was now singing "Dock of the Bay." We listened to the Otis Redding lyrics, then Gabrielle turned to me.

111

"Lyrics gave me a brainstorm. Remember Leslie?"

"The English girl who worked at the Glass Bottom Boat?"

"Yes, she married an American and wanted to get her Green Card. She will know what we have to do. If we can find her, she will give us all the info we need—"

"Perhaps I can help ..."

Gabrielle and I turned to the man sitting on the barstool next to Gabrielle. He was Latin and had silver hair. Sort of a Cuban version of Dennis Farina, but with the accent and sense of humor of Ricky Ricardo.

I gave Gabrielle a look. Just under a year ago, we had been duped by a man posing as a real estate agent and had been conned out of a $1000.

Gabrielle addressed the man: "We're all ears."

"What *you* want to do is go up to—"

Gabrielle interrupted, suddenly using a rather broad Texas accent: "It's for a friend. She's married to an American."

"Of course. What *she* wants to do is go up to the office of U.S. Citizenship and Immigration. It's up in Miami. Offices open at seven. I would plan to get there at four in the morning—"

"Four?"

"Yes, four, there'll already be a line, but you'll be near the front. At seven sharp the doors open. You will be led inside. Take your passport—"

"Let me stop you right there," Gabrielle said. "Let me guess, you're an Immigration Attorney and you want money for your sound advice?"

"No, just seen the two of you around. You look like good folk. Different than a lot of the types we get down here. You're minding your own business ..."

Our eyes bugged open.

"Seen you down at Mallory ..."

Gabrielle and I exchanged looks.

"Are you two married?"

"Yes."

"How long?"

"Ten years."

"There's what's known as a Stage One Right to Work Visa. Long story, short, it's a precursor to a Temporary Green Card."

"How come I couldn't find this on the Internet?"

"Have you tried to navigate the website for Immigration and Naturalization?"

"Yes."

"Did it have you pulling your hair out?"

"Yes."

This knowledgeable fellow downed the remainder of his whiskey and rose.

"Can I ask you one more question?"

"Shoot."

"What if *this person* has overstayed her Visa?"

"By how long?"

"About 162 days."

"Do-able."

And on that, Ricky Ricardo started off, then stopped and smiled: "You'll be okay."

"Sure?"

"Sure."

Gabrielle and I watched Ricky Ricardo exit the Bull, turn right and walk in the direction of the gay end of Duval.

"What was that all about?"

"Key West is a curious place. Lots of creepy people here. Lots of colorful people. Lots of good people."

"And which one was he?"

"He's one of the good people," came a voice from behind us.

We turned to see Popcorn Joe coming in the door which opens onto Caroline. Joe pulled Ricky Ricardo's barstool up and sat down. I ordered a Michelob for the Popcorn man.

"How do you know he's one of the good people?" Gabrielle asked.

"Remember, when the Pineapple Apartments were broken into and I told you I found out about it even though I was in Stanley, Idaho?"

"Because you know all the police in Key West ..." Gabrielle said.

"Oh, shit," I said. "Don't tell me he was police." I shot a glance over at Gabrielle.

"Oh, he's not police ..." Popcorn Joe said.

Gabrielle blew out her cheeks.

"... he's Border Patrol."

And I blew out my beer.

* * *

Gabrielle and I waited for Popcorn Joe to finish his beer, then we escaped out the side door and drove out to Chico's Cantina on Stock Island. We ordered fajitas, drank sangria and finally settled down. Popcorn Joe didn't have much more to say about the whole situation/ordeal/shit-your-pants interlude, but he was up to something.

"What?" Gabrielle said.

"Oh nothing."

Gabrielle and I looked at Popcorn Joe for the longest time. Then we looked at each other reading one another's subtext. Then we looked back at Popcorn Joe.

And his eyes were twinkling mischievously.

"You're up to something, Giuseppe," Gabrielle said. "You've got that twinkle in your eye."

Popcorn Joe just smiled back, held up his glass, and said: "That would be the sangria, Gabrielle."

But we knew better.

CHAPTER EIGHTEEN

The next morning I checked my email, I had two rejections from literary agents (one said my Glasgow-based crime novel had too much gratuitous sex and violence, the other agent said that sex and violence sells and I should put more in). Now in the correct aggrieved, aggressive and pissed-off state, we went to Mr. Tosser's office to tell him we wanted to stay at Villa Alberto.

The flatulent jerk wasn't there, but his secretary was. She was thrilled.

"Not everyone takes care of their place like you two have. I'm really glad for you."

"She gets a passport," Gabrielle said as we rode our bikes out of Truman Annex and back to Villa Alberto.

Wait! Let me interrupt this chapter for a moment and explain what "She gets a passport" means. As just stated, there are many nice people on this earth of ours, but there are also a fair share of insufferable pricks. Mr. Tosser being one of them. Gabrielle and I had been speaking with Popcorn Joe about this particular phenomena/irritating issue and we had decided that a new country should be formed called the **Republic of the Island with the Best Beaches**.

The **Republic of the Island with the Best Beaches** would be a sailor's paradise and a snorkeler's idyll. There would always be wind for the sailors and, curiously, always warm inviting gin-clear, glassy waters for those who love to snorkel or paddleboard (you would be encouraged to paddleboard with a dog onboard).

There would be a swim-up bar and a dog beach.

The barrier reef would allow the neighboring waters to be a fisherman's paradise and fine specimens of the world's most popular game fish would be pretty much hanging around down in the briny depths waiting for you to drop a line over the side of your fiberglass-composite Blackfin 34 TE with the nifty and highly useful transom door. The fish wouldn't discriminate as to which bait or lure you would be employing and would pretty much hit anything that moves. Catch and release would be strictly enforced so that we could load the boat up with beer and do it all again tomorrow. Before being released, these coveted marvels of evolution would oblige you time for a photo op.

The **Republic of the Island with the Best Beaches** would be easily accessible from the Great White North, San Francisco and Seattle, Galveston and the Jersey Shore (with low airfares that wouldn't be jacked to gouge travelers at school holidays and the like). You could travel commercially or … fly on "SALT AIR," the republic's very own charter airline. Despite being a charter airline, SALT AIR would adhere religiously to scheduled service. All flights would leave on time. No flights would be scheduled too early in the morning. SALT AIR would have no baggage restrictions and you could take humongous carry-ons onboard to accommodate things like snorkels, flippers, boogie boards and acoustical guitars. There would be lots of legroom and you would not be charged silly fees for things like coffee, soft drinks, alcoholic beverages, peanuts, Pringles, use of the overhead compartments or visiting the toilets. The entire aircraft would be fitted with first-class leather seats and your own entertainment system.

WiFi would be available to accommodate Dan Berger (who would like to get some work done), and others who would like to post travel pics on Facebook.

You would be offered seconds on peanuts with a smile, and you would always get your entrée of choice even if you were the very last person onboard to be served. The choices would not be CHICKEN or BEEF, rather LOBSTER or MAHI MAHI. If you did not fancy seafood, you would be able to choose from ANGUS BEEF or STRIPS OF SIRLOIN. You could substitute any of the above and create your own SURF and TURF, if you so wished. If you were a vegan or vegetarian or needed a low-salt or Kosher special meal, this would be accommodated and no one would make an embarrassing announcement where you would have to raise your hand. Your special meal would not be served before all the others in the aircraft to prevent those seated around you from growling.

The lavatories would not run out of TP or paper towels, and the mouthwash would not be the same color as the chemical you see swirling when you press the flush button. All the female flight attendants would look like Adrienne Coppola. And have her sense of humor.

The **Republic of the Island with the Best Beaches'** borders would be strictly patrolled and no assholes would be allowed in.

Only those with a passport would be allowed in for lengthy stays: All my friends on Facebook, for example, because they enlighten me and amuse me, Reverend Gweko and Mayor Gonzo Mays to perform marriages (we would need both on account of so many folk coming to the island to tie the nautical knot), and a few who don't get a mention as you choose to keep a low profile on account of political correctness or outstanding warrants.

All Parrot Heads would be granted a passport. They would be assigned the island's resident private investigator (who just happens to look like a young Tom Selleck, and he would work feverishly, and pro bono might I add, to finds that lost shaker of salt.

Salt! Salt! Salt!

Wait! Yes, wait again! Having said all that about the offending lost shaker of salt, would we really want to find it? Isn't it infinitely more fun to speculate about it … and if it really was cocaine in there?

No motor vehicles would be allowed on the island, only conch cruisers (or trikes).

There would be two golf courses: one a regulation PGA course, the other a nine-hole pitch-and-putt. Neither would have sand traps and there would be no Out of Bounds. For aesthetic purposes, there would be the odd water hazard, but none would have alligators over one-foot long. The clubhouse would offer "stadium dogs," and ice-cold beer would be served in personalized koozies, which you could keep as a souvenir.

Green fees would be minimal, or you could pay with the numerous beer vouchers that have been stapled into your Island Passport.

117

There would never be a line to get into the Ladies' toilets at any sporting event.

All animals would be welcome (except Burmese pythons and chickens that feel the need to cockle doodle doo and strut their stuff before ten in the morning).

Mute chickens would be welcome on a day-to-day trial basis.

All the mosquitoes would be summarily drugged and just not give a shit about us.

All establishments would display a water bowl out front for dogs.

Even the Sheelman Gallery.

Accommodation on the island would be patterned after the Eden House.

Folk who haven't as yet been granted a passport to the **Republic of the Island with the Best Beaches**, but are well-respected, nevertheless, would be granted Day Passes. A Day Pass would allow you access to the powder-sugar sands in the summer and the shuffleboard courts in the winter. During the summer months, along with your Day Pass, you would be allotted a ration card in order to purchase ice cream, Italian ices and Key lime pie. You would also receive a token which you could use to redeem bicycle rental from a branch of Key West Bike Shop or Key Largo Bike. Key Largo Bicycle Tours would organize excursions around the island including beery refreshment. In the winter, along with your Day Pass, you would be allocated a ration card for beef jerky. You would accordingly receive a token which could be used to purchase a meter of beer to wash down the beef jerky. If you didn't drink beer, then an adult beverage of your choice could be substituted. If you didn't drink beer or fancy wine or adult beverages, then you would be asked to leave.

The founding fathers (Popcorn Joe is one) would etch in stone, restrictive bylaws that no chain stores could open in the Republic. This would mean no Starbucks, Build-a-Bear, Hooters, Victoria's Secret or Holiday Inn Express (even though they do have hilariously appealing commercials).

Margaritaville would not count as a chain establishment and would be welcomed with open arms and fins to the right.

Kevin May would run the island's esteemed publishing house called INK, Inc. Since it's obligatory for writers to have a drinking problem (I'm not saying you do, Kevin, but let's meet for a beer later), the publishing house would have a Tiki Bar with a neon sign.

As the **Republic of the Island with the Best Beaches** is a hotbed of paranormal activity, David L. Sloan would head up the island's Ghost Hunt. He would also be in charge of the Key Lime Pie Festival. It would be a yearly event, and well-attended, but wouldn't coincide with the Key West Key Lime Pie Festival, so we could attend both.

The local newspaper would actually be called the *Mullet Wrap* as it would feature the Fishing Report, the Tides Chart and Happy Hour coupons. There would be no Crime Report, because we don't allow degenerate misfits or politicians or certain pro athletes on the island. Thus, no crime. The *Mullet Wrap* would be used by the island's one and only Fish & Chip shop to wrap the fish and chips when you get a takeaway (Styrofoam would not be allowed on the island).

Mayor Gonzo Mays would NOT be the Official Honorary Mayor here, she would be Prime Minister! This, of course, because it has a good ring to it: Prime Minister Mays.

And she's cool.

Popcorn Joe's company Pretty Good Popcorn would have stiff competition in the form of Damn Good Popcorn, but nobody would mind too much as Popcorn Joe would own this enterprise, as well.

The Republic of the Island with the Best Beaches would stay on Daylight Savings time all year long.

There would be free WiFi on the island, as the entire isle would be a hotspot, what with it being, well, hot.

The island's High Street would never flood after a combination of high tide and a downpour.

The form you would have to fill out to obtain your Day Pass would be exceedingly short and easily understood by a third grader (on account of being designed and authored by a third grader).

You would not have to give out ANY personal information or need a pin number.

The **Republic of the Island with the Best Beaches** would be gay friendly … and clothing optional (except if you were sitting on a bar stool).

You would be allowed to wear a parrot hat on your passport photo.

No one would ever go postal on the island – "only coastal," per JB.

The constitution of the **Republic of the Island with the Best Beaches** would state matter-of-factly and clearly, that if any of you reading this came up with anything else that should be included in its charter, it would immediately become law of the land (even on weekends … or Monday mornings … or Friday afternoons … or during Happy Hour).

Right off the top of my head, I would speculate that those who would be granted a Day Pass would be the Spectrelles (because they rock!), all the bar staff at the Bull, Rick's, Captain Tony's, the Cork & Stogie, the Desi Arnez Immigration Officer, and my mother-in-law.

You may well ask *"Who are we* to be doling out visas and passports, what with me harboring an illegal alien and Gabrielle being of scum-line immigration status," and I would have to respond that you have a very good point, indeed.

But we're working on it.

**AUTHOR'S OH-SO-IMPORTANT NOTE: The next time you are sitting in a bar somewhere and you see a member of the opposite sex, don't blurt out: "Check out her ass!" or "What a package!" just remark: "She gets a passport!" or "He gets a passport!"

You can still look at her ass … or his package … just be discreet.

CHAPTER NINETEEN

Two days later, Gabrielle and I were on the Greyhound bus at 5.30 in the afternoon as it pulled out of the depot at the Key West Airport. On account of Old Town logistics, we had to take a bus to get to the bus.

Might I mention right up front, and it's best if I whisper it so as not to denigrate and piss off GREYHOUND, but this is not to be recommended: taking the bus from Key West to Miami, I mean. The bus was filled with certifiable crazies, crackheads, down-and-outs carrying ukuleles, an older gent with a cat in a wicker basket, and someone who resembled my new dentist.

Did you know Greyhound serves over 3,700 destinations in the US, Canada and Mexico?

Did you know Greyhound is owned by the British transport firm, FirstGroup (of Aberdeen, Scotland)?

Do you even care?

The Greyhound is readying to leave. "Readying to leave" means the driver is stashing his Big Gulp off to the side so as not to break any company rules while keeping it well within reach, which breaks company rules.

Okay! Grab a seat, quick, and make sure you get a window seat!

The bus groaned as it swung out onto S. Roosevelt Boulevard and the Florida Keys Overseas Heritage Trail, and soon we were sweeping past the old houseboat row, in a puff of what smelled of "red" diesel.

We were nervous as, well, a nervous cat in a wicker basket. How would we be received by Immigration up in Miami?

With open arms?

Or closed doors?

Or locked cell doors?

Okay, we are just rounding the curve at the northern end of the island by the Days Inn and Waffle House. And, yes, I see you eyeing the Waffle House and thinking about the chocolate chip waffles, but this is not the time for gluttony! Focus! Plus, if you haven't noticed we are already careering onto A1A and the Overseas Highway and crossing over the Cow Key Channel bridge to Stock Island.

We are leaving Key West behind and we are not so very thrilled about it. Will we be returning to our adopted home any time soon?

Hang on a sec, look over there to the right. That's Chico's Cantina Mexican restaurant. That's where Popcorn Joe and John Rubin and Doris, and Gabrielle and I had lived *La Vida Loca* and weathered that ferocious tropical storm rendered *Fuck it!* unintimidating by vats of grape and kegs of grain -- and our tipsy waitress in the fruit-chapeau guise of Carmen Miranda. Do you remember that? That was great crack and we'll have to go back there one day.

Perhaps not under cloak of tempest.

Now, we are crossing the bridge which will put us on Boca Chica. Look out there to the right. Do you see it? That's the Naval Air Station Key West. Look! There's an F-18 taking off and slicing silently into the late-afternoon sky. The wind must be out of the north, and the F-18 is downwind, otherwise it would be slicing into the late-afternoon sky with one hellacious roar. If you happen to live in the area of the Naval Air Station Key West, you can save money and not buy an alarm clock. Most mornings at 7.00 am, the rumbling beasts roar into the streaky sky to perform secret maneuvers and shake the shit out of anyone who happens to be sleeping on Geiger Key. A woman we know was so outraged by being ripped from her sleep at 7.00 am, she actually had the ballsy wherewithal to ring up the commander of the Naval Air Station and ask him: "What's so important that has to be done at seven o'clock that can't wait till eight?" There was no response from the commanding officer, so the woman really figured she had posed a worthy question. That's when she realized that he had hung up on her.

On two different occasions, when riding our bikes out on the other side of the Naval Air Station, Gabrielle and I have seen a Learjet pulling a large white "target." The Learjet zips off somewhere toward international waters and then those early rising F-18 pilots do target practice on the trailing large white "target." Who gets to pilot the Learjet, I don't know, but he is not paid enough in my opinion.

Why have you moved to the back of the bus? What are you up to? The toilet? Alright, then, let me know when you're back, because I don't want you to miss anything.

Are you back now? Okay, quickly re-commandeer your set. The hippie girl with the piercings and the twelve-string guitar was eyeing it before she began chanting.

We are just passing Big Coppit Key now and the bus is really cold. Gabrielle is motioning over there to the right at Geiger Key. "Down there is where Tina and Patty's new house is. They've invited us to go paddle boarding ..."

Now Gabrielle is pointing just past Seaside (trailer park) down Old Boca Chica Road. Once again, dear Reader, you may remember that we rode our bicycles out here and went down to the end of Boca Chica Road, just before the nude beach. Boca Chica Road leads to the end of the runway of the Naval Air Station and this is where Gabrielle and I were straddling our bicycles ten feet from the fence and the end of the runway when an F-18 roared down the runway, hugged the runway (on purpose) and cleared us by 30 feet at most. This, also, is not to be recommended. We thought our brains would explode and then when the pilot rotated, the premier fighter jet sandblasted us and created a nifty wake in the clear, shallow waters.

Gabrielle is thinking what I'm thinking and she turns to me with: "Remember later that night we went to the Geiger Key Marina for a well-deserved bevvy, and our hearing had still not returned?"

"Oh, right, we were sitting at the Tiki Bar next to a friendly dog who kept eyeing you. That's the night we learned that the marina was built along the old US Highway 1."

"We did?"

"You don't remember the bartender telling us?"

"I remember his lips moving, but I still couldn't hear."

We motor on ...

Quick! Look out the window. Not down there by the water,

up there in the sky.

Is it a bird?

No!

Is it a plane?

No!

Is it Superman?

No!

IT'S FAT ALBERT!!!

This is Cudjoe Key, and we are gazing at the tethered eminence of the white radar aerostat lovingly known as "Fat Albert." There he is right there, glistening in the last of the day's dying rays. Fat Albert was originally constructed for use as a US Army missile tracking station during the Cuban missile crisis in 1960 and is now used for drug interdiction by the DEA. Did you know that on April 20th, 2007, a Cessna 182 went down after its left wing struck the "wire." The pilot apparently had not done his homework and read the navigation chart which clearly states the warning: "Caution: Unmarked balloon on cable to 14,000 feet."

A video record from the camera mounted on the TARS flight control building, which monitors Fat Albert, showed the lights of the Cessna coming this way. The Cessna's left wing struck the cable which had a payout of 8,000 feet that evening. The Cessna spun out of control and crashed in 3 to 4 feet of water in Kemp Channel on the bay side of the key. The plane had taken off from Key West just under 15 minutes earlier. There were three fatalities.

After the crash, Fat Albert was reeled in and the cable showed damage at its 4,533-ft cable payout level.

We are just passing Boondock Grille and Draft House on Ramrod Key now. This is where the incomparable Howard Livingston can be found on occasion singing one of his many hits like "Six Pack and a Tan."

Something we would all love to have.

At MM26, we pass a sign which reads: "Prevent Scurvy. Eat Key Lime Pie." Then, as we are motoring onto Big Pine Key, a TV falls off the back of a ratty old rust bucket of a pickup truck right in front of us and our bus driver has to swerve wildly to miss it. I'm concerned about the passenger who was in the toilet at the time of the slalom, a fucked-up dude, who won't soon forget this trip. Or the trip he was on. We pull over at the Big Pine Greyhound stop and the driver shuts down the engine with a shudder and hits the Big Gulp with a parched vengeance. About now, the dude in the toilet emerges and has a *What the freak look?* on his face and I think I hear him mutter: "Could've used a seatbelt." The image is frightening, so I quickly banish it.

Before anyone can de-bus, the driver physically ejects the two glassy-eyed freaks who resemble Leopold and Loeb. They were caught red-handed, or should it be tie-dye handed smoking a joint in the back of the bus.

Presumably, they got tossed because they weren't passing it around.

Hey! Check out the guy climbing on the bus. Don't you think he bears an uncanny resemblance to Truman Capote? Do you see what his "carry-on" luggage is? He's carrying a Styrofoam head with a pink wig. Jeez, I hope *he's* not going up to Miami for an interview with Immigration.

The bus driver fires up the refurbished MCI coach, and we are once again on our way.

Someone on the bus is snoring BIG TIME as we pass by Bahia Honda. There's the derelict railway bridge just over there, visible in the fading light. The snoring sounds like a train approaching and it adds to the effect of the railway bridge.

Have you ever been snorkeling at Bahia Honda State Park? It is a glorious beach to do so, isn't it? But you have to be cautious as the tide rips between both bridges, and remember that BIG FISH use that channel.

The snoring has taken on an enervating, sleep-apnea beat and we all fear for the man involved. At least we think it's a man. Why don't you just swivel around in your seat and tell me who's doing it. What? It's Truman Capote? I turn around to look at Truman and the bus is just a deep black hole illuminated only by reading lights over the seats of people who are fast asleep (the lights above the passengers trying to read, don't work).

Guess what? Guess where we are now? That's right, we are just starting the crossing of the Seven Mile Bridge (in reality it is 6.79 miles, and just slightly shorter than Flagler's original Overseas Railway bridge, but this is not the time to quibble).

Were you as horrified as we were, when in the movie *True Lies*, the bridge was destroyed? The flick which was filmed in the early 1990s, had a section of the old bridge being destroyed by missile strikes. The missiles were edited in, and the explosions were done on an 80-foot model of the Seven Mile Bridge. Other less explosive scenes were indeed done on the actual bridge, and the "blown up" segment was the former swing span, which had been removed upon completion of the new bridge.

You've probably read that after the devastating Labor Day hurricane of 1935, the Overseas Railroad sustained such damage that the railway line was sold to the federal government and they rebuilt the Seven Mile Bridge so that it could accommodate vehicular traffic. The old tracks from the Overseas Railway were dismantled, painted white and were then used as the guardrails for the "old" Seven Mile Bridge.

You would be able to look right out there and still see their rusted remains if it weren't so dark now.

I remember reading that the old Seven Mile Bridge's swing span was to allow for boat traffic. This span was situated adjacent to Pigeon Key. Pigeon Key was used as a work camp for the men toiling on Flagler's Overseas Railroad. When you drive on the current road and bridge (which was built between 1978 and 1982), the remains of the old bridge are still there used by fishermen and as access to Pigeon Key.

You probably know (in fact, you may have been the one who told me) that Pigeon Key or *Cayo Paloma* as it was once called, at Mile Marker 45, *mas o menos*, is also a historic district. The main construction depot of Henry Flagler's Overseas Railroad was located here. From here workers put in long hours to build the Seven Mile Bridge. During the Great Depression, Pigeon Key was a beehive of activity. Hundreds upon hundreds of unemployed veterans of World War I, descended on the island aboard the Florida East Coast Railway's trains. "The federal government set up the (New Deal) program to give them jobs. (They) were here working on the bridge system," says Kelly McKinnon, the foundation's executive director and the island's only year-round resident. But, he says, an attempt to move those men to safety during the 1935 hurricane went horribly wrong.

"Government officials found out the storm was coming and

sent down their biggest, heaviest locomotive and loaded all these men on it," he says. "It only got up as far as Islamorada and the train was lost over the seas."

The original Seven Mile Bridge was an engineering marvel and gives me goose bumps every time I see it. The historic remains are a time-gone-by reminder of Henry Flagler's "railroad that went to sea."

The bridge is listed on the National Register of Historic Places.

As it should be.

When you traverse the Seven Mile Bridge in daylight, as Gabrielle and I did when we first arrived nearly a year earlier, we were taken with the gin-clear waters, where you could peer down and just might see sharks, tarpon, sea turtles, and pelicans diving into the translucent waters.

Okay, the Greyhound is passing through Marathon now and I hope no one is getting on because I fear all the seats are taken. Well, all but one near the back, where some troglodyte has his corpulent ass sprawled across two seats.

Shit! The bus is slowing. No sooner did I think that, then we are making a stop. And, oh, oh, here comes a quintessential little ol' lady climbing onto the bus. She's the poster child for osteoporosis. She's dragging her carry-on behind her down the aisle (the carry-on is a black garbage bag) and is it just me or does she smell? We all watch in forthcoming and increasing horror as she schleps her hand luggage on a collision course with the snoozing cave dweller. Just at the moment of impact, when we all know the brute will wake up, pull out an assault rifle and go postal, the bus starts up, lurches and the ol' crone gently nudges the leg of the sleeping ex-felon. He wakes up, gets one whiff of the bag lady and jumps up from his seat. Now she has a choice: aisle or window.

We've been on the bus for two hours and have two and a half more to go.

Do you remember in my first book on Key West the part about the Cuban MiG scorching the beach at Fort Zach and the pilot landing at the Naval air Station on Boca Chica and defecting?

Are you thinking about that now?

I am.

Remember Marathon was where he took off from in that twin-engine Cessna, then flew at wave-skipping altitude and slipped under the radar entering Cuban air space, skimmed just over the roof of a bus and landed on the Veradero Highway almost right in the grill of an oncoming truck which had to slam on the brakes to avoid a collision. The truck stopped only 10 meters from the churning propellers. The pilot picked up his wife and two sons, turned the airplane around and headed back to freedom and a future.

Since recounting this tale, I have learned that the Cuban pilot, Orestes Lorenzo Perez, was a handsome 36-year-old Air Force major and combat pilot. When he first defected and flew under U.S. radar, buzzed the beach at Ft. Zach (twice) and then landed at nearby NAS Key West, he thought the Cuban government would be so embarrassed by his act (and antics), they would allow his wife and family to leave, happy to see their backs. But it was not to be. Over the nearly two years the Major was separated from his wife, Victoria, who was a respected dentist, and his two young sons, the wife was lied to and told at various times that her husband was a traitor, planning to marry a rich American woman, was a homosexual, and even that he was dead.

Eventually, she lost her job and the government repossessed her home.

Back in America, the Major tried every possible avenue to get his family released and brought over to America. Helped financially by cousins in the U.S. and by the Valladares Foundation, a Northern Virginia-based human rights group, the Major lobbied Congress and President Bush (#41), who during a campaign speech in Miami, urged Fidel Castro to let the family leave. When this didn't work (surprise), the Major resorted to a week-long hunger strike. It brought attention to his plight, but not success.

And then the story took a turn for the strange as life intervened: The Major was able to place a phone call to Havana, through Canada. He actually got his wife on the phone. After she spoke for a few minutes, she passed the phone to their little son, 6-year-old Alejandro, and Alejandro said these words:

"Daddy, you are a pilot, come get us in a helicopter. Fly over the house and drop down a ladder."

And from little Alejandro, the Major got his inspiration.

The first thing he had to do was learn how to fly. *What! He's the Cuban equivalent of Top Gun!* Well, it's this way: He had to obtain a US pilot's license, but language was not the problem, technology was. He may have been able to fly a sophisticated MiG-23 jet fighter, but he had to take lessons to learn how to fly a simple twin-engine Cessna. This is sort of like asking a teenager, who can hack into the Pentagon, to do simple math in his head.

Then he had to find a plane. He didn't want to rent one. He feared that if he was shot down on his flight to Cuba, authorities would think he had just wanted to steal the plane to get back to the island. Eventually, Valladares co-chairwoman Elena Diaz-Verson Amos, a wealthy Cuban-born widow, heard of the Major and his family and she put up $30,000 of her own money to buy an aircraft.

The plan: His wife was to make as if she were taking the two boys to the beach for a seaside outing. The Major would take off from Marathon, fly the 90 miles to Cuba at an altitude of **six feet** -- and under US and Cuban radar -- then he would set the twin-engine Cessna down on the congested Veradero highway, just yards from where his wife and sons would be enjoying a day at the beach and his wife and two boys would run for their lives.

From his days with the Cuban military, he knew he had a 40-second window before he would be targeted by missiles.

The Major would eventually tell friends in America: "Even I thought the plan was crazy, but I had to try. I would rather die than leave my family there."

The Major smuggled the details of his plan in a letter hand-delivered by two female Mexican human rights activists. When his wife received the letter, she knew it was the real deal and not some government ruse -- the Major had addressed his beloved wife by his pet name for her "Cuchita."

The two human rights activists also accompanied the Major's wife on a reconnaissance visit to the pickup site to do a mock run-through. Then they purchased international-orange shirts and hats for her and the boys, so the Major could spot them quickly upon touching down.

The entire preparation took nine months.

On the night before the mission, the Major was praying at a chapel. "This sister came to me and said, 'Don't be afraid. Your long trip will be a success.' How could she know about my plans? I believed that God was speaking to me then and that God would be with me."

The Major roared down the runway in Marathon in his twin-engine Cessna at 5:05 the next afternoon and stayed low over the aquamarine waters of the Florida Straits. He hugged the ocean and prayed that his plane would not be intercepted.

The Major's wife was watching as a dark speck skimmed the waters of northern Cuba and then fought to land just over a bus, and avoid a street sign and boulder in the middle of the road.

The Major's wife screamed to her children: "Run! Run! It's Daddy!"

And the 40 seconds began.

Tick. Tick. Tick.

The Major braked desperately to avoid hitting the approaching truck, which screeched to a halt and only just avoided hitting the propellers. The Major would later say he would never forget the bug-eyed look on the stunned truck driver's face.

Tick. Tick. Tick.

The Major had to turn the plane around in front of startled onlookers. Cars in the way pulled over and made a path out.

Tick. Tick. Tick.

His wife and children threw open the door and burst into the airplane. The boys were crying and hugging their daddy, forgetting that there wasn't time for that.

Tick. Tick. Tick.

Looking back on that day, the Major says the hardest part, was when his wife and kids jumped into the plane—and he didn't even have time to touch them. "They were crying. I had to say to the children, 'Shut up and sit down.' I had to fly the plane."

Tick. Tick. Tick.

With more rubberneckers stacking up, the Major roared

down the Veradero Highway, nearly clipped a wing on a car, lifted the nose of the twin-engine Cessna and once again hugged the waves as the sun set in the west.

Twenty-one minutes and 43 seconds later, they were out of missile range and entered U.S. airspace. "We did it!" the Major shouted triumphantly. "We did it!"

Still gives me goose bumps.

Safe on American soil, the Major will tell you: "I wake up every night at 4 a.m. I look at my wife. I kiss my sons. I watch them sleep. I cannot believe that they are here with me."

And his wife, Victoria, will add: "I knew he would come, I always knew it. I believe in him. I believe in love."

And perhaps most of us don't know how lucky we are.

CHAPTER TWENTY

Marathon.

The name Marathon dates back to the days of the Florida East Coast Railroad. "Marathon" was coined by the scores of railroad workers who were working their asses off night and day to complete the railway. On account of the unrelenting pace and increasing hardships brought on to complete the project, many of the workers complained that "the building of the overseas railroad was getting to be a real marathon." So there you have it, the name stuck for this island, and a railway stop along the great railroad that never was.

We all know that the overseas railroad was the brainchild of Henry Flagler. If you would like to know how Flagler came upon such a grand scheme, here's the short version, as that's all my brain can handle: Flagler (a founder of Standard Oil -- and not short of change) was living in the Great White North and his wife's doctor suggested they winter in Florida due to her failing health. Flagler chose Jacksonville as it was difficult to travel much farther south because the St. Johns River was in the way. Two years later, Flagler's wife died and, with some difficulty, he made his way down to St. Augustine.

He was taken with St. Augustine's charm, but felt the city was lacking a great hotel, so he built the 540-room Ponce de León Hotel. After he built the Ponce de León, he realized it was still difficult to get to his hotel, so he purchased short line railroads in what would later become known as the Florida East Coast Railway.

The Ponce de León Hotel, now part of Flagler College, opened its doors on 10 January 1888, and was such a success it gave Flagler ideas, big ideas, and he now wanted to create the "American Riviera," so he built a railroad bridge across the St. Johns River (do you see a pattern developing?), so he could gain access to all points south. Then he bought the Hotel Ormond just north of Daytona. And then he constructed the 1,100-room Royal Poinciana Hotel in Palm Beach (the largest wooden structure in the world, at the time). To ensure high occupancy, he went back to the drawing board and extended his railroad all the way to Palm Beach.

Flagler originally intended West Palm Beach to be the terminus of his railroad system, but in 1894 and 1895, severe freezes hit the area, causing Flagler to freeze his ass off and rethink his original decision. Sixty miles south, the town today known as Miami was untouched by the freeze.

Then the *coup de foudre* was spawned in 1905: Flagler decided that his Florida East Coast Railway should be extended from Biscayne Bay all the way down to Key West.

And now you know the rest of the story. (Didn't mean to sound so Paul Harvey.)

Everyone is asleep on the bus now as we pass the Marathon Veterinary Hospital, except Gabrielle, you and me. May I just take this sleepy, snoring, little interlude to once again stress that taking the bus to Miami is not to be recommended. The feeling is that of sleeping behind locked doors with all of God's twisted, certifiable creatures. Do you have weird dreams? I don't, but I'm sure I will from here on in. Perhaps this isn't the Greyhound Bus to Miami, perhaps this is really the bus from *CON AIR*, and we are being taken straight to the Krome Detention Center.

What? What? Is that you shaking me gently by the shoulder, or is that Gabrielle? Oh, I seem to have dozed off and I've been reassured that we are in fact on the Greyhound Bus to Miami.

Perhaps things aren't as I thought they were.

Perhaps they are worse.

Just after we passed the old Crocodile Road Kill Café, somewhere near Mile Marker 60 "You kill it, we grill it." ****BTW**: I think they should've added: "From your grill to our grill." I looked out at Florida Bay. Amazing to think that the average depth of this vast expanse is only three feet. The moon was peeking out from a rack of cumulus clouds and the bay glistened back in an inviting manner, middle of winter or not. Just across Florida Bay, the coast is rife with estuaries and thick with mangroves. If you don't know, let me be the first to tell you

133

that Florida Bay is actually part of the Everglades Watershed, and more than 800 square miles of Florida Bay is protected by the Everglades National Park. The freshwater which flows out of the Everglades and into Florida Bay creates an ideal environment for vast beds of turtle grass. Manatees, as well as sea turtles, dine on the turtle grass (thus, the, ah, term *turtle grass* one can surmise). Manatees spend the "cold" winter months in the warmer water of the bay, while female sea turtles return yearly to nest on the shores.

Now we are passing by mile marker 81.5 in Islamorada and the *stone memorial*. Day after day, thousands of travelers pass by this monument without even giving it a glance. This majestic 18-foot tall memorial is just there on the right-side of the road as you're motoring north. Within this memorial lie the cremated and skeletal remains of many of the 423 people who perished during the hurricane of 2 September 1935, which nearly wiped Islamorada, Upper Matecumbe Key and Lower Matecumbe Key off the mapwhen, as James McLendon put it: "the barometer dropped and dropped and from out of a driving rainstorm at the outer edge of the hurricane, a 200-mile-an-hour killer wind emerged from a barometer reading of 26.35 inches of mercury (892 millibars) the lowest ever recorded in the hemisphere. A 17-foot tidal wave crashed over the Keys and when it was all over, there was nothing but devastation. A rescue train, dispatched from Miami to evacuate local families in Key West, lay in a swirling mass of steel, its passengers dead, blown into the Gulf of Mexico or tangled in the mangroves. In all, 577 bodies were finally accounted for, but the true number of the dead was never known."

CHAPTER TWENTY ONE

We are just pulling into the Greyhound bus depot in downtown Miami.

I must have dozed off again, which is a bit unsettling as I wanted to tell you about Key Largo and as the name implies that it's indeed *long* ... the longest island in the Florida Keys at 33 miles.

And I wanted to point out that once hideously frightening 18-mile stretch of highway between Key Largo and Florida City ... and that body of water on the right where there is a sign saying **No Swimming Alligators**. Now I don't know about you, but I'm not going in there, are you? Yet there were people in there *swimming* when we came through on our drive down from Miami. Surely, there's a reason the sign is there. Alligators can't read, so that rules out that the sign is for their benefit. On the other hand, if you factor punctuation into the equation, since there is no comma, it could be taken as a *command* to alligators.

Something else to consider is that the water is not just brackish, rather pretty much full-strength saltwater, so are those alligators in there or crocodiles? There are crocodiles in Florida, you know, not many, but this is where they might want to pay a visit, here and near Homestead by the Turkey Point Nuclear Generating Station. And I'm not sure if you've been paying attention when watching the Discovery Channel, but alligators are mean sons-of-bitches and you really don't want to piss one off. But they aren't even in the same league with crocodiles. You do not want to fuck with crocodiles. Granted the ones hanging out in the Everglades are not the 20-foot-long, slavering Nile crocodiles which weigh one ton, or the killing machines quaintly known as "salties" (measuring 23 feet and weighing two tons) which frequent the Northern Territory of Australia, up by Cairns, mate, but they are crocs just the same and they grow to a toothy length of nearly 10 feet and can weigh close to 400 pounds.

**FYI: As I write this chapter, I'm reading (with toes curling) that three Nile crocodiles (these are invasive, by the way, and are not our own Florida crocs, which are less aggressive) have been sighted in Florida, near Miami, one at the Redland Fruit and Spice Park in Homestead. It is feared that these crocs were kept as exotic pets and were released when they grew too large by their irresponsible owners. It's hoped they won't enter the eco-system the way the Burmese pythons have. Wildlife managers have already issued a shoot-to-kill order.

**FYI ADDENDUM: Have you ever read Mark Terrill's Bike Guide about riding from Key Largo all the way down the Keys to Key West? This is a must read for anyone who wants to get behind the guidebook pages of the upper, middle and lower Keys. Mark is a bit of an historian slash comedian, and he runs Key Largo Bike. A man who knows what he's talking about: the Keys inside and out, from both sides now, every which way, but loose. I say all this because he not only talks in his Bike Guide about biking, smuggling, celebrities and murder, he talks about "Crocodolly." This is what he says: "Now about the 78 mile marker, you should cross over to the Bayside and get on the bike path before the last bridge. You will go over the shoulder of the bridge and land in front of Robbie's Marina. Some people like to go see the tarpon at the docks there. There have been crocodiles that started hanging out around here lately. They tried to move them, but crocodiles have great memories. They are not harmful to humans, but scare people however. There is one crocodile that has been named 'Crocodolly' who keeps coming back. She even has a Facebook page now."

REPTILIAN NOTE: Crocodolly and I are now friends on Facebook. *Just friends*. It says on her Facebook page that she's **In a relationship.

Just had a thought: Crocodolly's ancestors were here first, humans are the invasive species.

We are debussing now, and I would just like to point out that as frightening as the passengers were on the ride up from Key West, the low-lifes hanging out at the bus station in downtown Miami are even more so, say, the difference between alligators (passengers on the bus) and crocodiles (low-lifes circling at the bus station). And, no, that does not include you, Crocodolly. *You* are adorable!

I think it's best I bid you a temporary farewell here, dear Reader, and let you get on your way, or perhaps you want to stay on the bus and make the return trip to Cayo Hueso where life is good.

CHAPTER TWENTY TWO

It's midnight and Gabrielle and I are cowering in the bus depot in Miami, Florida, USA, the mainland, and things are not looking good. First of all the bus didn't go to the downtown bus station like we'd thought. Apparently it has closed or has been relocated. So we got off at the bus stop by the airport. That's all well and good, but we are a long distance from where we need to be. And the place is scary and looks like the bar in *Star Wars*. There's someone here who resembles Freddie Krueger, another person who could be Mommie Dearest, yet another who resembles Leatherface (*Texas Chain Saw Massacre*), Dr. Christian Szell (*Marathon Man*), that one vendor down at Mallory, and the scariest of all is the security guard, who has eyes like a chameleon which look in different directions at the same time. He's flirting with one of the girls behind the ticket counter. Giving her the eye, both, actually, although not at the same time.

What are the requirements to be a security guard in a bus station in a major city? Blood lust? Hellacious chip on shoulder? Ability to sneak short naps while sitting upright in front of a bank of TV monitors? Hormonal time bomb? I don't know and I'm not about to go up to him and ask. An announcement is made and it sounds like Hal 9000 is making it, so we scarper.

Gabrielle and I did not book into a hotel. We thought the hotels near the downtown bus station would be too expensive. Now, here, by the airport, they are even more expensive. We had planned to power nap in the bus station, one sleeping while the other stood guard, but there's no way we will catch any shut eye here. Not around this bag of loonies.

Then Gabrielle gets an idea: "Let's go find the Immigration building, so we know where we're going. Perhaps there will be a hotel out there, this is Miami after all."

Someone told me once that Greater Miami has more hotel

rooms than all of Australia, true or not, we don't know, but we feel our chances are good.

I like this idea. It's something I used to do before I had a big interview, not that I ever applied for a real job in my life. I would walk the route or drive the route so I would know where I was going the next day. It relieved the stress and many times I even made it to the interview on time.

Not that I ever got the job.

We took the city bus from Miami International Airport out to the Immigration building. It took us two hours and we had to change buses three times.

The building is quite impressive (even in the dark) and newer than we thought. And it's located out on a vast boulevard, a teeming thoroughfare with non-stop traffic.

"What time do you have, Gabrielle?"

"Midnight, just gone."

"Do you see any hotels around here?"

"No, just endless office buildings."

"If we take the bus back to the airport where there are hotels, it will take us another two hours to get back there, then we need to go to sleep so we can get up early feeling like shit to have the right to take the bus all the way back out here."

"You are presuming there are even buses running this time of night."

"Oh, crap."

Gabrielle and I were wondering what to do when we noticed a group of people over by the entrance to the Immigration building.

"Let's go ask them. They have to know more than we know."

"EVERYBODY has to know more than we know."

We approached the group of people. Curiously they appeared to be one large family: a single mother with a few young children and some grandparent types.

Gabrielle whispered to me: "What are they all doing here this time of night?"

"Wondering the same thing myself."

We greeted the group of people and explained our predicament, but no one responded. They just all stared back at us.

Gabrielle and I stood there, smiling, then finally Gabrielle grabbed me by the arm and led me a distance away.

"They don't speak English …"

"I was starting to think the same thing."

"What do they speak then?"

"I'm guessing Spanish."

"How do you know that?"

"I think I heard someone say *puta*."

Well … it just happened that Gabrielle and I knew nine words of Spanish between the two of us. That's including *puta*. Just enough to get ourselves in trouble. For example, we could ask for directions, but then wouldn't understand them once given.

We approached the group of people who were now huddled together like Meerkats and greeted them in our best *español*.

And guess what? They burst into grand smiles and relaxed and became wonderfully helpful. We used eight of our nine words of Spanish, they used their nine words of English, and that made seventeen words, a veritable lexicon!

Only problem was, that's when we found out: 1) there were no more buses running 2) there were no hotels this side of Little Havana 3) they were standing in front of the Immigration building because they were already in line for the next morning!

First come, first served.

"They're already waiting in line for the next morning?" Gabrielle asked me.

"Sadly, yes, they are all waiting to get their temporary Green Card. Just like you."

"What do we do?"

"We get in line."

Well, dear Reader, standing in front of the Immigration building in Miami in the middle of the night – in January – when the temperatures dipped down into the upper forties is not to be recommended. Although, we did improve our Spanish.

Just as the eastern sky was smearing with the hint of a new day, a friend or relative of the mother brought a gigantic thermos of coffee and plastic cups and the coffee was passed around and even shared with us.

And by the time it inched toward 7.00 a.m., and the doors were just about to open, there was such a long line of people behind us, we were glad we had stayed. Many of the people in the back of the queue would have to go back home and try another day.

For us, that had not been an option.

CHAPTER TWENTY THREE

At seven o'clock sharp, the doors swung open and we were beckoned in and entered the hallowed foyer of the U.S. Citizenship and Immigration Services.

We were both pretty wired (it had been a double-strength Cuban coffee) and we had to pass through a Security Check Point like you do at the airport. The officers only spoke Spanish, but at least we got to keep our shoes on, so that was a plus.

When Gabrielle went through the metal detector, she set off the alarm, and had to be frisked by a libidinous-looking woman who seemed to take unusual pride in her work.

Desperately needing morning ablutions, along with the brushing of teeth, we were led into a large room with about a hundred seats and took a number. Our number was #2, the same as our now immediate concerns.

We sat in the back row, waiting to be called. Everyone looked nervous. And rightly so. If anyone was looking at us, they would have said that we looked nervous. And rightly so.

Eventually our number was called and we were directed to a room bearing a letter of the alphabet that I had never seen before.

We knocked on the door and no one answered. We knocked again and still no one answered. Were we at the wrong door?

"May I help you?"

Gabrielle and I turned to see a woman standing in the neighboring doorway, blocking out most of the light coming from within. She waved us in and explained the procedure in heavily accented English. No one working for the Immigration Services in Miami spoke English as a first language. I wanted to dazzle the woman with my Spanish, but didn't know if I should leave the *puta* in or take it out, so I said nothing.

Eventually, I was asked to leave the room and Gabrielle was grilled about all sorts of personal things about her husband, *me*, and about where we lived and what we did and if we one day had a dog would we let him up on the couch, and would we feed him at the table, and if we were planning to go on the Internet and download plans on how to construct a thermal-nuclear weapon, and would we ever think about buying a pickup and park it on the front lawn, and if we chased beers with shots of tequila or whisky, and if I left the seat up, and did I snore (like a brown bear) and did I eat with my fork in the right hand or the left, and did we share a sock drawer, and did I know libraries were becoming a thing of the past, and did I litter, and did I finish the entire tube of Pringles in one sitting (like a brown bear), and was I afraid of spiders, and did I hold the door for my wife or just barge ahead, and did I pull out a map when lost or just try to wing it, and if I was invited to dinner and I didn't like the asparagus, would I hide it in the pockets of my blazer like a squirrel (*squirrels like asparagus?!*), and had I ever been in Facebook jail, and did I self-medicate with alcohol.

That's pretty much verbatim.

Then Gabrielle was sent from the room and I was asked the same questions … and I got lots of them right, but slipped up and exchanged wild boar for one of the brown bears. And I screwed up on the question about the sock drawer because I thought she had asked if we shared an *armoire*, not sock drawer.

Perhaps it was her accent?

Then she called Gabrielle back in the room, and without further ado grabbed a large officious-looking chrome stamp machine, stamped Gabrielle's passport and a few pieces of official-looking paper with a few prodigious whacks like a judge calling for *Order in the court!*

"Welcome to the US," she said, then she rose and ushered us out.

As we passed back through the waiting room, we saw the Cuban family who had been standing next to us in the line. They smiled.

Outside in the streaming sunshine, Gabrielle studied the stamp in her passport, and the sheet of paper we had been given.

"This is a temporary Green Card," she said bursting into a

wonderful smile. "I even have the right to work."

"Wonder why she didn't just deport you?"

"They want the people living and working in the country to be legal, so they will pay taxes."

"Let's go celebrate!"

"What do you have in mind?"

"Let's splash out and take a taxi back to the Greyhound Station."

"You're on! And I'll buy you the strongest *con leche*."

We flagged down a passing taxi. The driver was from Haiti and didn't speak English. We asked to go to the Greyhound depot ... and he took us to the greyhound track in Hialeah.

But we didn't mind.

Our dream, which had become a nightmare, was turning back into a dream again.

One glorious HD blissful, tropical Technicolor dream.

CHAPTER TWENTY FOUR

We were exhausted by the time we got back to Key West.

But insatiably giddy.

I wanted to get down on my hands and knees and kiss the marl upon which Key West stands.

But didn't want to be mistaken for a religious fanatic.

The Greyhound stopped at the Key West Airport and then we splashed out again and took a taxi back to Villa Alberto. Our cabbie got us to our destination and he spoke English as a first language. He was from Chicago and he had moved to Key West ten years earlier to get away from snow and family.

We waved goodbye to the cabbie and looked over to see Mr. Leroy standing there, waiting for us. He had a sour look on his face. Cats know when you've been gone and didn't tell them. We figured that's why he was upset.

Then Gabrielle grabbed my arm. "Notice anything different."

I looked up at our tin roof where we always had a leak. It hadn't been fixed, so that wasn't it. I glanced at the back gate, where the whole fence was starting to sag. It was still sagging, so that wasn't it. I looked under Villa Alberto where there had been an old pile of boards which attracted rats. They were still there, so that wasn't it.

I turned to Gabrielle: "What?"

"It's not what's *there*, it's what's *not* there ..."

"What are you talking about?"

"The FOR RENT sign is gone."

CHAPTER TWENTY FIVE

Gabrielle and I went inside Villa Alberto and it was obvious to us that uninvited scourge had been in our home.

We did a quick reconnaissance of our home.

"Someone left the seat up!"

"Someone sat on the bed!"

"The fridge is not shut properly!"

"It never shuts properly ..."

"Oh."

"They didn't even have the courtesy to ring and ask if they could show it, they just came in and ran rampant while we were gone."

I tried to calm myself down, but it wasn't working, so I checked my emails: I had three rejections from literary agencies. Remember that Peanuts cartoon? The one where Snoopy has written "It was a dark and stormy night?" He's sent his manuscript off to a publisher, and the publisher sends back this note: "Dear Snoopy, please find enclosed TWO rejection slips. One for the manuscript you sent us, and another one for anything you may write in the future."

THAT, coupled with the missing For Rent sign out front of our home! I was, in this order: Incensed. Livid. Furious. Pissed. Fucking ready to explode. I grabbed Gabrielle and we hopped on our bikes and pedaled (with our feet to the metal) over to Mr. Tosser's office. We entered the building and were hit by the indigenous fugue of cigarette smoke. This was his wife's (the hydra) doing. Why was she allowed to smoke in the building? Because she and her dickhead husband owned the building, that's why. They both needed a swift visit to a wood chipper.

We climbed the stairs to the second floor and approached Mr. Tosser's secretary. Right off, we knew that she knew we knew."

"Did he rent it?"

Before, she could answer, Mr. Tosser strode out of his office and approached us. He looked like the type of person who was about to give bad news and derive joy from it. *Schadenfreude*.

Gabrielle began the assault: "We'd like to stay in our place."

"Thought you were leaving."

"Things have changed. We'd like to stay if we could."

"I've already taken a deposit."

"You can give it back."

Gabrielle's firm aggression seemed to render Mr. Tosser speechless for a moment. "Guess, I could."

"Please," Gabrielle said. "It would mean a lot to us."

I shot a look at the secretary and for some reason she had a look on her face of impending doom. How could that be? We were going to get to stay at Villa Alberto, right? Villa Alberto had become our home. It had become Mr. Leroy's home. It was a short commute for him to Cowboy Bill's.

"Alright, you can stay."

We couldn't believe our ears. Had Mr. Tosser lapsed into civility? Gabrielle wasn't going to get dragged off to the Krome Detention center AND we were going to keep our home!

Gabrielle and I turned to leave, but were stopped with: "Have to raise your rent, though ..."

We froze. "Excuse me?"

"I'll have to write you up a new lease. The couple that was planning on taking it was prepared to pay more."

"We can't really afford to pay more."

"Then don't stay. I'm not holding a gun to your head."

Insensitive leech! "But if we stay, you won't have to spend money to get the place cleaned."

"Wasn't planning on doing that anyway. That was to be your job ... or you wouldn't get your deposit back."

"How much will the new rent be?"

"Thousand a month."

"You're raising the rent by four-hundred dollars a month?"

Mr. Tosser actually snickered. "That's Key West for you..."

Gabrielle and I were stunned. I had been silent up till then, Gabrielle was always better in these life-or-death situations than I was. I looked over at Gabrielle and she was patently upset, and the great protector in me came out -- and I sort of snapped.

"Y'know, I could stoop to your level and tell you what a pompous fucking asshole you are, but what would that achieve?"

Mr. Tosser exploded: "YOU JUST LOST YOUR DEPOSIT!"

Gabrielle quickly shot back: "You might want to rethink that or the place won't be fit for renting anytime soon."

CHAPTER TWENTY SIX

Gabrielle and I pedaled away from Mr. Tosser's feeling good for once. Feeling fucking great!

Sometimes you have to stand up for yourself. Sometimes you have to strike back. Sometimes you have to level the playing field. Sometimes you have to do the right thing. Sometimes you have to run through all the clichés in your arsenal.

And we were glad we did.

We went over to Popcorn Joe's and sat out on the back deck with the popcorn man. We told him about Mr. Tosser and what a bumfuck Mr. Tosser was. And do you know what Popcorn Joe did? He scurried downstairs to the Caroline Street Market and brought back three steaming *con leche*s.

"Nice to hear that someone stood up to that asswipe. Everyone in Key West laughs at him behind his back."

I glanced over at Gabrielle. Then: "Hey, Giuseppe, if you hear of any places for rent, let us know. We will be without a home in less than a month."

"Difficult this time of year. It's high season as you know. Rents are up, folk are gouging."

"Crap," I said. "And we don't have enough seniority to get on the pier. We won't be making any money, any time soon."

We sipped our *con leche* in silence and watched the resident parrot flit about in the palm tree out behind Popcorn Joe's pool. Then Chubba came up to Gabrielle and rubbed up against her leg. Then BC made an appearance and jumped up on Gabrielle's lap. "Where's Scaredy Cat?"

"Here somewhere, keeping a low profile. The three mus-*cat*-eers always come to say hi when you come over."

We turned our attention back to the parrot in the palm tree.

We were silent and decidedly down, drifting in and out of the reality that we were homeless, jobless and basically fucked.

CHAPTER TWENTY SEVEN

Gabrielle and I heard about a houseboat for rent on Stock Island.

Have you ever been to Stock Island? I'm talking about, said with a whisper, *Stock Island*, not Chico's Cantina, not Boyd's Campground, not a few other fine establishments, but deep in the lower intestine of Stock Island. There are places where feral cats just won't venture. I don't want to offend anyone who calls Stock Island home, but you have to admit there is a bit of a rough side in that one area.

So this is what we're thinking about as we bike across the Cow Key Channel bridge and pedal doggedly onto Stock Island. Perhaps Stock Island is like most places: some great areas, some not so great areas. Perhaps.

We turn right on a street where the street sign had been plowed down and was lying flat on the ground and eventually pass a group of rough, surly men picking their teeth with knives. They leer at us from a down-market section of a down-market trailer park.

We pick up our pace and I look over at Gabrielle, and she mutters six words: "Does *Mariel* mean anything to you?"

"It means a lot to me ... Remember back during the boatlift, Cubans came in droves and a fair amount were criminals? Some of those criminals ended up on Stock Island."

"As did a lot of good, hardworking Cubans."

"Indeed."

**El Tidbit de Info: Back in April of 1980, relations between Cuba and the United States were finally warming. President Carter established an Interest Section in Havana and the Cuban government immediately reciprocated by establishing an Interest Section in Washington, D.C. (Sort of like you "Liking" someone on Facebook, because they just "liked" you.)

150

Shortly thereafter, in a mood *muy bueno*, Castro agreed to the release of scores of political prisoners and allowed Cuban-Americans exiles to return to the island to visit family and loved ones.

Everything was progressing nicely in *los Estados Unidos*, but in Cuba, things weren't going so very well. There had been a marked downturn in the economy, and this spawned internal tension on the island, so much so, five disenchanted Cubans came up with a plan that would have explosive consequences worldwide, and for years to come. They decided to leave Cuba, but they weren't about to board a ramshackle raft and try to make it to Key West. One of the dissidents was a bus driver, so he dutifully went to work. As his bus approached the posh Miramar section of La Habana, where Embassy Row was located, he brought the bus to an abrupt halt and told all the passengers onboard that the bus had broken down and they would have to debus. Only all didn't get off the bus, four remained, including Hector Sanyustiz who had hatched the plan. Our driver fired up the bus, accelerated, drove it at a high rate of speed and crashed through the front gates of the Peruvian Embassy. Cuban guards stationed out front opened fire. One guard was killed by friendly fire. Castro immediately condemned the brazen attempt and said the guard had been *murdered* by the five men as they stormed the gates and blasted away with their weapons. Castro demanded that the five be returned to Cuban soil to stand trial. The Peruvian diplomat (who had prior knowledge of the attempt) refused.

But Fidel Castro was always wily and never a man to be fucked with. He simply opened up all the prisons, asylums and mental hospitals and announced: "Any *scoria* (scum) who want to leave Cuba can do so by going to ... the Peruvian Embassy."

Ten thousands Cubans did.

And this overwhelmed the embassy.

Soon after, there was a cry of foul from the Americans, but Castro wasn't too bothered, he simply opened the port of Mariel to anyone who wished to flee Cuba to America.

Over a protracted and enervating five-month period, 125,266 disenchanted, dispossessed Cubans came across the Florida Straits. Somewhere in the neighborhood of 20,000 to

151

40,000 were criminals, mental patients or other undesirables.

Upon arrival in Florida, most Cubans were bussed up to the Orange Bowl, but some slipped into Key West.

And others onto Stock Island.

The Mariel boatlift created a logistical nightmare for Miami. Cuban refugees were shipped to points north. Oddly, so many Cubans ended up in Union City, New Jersey, it became known as Havana on the Hudson.

Thousands of others were relocated to Arkansas, of all places. Don't ask, because I don't know.

Back down in Miami, Cubans who did not have any family members in Dade County were not received with open arms. Until 1980 most exiles from Cuba were of the upper or middle classes and predominantly white. Are you getting the picture here?

In Miami's South Beach, then a depressed neighborhood, Mariel criminals preyed on fearful Jewish retirees. Mentally ill refugees wandered the streets in Little Havana. Unemployed Mariel refugees hung out on corners. Think Al Pacino in *Scarface*. His violent, cocaine-crazed character, Tony Montana was a *Marielito*, a Mariel refugee. Most *Marielitos* had been military-trained due to Cuba's mandatory three year military obligation.

America was repulsed.

Voters incensed.

One of the reasons then President Jimmy Carter wasn't re-elected.

One of the reasons then Governor Bill Clinton of Arkansas wasn't re-elected.

So am I saying that crime on Stock Island is related to the Mariel boatlift? Nowadays, perhaps a drying-up trickle, but back then it had a huge influence.

Again, so as not to piss off all the wonderful, deserving Cubans who were part of the boatlift, Miami and South Beach are partly the glorious destinations they are today because of them. You see, in Fidel's prisons were not just criminals. Miami had been a cultural wasteland. "The boatlift infused Miami with scores of artists, writers and musicians oppressed under Castro and now eager to practice their art without fear or repercussions or oppression -- and South Florida's culture -- was greatly enriched by the artists, musicians and actors who came on those boats," said painter Andres Valerio, who arrived in the boatlift with his wife.

"Mariel nudged Hispanics close to a numerical majority in Miami. It also laid the foundation for today's local Cuban-American political dominance. Some contend that the boatlift can also claim some credit for Miami's current economic and cultural resurgence."

Along with Miami's cultural revival, came Hollywood in the form of *Miami Vice*, and even though *Miami Vice*, glamorized the *Marielitos*, it helped lure visitors to nourish the revitalization of South Beach.

Gabrielle and I stopped our bikes and looked at the houseboat that was for rent. A real estate agent driving a late model caddie pulled up. He showed us the houseboat. It was downstairs and upstairs. It smelled of mold and was damp. Every time a small boat passed, it rocked back and forth.

But the price was right. Just $600 per month and that included water and electricity.

"We will have to buy a car to get our stuff down to Mallory each evening."

"Didn't think about that. A car means parking and parking is a nightmare with three acts and a bad ending in the Old Town."

We thanked the real estate agent and pedaled our bikes back past the Cubans picking their teeth with knives and headed back to Key West.

For reasons unknown, we tooled down Truman, then hung a right on Simonton. This was not our usual route. Traditionally, if we came anywhere near Francis, we pulled up in front of the Eden House to gaze at its architecture. Anyhoo, on account of riding down Simonton, we rode to the water's edge by dirt-bag beach (now transformed into the supremely appealing Lagerheads Beach Bar and Watersports). A transient with good taste in trikes was sitting in the shade of the Simonton Street Beach sign. He had his worldly possessions in a large garbage bag and was rooting through the equivalent of his sock drawer.

We pulled our bikes up, climbed off and shaded our eyes from the sun as we gazed out at a rather old, yet funkily romantic wooden cruiser anchored out by Christmas Tree Island.

Gabrielle nodded at the old wooden tub. "Isn't that yacht for rent? I thought I read that somewhere."

"You did. I saw it in the Mullet Wrap. Wait here."

I went over to the waste bins where the shower used to be and found a lonely copy of the previous day's paper. But the Classifieds were missing. I went back to Gabrielle.

"Found the Mullet Wrap, but no Classifieds …"

Gabrielle was punching numbers in her cell. "Don't need it. I found a notice tacked to the telephone pole over there."

Someone on the other end answered immediately. Gabrielle asked if the tub was still for rent, received an affirmative and then she rang off.

"The owner's coming to pick us up."

"Now?"

"Right now. Lock up the bikes."

We handcuffed our bikes, and almost immediately a rusted-out black Ford Ranger pulled up and parked illegally in the Handicap Parking space. Gabrielle and I exchanged looks, as a rough cowboy type aimed for us … then walked on by and over to the corner of the Hyatt. The cowboy grabbed a hold of the railing of the ground floor balcony and swung a leg up and over and disappeared.

What was that about? Pizza delivery? Late date? Meals on Wheels? Cowboys on cowgirls?

Gabrielle's cell phone rang. "Hello? Okay." Gabrielle put her hand over her cell and whispered "He's here."

"Where?"

"There."

Gabrielle gestured to a dinghy just pulling up to the sandy beach.

"That's him?"

"That's him and that's our ride."

We greeted the owner of the tub, gingerly climbed in the dinghy, and he whipped it around and headed out through an ebbing tide toward Christmas Tree Island.

"Y'all can use this here dinghy, if ya wanna. It's even got oars in case the outboard doesn't start."

Gabrielle and I exchanged looks again.

Soon we were tying up to the tub and climbing up onto a swim platform and clambering over the transom.

"How many feet is she?" I asked, trying to sound nautical, and most assuredly not.

"She's just under eighty. Sleeps twelve ... or 24 close friends," he said, then laughed at his own joke.

"And the rent's just four hundred a month."

"That's right, ma'am. Let me show you around this palace."

Well, we just knew this old yacht was going to be rusted and weather-beaten and a sea of peeling paint and varnish, and anything but a palace, and we weren't disappointed.

"Let me show y'all's stateroom."

Well, I don't know about you, but "stateroom" sounds pretty romantic and cool. And it was. The owner led us "below" (more nautical terms), where it was a bit hot and stuffy, and into a rather enormous stateroom. Much wider and higher than we would have believed.

"This is where you'll sleep, and now let me show you the galley."

The owner showed us the galley and then a lounge of sorts which was back up on the main deck where it caught the breeze and there was good light for reading. It smelled of stale smoke and we spied an aging roach in an ashtray.

"So what do you think?"

I looked at Gabrielle and I could see we were on the same wavelength. "It seems ideal. What do we do if the seas are rough or there's a storm coming in and it might be dangerous getting back out here?"

"You mean: what if you're fall-down drunk and can't make it back out here?"

"Yes."

"*Compadres!* I always recommend that you have some place on the island to crash."

"What about laundry?"

"You'll have to go to the Hilltop Launderette on the corner of Elizabeth and Eaton, but you're welcome to hang any other laundry out on the bow ..."

I nodded my assent at Gabrielle.

"… that's what Henley does …"

"Henley?"

"Yeah, she's one of the live-aboards …"

"Other people rent here?"

'Hell, yeah. There's always someone coming and going. It's one big revolving door!" He laughed.

Gabrielle gave me a look.

"C'mon, I'll introduce you."

"She's here now?"

Gabrielle gave me a panicked look.

"Should still be here. She tends bar … does a little bit of crewin', tries to pick up a bit extra in mini-lobster season."

The owner led us forward and up on the bow, sunning herself was Henley. Henley was the roughest woman I had ever seen in my life. Even rougher than that mad old bat who used to work at the Owl Market. She was tanned black, had the skin and fingers of someone who had been chain smoking since they were twelve, make that eleven – and she was topless. Shudder.

"Henley! C'mon over here and meet your new neighbors!"

Henley bounced up and stuck out a claw. "Y'all thinking of moving onboard. Shoot, we're gonna have us some parties!"

"How many live-aboards are there?" Gabrielle asked the owner.

"At the mo, just Henley and Crack-head Frankie …"

"Crack-head?" Gabrielle asked.

"Oh, not like that … Frankie's tall, six-six and he keeps cracking his head when he goes below …"

I looked at Henley and she was looking at Gabrielle the way a cat looks at a bird. You know, that involuntary chattering of the teeth.

Check, please.

156

CHAPTER TWENTY EIGHT

The owner of the yacht/palace/mental institution, PUTT-PUTTED us back over to dirt-bag beach and we thanked him for his time, then we fled over to Popcorn Joe's and told him of our misadventures.

Popcorn Joe was always the coolest of the coolest, and he quickly soothed our feverish brows by plying us with nuclear-strong lattes.

There was always something serene and relaxing about sitting up on the back deck at Popcorn Joe's. We watched the resident parrot flit about the palm trees next to the pool, and then another parrot of similar ilk appeared. He had a friend! Then Chubba came over and jumped up in Gabrielle's lap. She started to purr immediately. I'm talking about Chubba.

Then Popcorn Joe spoke: "Well, have I got news for you. Lois is going back to England, and Nina can't come down and cover this year ... sooo ..."

"You've got our attention," Gabrielle said.

"Sooo, how 'bout you come back and work for me and live upstairs?"

"Are you serious?"

"You both know how it works around here and you need help and I need help. Plus the cats like you."

We couldn't believe it. Popcorn Joe was going to save us from peril yet again.

Then Gabrielle thought of a problem: "What about Mr. Leroy?"

But Popcorn Joe had the answer. "Aronovitz Lane is his home, sure he hung out at your place, but the lane is where he belongs. Talk to Mrs. Grace across the lane. She'll look after him. I've often seen him sleeping on her porch. You can visit him whenever you want."

Well, this was all sounding pretty good. Then it suddenly got better.

"Gabrielle ..." Popcorn Joe sang, "Remember when we were over at the garden talking to Alberto?"

"Yessss ..."

"We watched him painting his 'Tropical Lettering'? If you could learn to do that as Alberto had suggested, and find a small nook on Duval, you wouldn't have to worry about if you get on the pier or not..."

CHAPTER TWENTY NINE

Less than a month later, we were ensconced back upstairs in the attic, and it felt *marvelous* (as Billy Crystal would say) to "be back home."

And shock of shock, Mr. Tosser had given us our deposit back. Perhaps he was motivated by the presumptive tenants he was losing every time real estate agent Bob tried to show the place. We didn't need to enlist our neighbor Snake's help, but the threat of the scorpion infestation and the eviscerated dead rat on the front stoop always worked a miracle. We blamed it on the "pack of mange-festering feral cats which ran amok in the lane late at night while you were sleeping."

The one good thing about Villa Alberto was that it was always easy to find a dead rat on the property. The "pack of feral cats" had to be borne out of Mr. Leroy hyperbole.

The attic was much as it had been before: the window at the top of the stairs was always kept open -- all year long -- the hatch which looked out on to the bight and the masts of the sailboats down by the seaport had a new stick holding it open (so we didn't look at the move as a step backwards ... it was a *stick* forward). The stick looked like a sexual adjunct of some sort, so we knew this must have been Lois' doing. I'm talking about her sense of humor. The small TV on the desk/table in the bedroom had a new sheet of tinfoil being used as an aerial, which was good as we would have better reception when watching *Local on the 8s*. When you live in Key West, you always have one eye on the weather.

And the other eye on your favorite barstool.

The toilet and shower in the middle of the living room had a new curtain. One with a sailboat on it like Gary Cairns lusts after. Someone in the U.K. once told me that sailing was like standing in a cold shower and ripping up ten-pound notes. With this beautiful example (the real yacht, not the one on our shower curtain) this certainly would not be the case, this would definitely offer the hot shower.

Life was good.

As you know, high season in Key West is in the winter and the Pineapple Apartments were booked solid. Many of the guests we knew from the previous winter, even the nuns, so it was deeply enjoyable being back working for Popcorn Joe.

One sunny afternoon, after finishing our chores around the guest house, which included removing two coconuts and one corn snake (very alive and very unhappy) from the swimming pool, Gabrielle and I walked the two blocks over to Duval and paid a visit to Alberto.

"Heard you get to stay in Key West. And heard you moved out of villa."

"We loved it there, but life's too short to deal with a landlord who's at the bottom of the creeps-R-us food chain."

"Tell me about it. I have small atelier in his building and his wife smokes so much it seeps through the walls. I'm paying good money for rent, then trying to find reason not to paint. I'm going to have to build a small artist studio at my new house."

"How is the new house?"

"*Fantastico!* I'm building swimming pool. Pool costing fortune. Not so easy to dig down into ground that is rock-hard."

Alberto moved one of his paintings out of the way and made room for Gabrielle and me to sit.

"Who's up for a smoothie?" I asked.

"Strawberry," Gabrielle said.

"Banana, raspberry, coconut juice, papaya, guava … and a splash of rum," Alberto said.

"Do you have something to write that down with? You lost me at banana."

Alberto fetched a piece of paper and the coolest looking artist's pen I'd ever seen and I wrote down his requirements.

I went over to Fat Tuesday just across the street from the garden. There was a queue, so I lined up. I looked back across the street at Gabrielle and Alberto and I saw Black T-shirt Guy walking by, **THE RULES FOR DATING MY DAUGHTER** emblazoned on his back. What was he still doing in Key West?

Was he a touron who had overstayed his welcome (which, in fact, is anything over about an hour for tourons in regard to overstaying their welcome), or was he a snowbird down for the entire season? What was the draw? What was keeping him in Key West? Or ... did he live up in Miami or West Palm or Atlanta and just made frequent appearances? And why always the same shirt?

I would have to get to the bottom of this conundrum.

"May I take your order?"

I turned and looked at the girl working the counter. Big blue eyes. Like the peery boulder marbles we played with as a kid.

I ordered the smoothies, and watched the girl. She must have come to Key West to get a job at Hooters when it was here, then lost out on close-but-no-cigar reasons and took the job at Fat Tuesday. She churned up our beverages, from an anatomically safe distance, then I paid and slipped back across the street, narrowly avoiding being flattened by an androgynous soul piloting a pedicab.

I handed over the smoothies to Gabrielle and Alberto, and Alberto said: "Where were we?"

Gabrielle quipped: 'You were sitting there, we were sitting over here."

Alberto laughed.

Alberto has a wonderful sense of humor and a laugh that's so infectious, the Department for Disease Control up in Atlanta should be notified.

"So, *porca miseria*, swimming pool is costing me fortune," Alberto said. "But forget that, let's learn Name Painting together."

Alberto went over to his easel and placed a sheet of heavy paper, almost card quality up on a piece of Perspex 12-inches high and 3-feet wide. Then he opened a plastic "bait box" like the fishermen down at Mallory keep their lures, and unmentionables in. Instead of lures and unmentionables, Alberto had 10 small containers of paint and 10 handmade brushes.

"This art come from Asia. Over two-thousand-years old. Brushes handmade of leather. Paint Venetian Aquarelle."

"Leather?" Gabrielle picked up one of the brushes and had a closer look. The brush was really not a brush, rather a small piece of leather about one-inch long and half-an-inch wide. And the leather was encased in two strips of copper and then wrapped with red electrician's tape to hold it all in place.

"Where do you get the leather from?"

"Cow, then I cure in saltwater and wash with baby shampoo. Have lots of baby shampoo at home. Watch."

Alberto took one of the brushes and dipped one edge of the tip in red, then the middle of the tip in blue, and then the other edge of the tip in green. Then he made a slicing motion across the page, then many short stabbing motions and within only a matter of seconds, he'd painted a beautiful, colorful palm tree. We watched with now *our* mouths hanging open like baby birds as Alberto proceeded to paint the letters ABC by using tropical icons such as flamingoes and dolphins and palm trees and butterflies and lighthouses and a whole host of other tropical creatures that we had seen before.

"Have new animal," Alberto said, and he painted an alligator.

When he was finished, he put down his brushes and turned to us. "What you think?"

"What about the rest of the alphabet?"

'Haven't learned yet. We learn together, okay, Gabrielle?"

"Where can we find a cow?" I said.

"How much do you think we could charge?" Gabrielle asked.

"Three dollars per letter?"

"Three dollars per letter? That's all for a personalized piece of artwork?"

"*Si*, better to be busy. Plus, cruise ship folk are cheap."

I looked over at Gabrielle and her eyes were as big as coconuts again. If Gabrielle could learn how to do this, it would be another welcomed avenue of income.

And that, dear Reader, is *sooo* Key West.

It's a tough place to make it and it's an expensive place to live. Many people hold two or three seasonal jobs and many people end up doing things that they would never consider doing for employment back home. Look at the Joke Man, for example, only in Key West could you walk down the street wearing sandwich boards, trolling for tourists, charging 25 cents

162

for a joke.

Or how about David Sloan and his ghost tours or Lloyd and his bike tours or Popcorn Joe. Folk, who were successful businessmen and women up in the Great White North, come to Key West and become entrepreneurs or work as taxi cab drivers, or power a pedicab, or tend bar (sounds pretty good) or work in an adult bookshop, or make and sell their own jewelry or take jobs as maids or become crew on a Sunset Cruise or even end up down at Mallory Square playing the guitar, doing Tarot card reading or selling Sunset Photos.

In many ways Key West is the American Dream.

But, for many turns into the American Nightmare.

Key West is such an expensive place to live, it may drive you to dig deep down inside and find that unknown talent or skill that you didn't know you possessed, or it may drive you off the deep end trying to pay the rent, a bar bill, or support a drug habit. Key West is paradise, indeed, but it is also the great leveler of the playing field. You have to be tough, flexible and creative to survive here.

You have to have your head screwed nice and tight.

CHAPTER THIRTY

Alberto showed Gabrielle how to make the brushes from "cow," and where to get it, and he gave her the name in South Beach of his supplier for his paints, and he told her about an easel available at the Liquid 8 Pawn Shop across from the Garrison Bight.

So we went to the pawn shop.

If you've never been to a pawn shop in Key West, might I suggest that you hop on your bike and belt on over. It's great, cheap entertainment, and you might even find something of interest. All those people who can't pay the rent, or the bar bill, or support that new drug habit, have come and dumped many a good item. It can be a veritable treasure trove. Remember I found all my camera equipment at the pawn shop? Do you remember the sign on the front door? ALL OFFERS CONSIDERED ... SOME FOR LONGER THAN OTHERS.

The pawn shop had that intriguing aroma that only a pawn shop can and it had on offer: gold, silver, precious gems, a vast array of jewelry, musical instruments, power tools, and just about everything else under the tropical sun. We found the easel in a corner up by the front window, right next to a nearly new set of Ping golf clubs, a bunch of fishing rods and a still-in-the-box microwave (Emerson). There was a price tag on the easel: $75. Ouch, a lot of money, but the easel was well-worn and splattered with lots of various paint colors, so that was a plus. Hard to flog your artwork to the public if your easel is all pristine and virginal. It doesn't have that same "spent years in the atelier appeal," or in the narrow lanes of Montmartre.

A man at the counter, wearing a Hawaiian shirt and a Boston Red Sox baseball cap, greeted us. We talked to him for a bit and he told us that he used to live in, yes, Boston and had worked for a broker selling hedge funds. He had made bags of money and "had it all," a 30-year mortgage, a live-in illegal maid, a love child, a divorce, an irregular heartbeat, eczema and a 45-minute commute, so he moved to Key West and now commuted five minutes by bike from a houseboat ... and was off the meds.

AUTHOR'S NOTE: I rail at the usage of the term "meds."

Mr. BoSox Fan went on to tell us -- even though we didn't ask -- that he had fallen into the usual traps growing up: He had to acquire a frightening student loan to go college (Vermont), he married his college sweetheart (from Stowe), she wanted a big house, with a maid who spoke Spanish, so the kids would learn a second language, they lived in Marblehead (a 45-minute commute into Faneuil Hall, when you hit the lights), he sometimes had to work late, so he'd purchased a small pied-a-terre near Fenway Park, and it was here at the pied-a-terre that he started to cheat on his wife *and* the live-in maid. On the nights he didn't come home his wife started cheating with two different guys: one was her trainer at the gym, the other worked at her tanning salon called Electric Beach. Our fellow joined the country club, so he could learn golf and show off his trophy wife, and so that the little ones could get into junior golf.

I looked over at Gabrielle. All we had done was come into the pawn shop to buy an easel and now we knew this man's intimate life story. But we didn't mind, and that's another aspect of Key West, so many people who live there come with baggage or they are damaged goods, and that makes for quirky camaraderie. It's like seeing everyone naked. Hard to explain, but I think you know what I'm talking about. For the first time in their lives, folk don't need the pretenses. They can be more open, shed that disagreeable past and just be themselves. This host of individuals is part of what makes Key West so special, you get a lot of colorful folk and a lot of crazies, but you also get a lot of people who are just able to be their true selves for the first time in their lives.

And we like that.

We bought the easel. Our new-found friend, Mr. BoSox Cap let us have it for fifty dollars if we promised to buy him a few beers if we ever saw him in the Bull.

We were excited for Gabrielle to start learning her new art

form.

"What should we call our new business," I asked.

Gabrielle thought for a moment, then said: "How about TROPICAL LETTERING?"

"Great name," I said. "Any other thoughts?"

"Just one."

"On you go …"

"Let's go visit Mr. Leroy."

CHAPTER THIRTY ONE

We pedaled over to Aronovitz Lane and found Mr. Leroy asleep on Mrs. Grace's front porch.

When he saw us, he looked at us for a long time, then came over and nudged his head against Gabrielle's face.

Mrs. Grace came out on the porch and sat in her rocking chair. Mrs. Grace you may remember was of Cuban descent and "she knew all that went on in the lane." She had winked at me when *some vile cur* had spray painted her bitch-bovine neighbor's car for being a pompous pain in the backside. Mr. Leroy crawled up in Gabrielle's lap and we sat there for a while talking with Mrs. Grace.

"New people have moved into Villa Alberto," she said.

"What are they like?"

"Loud. They come home drunk every night from the Duval Street bars and then sit on the front stoop right over there and smoke marijuana. They are not endearing themselves in the lane."

"Because of the weed?"

"Oh, God, no, everybody in this lane smokes, it's because of the noise.

"Does Mr. Leroy go over there?"

"No, he stays here with me until it's time for him to start his shift at Cowboy Bill's. I think he doesn't like the new neighbors..."

"How's that?"

"He leaves them little notices of eviction on the front stoop."

"Good boy!" Gabrielle said, and stroked Mr. Leroy.

Mr. Leroy purred gently back.

* * *

Gabrielle and I bid Mrs. Grace and Mr. Leroy farewell,

promising to return soon, then went back to the Pineapple Apartments.

We climbed the steep stairs to the attic and looked out the "hatch" and over at the masts of the sailboats, then we climbed back down the stairs and made a cup of tea on the two-burner hot plate that functioned as our kitchen.

"Once you've learned how to do this name painting, we will need to find a place for you to paint."

"What about down on the pier during Sunset Celebration?"

"I was thinking of that, as well, we'd have to get you juried…"

"I don't think artists need to be juried. They are like musicians and performers. If there's an available pitch, they get on—" Gabrielle stopped. "It's still high season, so there's no way I'm getting on until things quiet down."

"Well, then let's find you someplace on Duval?"

"Duval is where I'll need to be, but everyone is going to want a gi-normous rent."

Gabrielle and I sipped our tea some more. Chubba came up to Gabrielle and jumped up on her lap and settled in.

"I have an idea," Gabrielle said. "Perhaps we won't have to pay so much rent. Do you remember when we were in Italy, in Rimini, on the Adriatic? Remember how all the street artists and musicians set up in front of sidewalk cafés and their mere presence help draw patrons?"

"But that's the Continent. That's a different culture over in Europe. There they embrace the street artist. Here, they often call the police, plus we'd need to get some awful permit from the city or we would have Code Enforcement breathing down our necks. Just when you've got Immigration off your back, you don't want the other end of the nightstick jammed up your bahookie."

"True, but what if we are not on the street directly, but just on the edge of the property of a restaurant or hotel?"

"Then, we're dealing with a huge rent. Do you know what that guy who sells 'Cuban' cigars out of the open doorway pays for rent?"

"No."

"He pays a $1000 a month for the right to stand in an open

168

doorway selling unauthentic product."

"Jeez, Louise."

"But he's on Duval."

"Yeah, but he can just hand over cigars all night long. I'm going to have to paint each and every letter. I will only be able to paint so many each evening."

Gabrielle and I were subdued for a moment. We had stumbled on to a great new avenue, we just weren't able to find a way to drive down it yet.

Then Popcorn Joe came home. We heard his moped coming down Peacon Lane, then the back gate of the Pineapple Apartments squeak open.

The popcorn man climbed the back stairs up to the deck and pulled up a seat. We told him of our dilemma.

"R&R," Popcorn Joe said.

"Rest and relaxation?" I said.

"Nooo, *research and reconnaissance.* Do the Duval Crawl. Go sit in every bar, restaurant, café, courtyard, hotel lobby, and available hole-in-the-wall between Truman Avenue and the Sunset Pier.

See where you can find a space big enough to set up your easel. Then you will need a small space to keep one of those big plastic buckets—"

"For?"

"For your paper and back-up paints. And then you will probably get a crowd watching, so you have to be somewhere where you won't piss off a lot of people ..."

"What about setting up in front of the Bull? You are often out there of an evening selling your popcorn?"

"Good thought, masked man, but I have a mobile vendor permit from the city. They're not easy or cheap to come by, and even if you got one, you'd be crushed by the wave of ripped humanity that sweeps down Duval each evening."

"How do you avoid it?"

"I get crushed every evening. Say, let's meet for beers later. Becky's coming into town."

* * *

Gabrielle and I waited until five in the afternoon, about the time of the day she'd be setting up her easel and trolling for business,

169

then we began our foray. It was lovely and warm out and we started at Truman and Duval as Popcorn Joe had suggested. The first place that had potential was near Croissants de France. They had just enough space, and they were French, so perhaps they would understand the need for an artist taking up a bunch of the high-rent space who was willing to offer little in return in the form of remuneration.

"Should we go talk to them now?"

"No, let's wait until they're not busy. Let's carry on."

"Wait!"

"Wait, what?"

"I'm getting two *pain au chocolat* to go. They are *superbe* here!"

The next potential spot was the Southern Cross Hotel. The space would be a bit tight, but Gabrielle would be almost right on the sidewalk.

"What do you think?"

"Tight, but do-able. But, I've just noticed something."

"What's that?"

"The farther down Duval we go, the busier it gets."

"Which means?"

"I think we need to be more smack in the middle of the carnage."

"We strolled down to Fat Tuesday.

"This could be ideal here," I said. "A perfect location and lots of drunks. Let's stop and order a frozen concoction."

"Do you mean as in alcohol?"

"Absolutely."

"But you will write a sequel to your first Key West book and everyone will read this and they will think that you drink like a fish."

"Well, then I won't mention it in the seagull, I mean, the sequel."

Gabrielle and I entered the domain of Fat Tuesday. There was barely a seat to be had. Folk drink early in Key West. It wasn't even 5.30 p.m. yet and they were already knocking it back. The Hooters' wannabe was on duty.

"That corner right over there by the Hard Rock Café would be really good."

"Indeed, then the rich folk willing to put out seventeen

170

bucks for a cheeseburger would see you as well."

"This could be a perfect place," Gabrielle said. "We'll, find out who the manager is tomorrow and see if we can catch him in a good mood."

"Oh, you're not hoping to find the manager of a restaurant on Duval in a good mood, are you?"

"Hope springs eternal ..."

"Bugger."

"What?"

"Look across the street. What do you see?"

"A gigantic banyan tree."

"Correct. What else do you see?"

"The Porter House..."

"Correct, and thank you very much for that bit of history. WHAT ELSE DO YOU SEE!"

"The Porch restaurant."

"Correct. WHAT ELSE DO YOU SEE?"

"Shit!"

"Exactly."

Standing in the garden, in front of his Gallery Uno, was Alberto.

"Alberto has customers."

"He's painting their names."

"We would be right in his face."

"Not so very friendly."

"Not after him helping with the whole thing."

"What should we do?"

"Escape, I'm getting brain freeze from this smoothie."

We exited Fat Tuesday, stage right, and crossed over to the Bull. We took a seat in the open front window by the front door. It was getting dark and Duval was getting busier. Now, you, dear Reader, probably think I've chosen to patronize the Bull in order to procure alcohol, to get wasted, but no, we have unfinished business to take care of.

"Check out where Hooters used to be across the street," I said.

Gabrielle had a peep over across the street. "Every square inch has a table or chair on it. No room for me there ..."

"By the way, why did the city council allow Hooter's in here

171

in the first place? I thought Key West was trying to avoid the chain establishments. Glad they're gone."

"Starbucks is still here."

"Forgot about that …"

"What would you rather have when you come to Key West, a Starbucks Pike Place, or an authentic Cuban *con leche*?"

"Right, how does Starbucks keep Key West quirky and original? If you sit in there with your back to the window, you could be in Seattle, or Buffalo, or Fargo."

"Fargo has a Starbucks?"

"They have three."

"Now how would you now that?"

"Not important. Let's bolt."

"Where to?

"Down Duval. There's got to be some little nook or cranny where you could paint."

"*Vamos* …"

We exited the Bull, stage left, and cut over to Sloppy's, then back across to Rick's. We waved at Al Subarsky, then headed down to the Hog's Breath.

"All we would need to do, is get the management of Sloppy's or Rick's or the Hog's Breath to remove one barstool and that would give you enough room to set up your easel."

"And how much rent do you think they would charge me?"

"Perhaps none. You would draw customers, and you could listen to Al Subarsky when he was on—"

"Oh, oh …"

"What?"

"Just thought of something. How much does one barstool in Rick's bring in, daily?"

"Are you talking 'bums on seats'?"

"Yes."

"I see where you're going with this. We couldn't compete against those kinds of numbers."

We walked on.

When we got to the corner of Front Street and Duval, Gabrielle got an idea.

"How about setting up where the Old Town Trolley stops? It would be a great venue and there's lots of space."

"Let me just say two words to you …"

"Shoot."

"Ed Swift."

"Who?"

"Ed Swift. It's part of his empire."

"And that's a bad thing?"

"No, it's a good thing, but just for him."

"Crap. We are going nowhere, and fast. We have a great new idea, which would go down a bomb, but nowhere to set up…"

"Without forking out a fortune in rent."

"That's Key West for you."

"And that's why so many businesses fail here. People come down from the mainland, find a little place, sign a long lease with a hefty deposit and extortionate rent, and they do well in high season, then die on the vine during off season …"

"Or when a hurricane hits and it kills off tourism for a month."

"Don't remind me."

"We need someone with a vision."

"Huh?"

"Someone with vision. Someone who wants to add a bit of color to her/his establishment and doesn't feel the need to gouge the little folk."

"Want to walk out on to Sunset Pier and look down at the tarpon?"

"How does that solve our dilemma?"

"It doesn't, but I like watching tarpon."

The temperature was in the upper sixties, but the humidity was high and it felt warmer. Just a beautiful night to be walking around in shorts instead of shunting a snow blower through your driveway, with drips of you-know-what hanging frozen off your nose.

And your moustache.

I'm talking about the men.

Take a gander at these temperatures:

Key West: 68

Jersey Shore: 30, with a wind chill that would freeze your nuts off (and break guitar strings)

Wall, New Jersey: 30, visibility 15+, VFR

Galveston: 38

Alexandria, VA: 35, with sleet

Harvard Yard: 31, flurries

Livingston, Montana: 7, black ice, cold beer

Colonie, New York: No one home, everyone at the Jimmy Buffett concert in Boston

Scottville, Michigan: 24, lake effect snow ... lots

San Francisco: 52, and fog pouring down Hurricane Gulch in Sausalito, but the sailing's still great out on the bay. Hairy current as you near Alcatraz, so you need to be on the toes of your Topsiders

Seattle: Not reporting, still celebrating their Super Bowl win

Conshohocken, PA: 29, blowing a gale, but there's dancing at the hall, so no one minds

East Greenwich, Rhode Island: Colder than a witch's, but Chip's taken the twins, Matty and Danny, skiing at North Conroy and life is good

Dolgellau, Wales: 5°C, estuary flooding, wheelbarrow floating

Glasgow, Scotland: 3°C, pissing

Falkirk, Scotland: not reporting, away on holiday, winter sun

And did I mention, **Key West**: 68, balmy, shorts, tropical drinks, Duval Crawl, windows open, music pouring forth?

We crossed over Front Street, walked in front of the Ocean Key Resort and out on to Sunset Pier. We could smell the salt in the air. Lights were twinkling back from the houses on Sunset Key. We leaned on the railing and looked down into the crystal-clear water of the marina and there were fish everywhere.

"Look, there's a permit."

"And a mullet."

"A snook."

"Are you sure that's a snook?"

"Yes, he has an under bite just like Uncle Lou."

"How do you know it's a 'he'?"

"Uncle Lou?"

"No, the snook."

"Don't."

"Then why did you say 'he'?"

"I get your point ... says a lot about, well, a lot."

"Indeed."

Then we saw our first tarpon.

"Wow, they're big. He must be four feet long."

"Remember when we first got to Key West and we came down here early one morning to explore?"

"And we saw a manatee in about three feet of water."

"Right over there by the glass-bottom boat."

"Wonder if we could see one now?"

We walked back along the few charter boats and then past the Jet-ski rentals to the foot of Duval. We looked down in the water, but it was difficult to see anything as there were no lights shining down in the water like back out on Sunset Pier.

"I don't see anything, do you?"

"Nope."

"Perhaps it's past a manatee's bedtime. They're so cute, I can't imagine them staying up late."

"Party animals they are not ..."

"I scored on some lettuce! PAR-TAY!!!"

Gabrielle gave me a look.

"Want to hit the Bull?"

"Super, but you are not allowed to get clinically drunk in Poland..."

"What about Kazakhstan?"

"Perfectly acceptable."

We started to walk off, when Gabrielle stopped me with "Wait!"

"What?"

"Look!"

"A manatee?" I searched the water of the harbor.

"No, not down in the water. Over there."

Gabrielle was pointing right behind us at the veranda of the Ocean Key Resort.

"*Jesus Cristo.*"

"You took the Spanish words right out of my mouth."

We walked over to the veranda. It was the perfect place for Gabrielle to set up her easel.

"Look, the veranda is raised ..."

"So people can easily see me painting."

"And it has a railing …"

"So people don't get too close and spill beer on me."

"And you are undercover …"

"So it won't rain on me …"

"Or birds shit on you."

"Wait."

"What?"

"It's a bit dark. I'll need a light attached to my easel that shines on the paper. Let's see if we can find a socket."

Bugger. We looked everywhere, but there was no socket. No outdoor outlet.

"Can't believe it, this place would have been perfect."

"Why don't we do what we did at Mallory?"

"Use a marine battery?"

"Right."

"Great idea, but I fear you'll be putting in more hours here than at Mallory, and the marine battery just won't have enough juice."

Gabrielle and I were having an *Oh, shit! … what if* moment, when something caught Gabrielle's eye.

"What's that?"

"I would say that is a small palm tree in a great big plant pot. Help me move it."

We grabbed a hold of the beast and tried to shift it. Did you ever try to move a gigantic plant pot? No easy trick, huh? Finally, two strapping, rippling-in-muscle lads in bicycle shorts and tank tops which read PROVINCETOWN walked by and Gabrielle enlisted their help and we shifted the palm.

And there, right before our eyes was the most glorious sight imaginable.

An outdoor socket with the little silver flap.

Before we went to the Bull to celebrate our discovery, we went into the Ocean Key Resort and up to the front desk. A young lady, whose hair looked like she had been dragged backwards through a privet hedge, greeted us.

"Welcome to the Ocean Key Resort and Spa."

"Evening," Gabrielle said, smiling back. "You wouldn't happen to know the name of the hotel manager, would you?"

"Of course, want me to write it down for you?"

Mlle. Privet wrote down the name of the manager. We thanked her and went back out onto the veranda. We watched as a steady stream of bodies moved out to the Sunset Bar for victuals and grog, and we watched as others who were just walking Duval strolled past.

"This veranda is ideal. It's got Libation. Libation. Libation."

"Do you mean 'Location. Location. Location'?"

"In Key West it's much the same."

"Let's just hope he doesn't want a fortune for it."

"Can't hurt to ask."

"My mother always said 'there's always room for one more'."

"Mums know best."

CHAPTER THIRTY TWO

We were at the Bull with Popcorn Joe and Becky.

Becky and Gabrielle were drinking Merlot.

Popcorn Joe and I were drinking Piña Coladas.

Just so you know (and many of you do), I don't drink Piña Coladas, or Singapore Slings or Screaming Orgasms or Quick Fucks. They are all too sugary sweet for me, except the Quick Fuck, which makes me want to light up a ciggie and I don't even smoke. Never quite figured that one out. But tonight was different, everything felt so tropical and far-flung down here at the end of the world. Gabrielle and I were in a buoyant mood, and nothing could rip us from the revelry of our new found hope.

Soon thereafter, Don and Shirley strolled by and spied us sitting in the open front window.

"You're still here!" Don said.

"Well spotted," Gabrielle said. "We decided to not go back to Scotland after all."

"That's great news!" Don said.

"We have great news, as well," Shirley said.

"Fantastic," I said. "What is it?"

"We've been juried and accepted on the pier."

"Doing what?"

"Sunset photography."

CHAPTER THIRTY THREE

After Don and Shirley moved off down the street, I turned to Gabrielle and whispered: "Oh, shit. When high season is over and we get back on the pier, we will have competition in the form of Don and Shirley's sunset photography."

"No big deal. They're a nice couple ..."

"Indeed they are, but it will cut into the amount of money we will be able to earn. There's such a narrow window for business down on the pier, two hours before sunset and two hours after sunset."

"Well, we'd better go see the manager of the Ocean Key Resort tomorrow and hope he has *vision*."

Gabrielle and Becky ordered another Merlot, and Giuseppe and I reverted immediately back to beer. I picked up a rogue newspaper off the bar and perused the articles. Then my eyes grew stalks. "Check this out." I pushed the newspaper across the table to Gabrielle. She read the article and muttered something which sounded a lot like "Holy crapshit!"

The article went something like: In Georgia, a young man in his twenties had "raised a Burmese python from an egg." He had built a "tree" in his bedroom so the python could crawl up in it at night and sleep. The python was gentle and docile. The young man purchased frozen rabbits from the pet store, then thawed them out in the microwave and fed the snake. And the snake grew.

And grew.

And now he was missing.

All seventeen feet of him!

Authorities fear if not captured, it will eventually find a mate and reproduce. Burmese pythons are survivors -- they can live up to 25 years in fresh or saltwater, go months without eating, and females can lay up to 100 eggs at a time. Living near the top of the food chain, their numbers have swelled up near 100,000.

You may have heard about the Burmese python problem in the Everglades, but the little slithering blighters are also making inroads in the Florida Keys. FedEx and U.S. Postal Service drivers were the first to spy the pythons in the Keys. The drivers' domain is the highways, and pythons just love to warm themselves on the sun-drenched asphalt.

There's much discussion where these Burmese pythons came from, yes, Burma, to start, but that's not what I mean. Some folk blame it on Hurricane Andrew, which destroyed a reptile-breeding facility near the Everglades when it roared through South Florida in 1992. Some also blame the A DOG IS NOT JUST FOR CHRISTMAS syndrome, where irresponsible pet owners, who think there's nothing cuter than a little Burmese python egg or one-foot serpent squeezing the shit out of your thumb, are not so very enamored with the reptiles when they grow up to twenty-three-feet long and they realize they would have difficulty flushing these constricting machines down the toilet, so they release them in the boondocks. It has been theorized that some unscrupulous pet dealers may even intentionally release them into the wild to create a breeding cash crop that they can come and collect later.

But here's the proverbial rub: In Florida, the boondies or the "wild" almost always means the Everglades. And the Everglades possess the perfect environment for the pythons to hide, feed, reproduce and thrive. Since the arrival of the Burmese python, the number of Florida panthers has continued to dwindle, as has most of the population of the 300 different species of birds. Raccoon populations in the Everglades are down -- get ready for this -- by 99%.

The steamy, mosquito-infested Everglades lie about six inches below sea level and the system begins just south of Orlando. At the Kissimmee River. This doesn't get a mention in any of the Disney brochures.

The Kissimmee River then flows into Lake Okeechobee. The water which seeps out of the lake in the wet season creates a slow-moving "river" 60 miles wide and over 100 miles long.

This river flows in a southerly direction over a bottom of porous and permeable limestone all the way to, yes, you've guess it: Florida Bay – and the not so distant Florida Keys. The state had held out hope that bays, inlets and the open sea would form a natural barrier, keeping the pythons from spreading to the Florida Keys. But that might not be the case.

A report in the January edition of the *Journal of Experimental Marine Biology and Ecology* says "research shows that open ocean, bays or shorelines aren't necessarily the protection against further python migration that state officials had hoped they would be. The paper is the first rigorous scientific research to document what's been known anecdotally for some time: Burmese pythons don't mind taking a dip in the ocean."

"A few weeks ago, one was seen swimming across Florida Bay," says Gordon Rodda, a research zoologist and snake expert with the U.S. Geological Survey.

"Research has also shown that snakes often prefer to swim rather than crawl because it uses less energy. One group of pythons that had been radio tagged in the Everglades stayed put for months until the water levels rose enough that they could swim and then they took off," Rodda says. "Swimming is a very efficient way to get around, and they will use it."

Pythons are constrictors and they kill their prey by squeezing the *you know wha*t out of them until they die from asphyxiation. Pythons have jaws which disengage, so the prey is swallowed slowly and whole. This past October, workers in the Everglades came upon a python that had just swallowed a 76-pound deer. If they can eat a deer of that size, or an alligator, there are 31 endangered species in Florida which fall into that bite-size.

If you live in Florida, give this some thought, if a python will go after an alligator or Florida panther, and it can't find some other four-legged animal to gobble up, it will come looking for your dog -- or your toddler. These Burmese pythons have street smarts. And they aren't afraid of humans. A 17-foot python will not think of man as a predator. He will think of him as lunch. Pythons have already reached Key Largo where they are decimating the endangered Key Largo wood rat population.

"All snakes swim," Rozar explained. "They might not be happy in saltwater, but they can navigate from Florida City, where there is an established population, to Key Largo. And

181

before U.S. 1 was fenced in, we found python road kill. Snakes are attracted to the heat of the asphalt."

The first python discovered in the Florida Keys was in 2007 when researchers checking on the status of a male Key Largo wood rat wearing a radio transmitter noticed that it was no longer in its original habitat. The researchers -- a University of St. Andrews (as in Scotland, where Prince William attended) graduate student and a volunteer assistant studying the endangered Key Largo wood rat -- followed the signal and eventually found the wood rat: inside a 7 1/2-foot Burmese python sunning itself.

Recently, a 10-foot python was found flattened on U.S. 1 at Mile Marker 112.

Just something to think about the next time you are standing in your bare feet in the backyard, barbequing: Six other constrictors, averaging just over seven feet in length, have been found near the Key Largo School, the Card Sound Road Bridge, and in the Dagny Johnson Key Largo Hammock Botanical State Park, across C.R. 905 from the Crocodile Lake National Wildlife Refuge.

There are only 200 Key Largo wood rats left in the world, 199 if you factor in the Key Largo python.

Residents of the Lower Keys reckon the pythons would have great difficulty navigating the 42 bridges all the way down to Key West.

Okay, dear Reader, you may wonder why I went on this python rant while sitting at the Bull knocking back a bevvy or two, as I write this book, I've just learned: In October 2012, a 10-foot python was found in the grass near the edge of the commercial ramp at Key West International Airport.

It may not just be a pop-top that you step on the next time you blow out a flip flop.

I took the newspaper back to the bar and slipped it in onto the transom in front of an older dude who was romancing a whiskey. Then I returned to my seat and told Gabrielle, Becky and Popcorn Joe the entire story, finishing with: "Pythons in Key West ..."

"They will never be as much of a threat as developers," Popcorn Joe said.

And Popcorn Joe just might be right.

* * *

You may have heard about it.

Florida wildlife officials are trying to fight the aforementioned explosion of Burmese pythons that have colonized the Everglades, by hunting them down. The hunt is sponsored by the Florida Fish and Wildlife Conservation Commission. The public and python permit holders have a chance to compete to see who can harvest the longest and most Burmese pythons.

The FWC plans to hand out $1,500 to the hunter who snags the highest number of Burmese pythons and $1,000 to the hunter/novice/delusional-opportunist who is able to wrestle into submission the *longest* snake. To date, the longest python ever captured in Florida was, are you ready, 18 feet 8 inches. The following came off the FWC website: "No hunting license is required, but participants must be 18-years or older as well as pay a $25 entry fee and complete a 40-minute online training course called REDDy, which stands for Introduced Reptile Early Detection & Documentation. The course helps people recognize pythons and other non-native species they're not supposed to kill in this hunting contest."

Kristen Sommers, head of the FWC's Exotic Species Coordination Section explained: "The FWC is encouraging the public to get involved in helping us remove Burmese pythons from public lands in south Florida. By enlisting both the public and Florida's python permit holders in a month-long competitive harvesting of Burmese pythons, we hope to motivate more people to find and harvest these large, invasive snakes."

Some of the contest rules are worthy of note:

--You will be disqualified from the competition if you harvest and turn in a snake that was once originally possessed as a pet or a snake taken from a location other than the WMA locations. (*Your neighbor's snake-quarium*)

--You will be disqualified for posting inhumane photos or videos or for posting photos or videos of illegal activities on social media. (*You, out there with the boys, snake-snot drunk*)

--Road kill will not be eligible.

"It's very difficult to find these animals and we don't really have a good strategy on how to contain this population," said Linda Friar, spokeswoman for Everglades National Park. "This is a pilot to see if it will gain public interest in areas that you can hunt so that they would be able to remove and capture these snakes."

CHAPTER THIRTY FOUR

The next morning, we had a checkout at the Pineapple Apartments.

An elderly widow from the Great White North had been coming every year for the past ten years and she stayed for January and February and most of March, then went back home in time to spoil the grandkids and get them wired on chocolate Easter eggs.

When a guest stayed for most of the winter in one of the apartments, Gabrielle and I would have to lay siege and pretty much refit the unit. Few guests ever left the apartments tidy, and many left them in a miserable state. And I'm not just talking about dirty dishes in the sink. I'm talking about a toilet that was rarely flushed, sickly sweet, sticky-food splashes and drips beckoning an army of ants and servicing a cockroach breeding farm, used pregnancy test kits and spent condoms. Even cocaine hidden so that nobody would find it. You can see the problem here, can't you? The blow was so well hidden, the person doing the hiding had been too fucked-up to remember where she/he had hidden it.

And, no, you don't need to even ask the question.

Anyway, back to the present problem at hand, the woman, we will call her Mrs. Horowitz (as that was her name), had been staying in 710 down-rear, for the winter, so we grabbed the spare key, went around the back, unlocked the door, and stared in gobsmacked disbelief. Mrs. Horowitz was placing a tray of cookies in the oven. We quickly shut the door.

"Do you think she saw us?"

"No."

"She's making cookies!"

"Chocolate chip?"

"Focus! How can she be making cookies if she's supposed

185

to have checked out already?"

Gabrielle and I went back upstairs to Popcorn Joe's. The doors were open, so we yelled out his name. No answer. We yelled louder. Still no Popcorn Joe.

"He's got to be here," I said. "The doors are wide open."

"Perhaps not. Remember Giuseppe often leaves the doors open while he runs an errand. He can't be far."

"Let's check the bookings. Maybe we misread the chart."

There was a flow chart, of sorts, on the counter between the kitchen and the living room. It's where we penciled in a reservation or checked dates to see if a requested unit was available. Chubba was asleep on top of the flow chart, so Gabrielle picked her up and slung her over her shoulder. Gabrielle often did work around the Pineapple Apartments with Chubba riding shotgun on her shoulder.

"Look, there she is right there, Mrs. Horowitz came in just after Christmas and she's supposed to be checking out today. She should have been gone already."

"What should we do?"

"Let's go talk to her. Perhaps she's spaced out her check-out."

We went back down to 710 down-rear and knocked on the door.

"Who is it?" came a cry. Mrs. Horowitz sounded like Howard's mother on the *BIG BANG THEORY*. We thoroughly expected her to continue with: "Are you a sex criminal?"

We opened the door a crack and peeped in.

"Morning, Mrs. Horowitz ..."

Mrs. Horowitz was sipping a cup of coffee, the sink was filled with dirty dishes and the place strewn with bags of groceries and other bits and bobs. In fact, it looked as if she had done some redecorating. The TV had been moved, the couch had been shifted, and there was a new painting hanging on the wall. It looked suspiciously like one of Alberto's.

"Aren't you checking out today, Mrs. Horowitz? We can come back?" Gabrielle said.

Mrs. Horowitz looked at Gabrielle. Then at Chubba on Gabrielle's shoulder, and then over at me, and said these chilling words: "I live here now."

"Sorry?"

"I live here now. Popcorn Joe sold it to me."

"But Popcorn Joe didn't tell us anything about this ..."

"I know, he's so sweet. He wanted to keep it a secret."

"But you live in the Poconos, Mrs. Horowitz. You have family there."

"They can come and visit. I just love Key West, don't you?"

Earth to Mrs. Horowitz. Mrs. Horowitz was not answering.

"We'll leave you to your coffee," I said, and Gabrielle and I fled.

Out by the pool, Gabrielle and I stopped.

"Holy crap, Mrs. Horowitz has gone off the deep end."

"Let's call Popcorn Joe. He'll know what to do."

We went upstairs to Popcorn Joe's. Since we didn't have a phone, we used his. He picked up on the first ring.

"Wassup?"

"I know this is a silly question, Giuseppe, but did you sell 710 down-rear to Mrs. Horowitz?"

"Oh, shit. I knew this day was coming. I'm on my way. Meet me in front of the market."

Gabrielle put Chubba back on the flow chart and we hurried down the back stairs, past the pool, past the efficiency and went out the gate by the Caroline Street Market.

"There's Giuseppe!"

Coming down Caroline, fast, just passing B.O.'s and the Red Doors Gallery was Popcorn Joe. He was on his rollerblades.

"Speak," he said, as he did a little full spin and came to a stop.

We spoke. We told Giuseppe about what transpired. And he gave all this some thought.

"Shit on a stick. We've got three nuns checking in there tomorrow."

We went back to Mrs. Horowitz's door and politely knocked. There was no answer. Popcorn Joe looked at us. "Christ, let's hope she hasn't kicked the bucket in there."

"You go in and tell me what you see ..."

"No, you go in ..."

"I'll go in," Gabrielle said.

Gabrielle opened the door a crack. Popcorn Joe and I

187

peeked over her shoulder.

"I hear water running. I think she's running the bath. I'M GOING IN!" Gabrielle shouted like the SWAT TEAM does when they're entering a decidedly un-secure environment.

Gabrielle returned. "It's not the bath, it's the TV, she's watching a show about dolphins."

"Did she see you?"

"Yes."

"Say anything?"

"Yes, she asked if I do pedicures."

"What did you say?"

"I said, I DON'T DO PEDICURES."

"Oh, my God," Popcorn Joe said, "The train's left the station and she's not on it. I'm going to have to talk to her."

Popcorn Joe and Gabrielle and I went into the living room and sat on the couch across from Mrs. Horowitz. And Popcorn Joe was good and kind and gentle with her.

"Your family back up in Pennsylvania will be expecting you."

Silence.

"Gabrielle and Jon will help you pack, then I'll take you to the airport."

Silence.

Popcorn Joe smiled in an avuncular sort of way and then pulled out his cell phone. He ran through his contacts and then thumbed a button. He listened, then spoke: "Is that Rachel? Hi, it's Joe Bement down in Key West. No, no, nothing like that, she's fine. Perhaps you could speak to her, yes, yes, that's exactly what's happened."

Popcorn Joe handed his cell phone over to Mrs. Horowitz and she greeted her daughter and listened. She listened for a long time and then said "Okay," and hung up. She looked over at us.

"Can't offer you any cookies, I have to go home. My daughter needs me."

We all looked at one another.

"My daughter said I have to be good now and come home or she won't let me come down to Key West again. I want to come back ... so I'll go ..."

I looked over at Gabrielle. That sort of logic reminded me

of the line in *BUTCH CASSIDY AND THE SUNDANCE KID* when Paul Newman says to the gunslinger: "Invite us to stay ... and we'll go."

Popcorn Joe said Mrs. Horowitz could keep the painting she'd purchased from Alberto on the wall in the living room, and that he would pencil her in for next winter. Then Gabrielle and I helped Mrs. Horowitz pack.

And Popcorn Joe took her to the airport and got her safely on her plane.

The last flight out for Mrs. Horowitz.

CHAPTER THIRTY FIVE

It took Gabrielle and me five hours to get the apartment ready for the nuns arriving the next day.

Have you ever cleaned an apartment for nuns? You don't cut corners, I'll tell you that right up front. You truly endeavor to do a five-star, captain's-cabin job. Perhaps it's the respect factor. Or perhaps you don't want to get your knuckles rapped with a ruler.

Then we went down to the Ocean Key Resort to see if we could find the director.

When we got to the Ocean Key Resort, we came in through the car park on the Mallory Square side. Some man who looked as if he had once played football was walking through the car park.

"Let's ask him if he works here."

"Excuse me, sorry to bother you, but do you work here?"

"How can I help?"

"We're looking for the management offices."

"I'm going that way. I'll point you in the right direction."

As we walked along through the bowels of the Ocean Key Resort, I asked: "So what's this director like? A man or a woman?"

"A male, and in my humble opinion, a good man who treats everybody fairly."

We walked on. The football player turned to us. "Glorious night! Love it down here this time of year!"

We agreed, then Mr. Pigskin spoke again: "What do you want to see the boss about? Don't think we're hiring."

Gabrielle told this fellow about her Tropical Lettering. And about how it was a great thing for kids and there wasn't so very much for kids to do in Key West and about how the veranda would be a perfect place for her to set up her easel and how we were worried that the director would either say no or would want a bunch of money to rent what was essentially a dead spot.

This kind man listened and smiled and thought it was a great idea, and when we got to the management offices he even held the door for Gabrielle and me. We hoped that perhaps he would make an entrée for us, but he didn't, rather he said: "Why don't you bring your easel down and start as soon as you're ready. Plan on starting around four or five in the afternoon. There will be a lot of traffic when the masses stream down for sunset. This is exactly the kind of thing we need."

"You're the director?"

"The one and only."

And Gabrielle and I stared at each other in holy-shit wonder.

Sometimes it helps to have a bit of luck in life.

And someone with vision.

CHAPTER THIRTY SIX

Are you sitting down?

We've just run into a friend of ours. We were sweeping the sidewalk in front of the Pineapple Apartments and he rode by on his bike. Our friend's name is Atsushi. He's from Japan. He somehow ended up in Key West selling T-shirts down at Sunset Celebration. Atsushi wants to become a musician and he's making great strides in improving his English. When it's slow on the pier, he comes over and asks us to help him with the curiousness that is the English language. Example: why is "wind," as in blowing in the wind, spelled the same as *wind*, as in winding your watch? Spelled the same, pronounced differently. And in an allied area, what about blew and blue? Tow and toe? Steal and steel? I could go on and on, but if I do, you will surely start to groan.

Atsushi knows lots of words in English.

We now know nine words in Japanese.

But that's not the interesting part of the story.

The interesting part is that Atsushi lives in an old conch house near the cemetery, on the second floor (of the house, not the cemetery). He has a balcony which looks out on to the graveyard. He often sits out on the balcony and practices the guitar (no one to disturb?). Just above where Atsushi sits on his balcony, is a cage hanging from the beams. Inside is his beloved pet "blue-fronted Amazon parrot" that speaks only English. More than nine words.

Last night when he came home from the pier, his pet parrot was gone. In its place was a five-foot-long Burmese python. Asleep. Atsushi ran into his kitchen to get a butcher knife to kill the snake.

When he came out, the Burmese python was gone.

Sweet dreams.

CHAPTER THIRTY SEVEN

Gabrielle painted and practiced and perfected her tropical art for the next few weeks, day and night. And on a Wednesday, at four in the afternoon, we schlepped Gabrielle's easel down to the Ocean Key Resort and set it up on the veranda.

"Let's turn the light on," Gabrielle said.

"But the sun hasn't set yet."

"Well spotted, but just like moths, the punters will be attracted to the light."

"You are so smart."

"I'm all about moths."

It took us only a minute or so to get Gabrielle's light sorted.

"Want a *con leche*?"

"No, I'm wired enough as it is. I don't feel so very comfortable painting in front of people. What if somebody actually orders a name, I'll be a wreck if they stand there and watch me paint it."

"Tell them you're backed up a bit and ask them to come back, then you paint it when they're not here."

"Great idea. Think I'll chum ..."

"What?"

"Think I'll chum, it worked in *JAWS*."

"Huh?"

"You know, paint a name and see if I can draw a crowd. No pun."

"What name are you going to paint?"

"I'll paint KEY WEST."

Gabrielle started to paint KEY WEST using flamingoes and dolphins and palm trees and even the Key West lighthouse.

"That's really good work!"

We turned around to see the director of the hotel standing there with a big smile on his face.

193

"Do you have any kids?" Gabrielle asked.

"Yes," the director said. "Isabelle and Chantelle."

"I'll paint them for you."

"How much will that cost?"

"There's no charge ... for nice people."

"That's very kind."

"No, *you're* very kind."

The director took his leave and Gabrielle turned toward me.

"Isabelle and Chantelle! That's going to take me all night. I was hoping for 'Jo' and 'Jen'."

Gabrielle had just finished painting KEY WEST, and it was still up on the easel, when two brick shit-houses in tank tops stopped by and studied the painting.

"How much for that KEY WEST?"

"It's three dollars a letter, so that would be twenty-one dollars."

"We'll take it."

Gabrielle gave me a look, then turned back to the brick shit-houses. "Really?"

"Yes, and we would like you to paint another name for us."

"I can do that," Gabrielle said, not believing her good fortune. Just setting up and already knocking them dead. "Here." Gabrielle handed one of the gentlemen a clipboard. "Just write down the name you want. I paint in all capital letters."

One of the boys, the one with the short-shorts and the bulge, took the clipboard from Gabrielle, plucked the pen from under a rubber band and wrote down the name he wanted. He handed the clipboard back to Gabrielle.

Gabrielle studied the name. It read "PEANUT."

"Is this for a boy or a girl?" Gabrielle asked.

"It's for our dog."

"O--kay, is your dog a boy or a girl?"

"A girl."

Gabrielle took a fresh piece of white paper 12 inches by 36 inches out of the plastic "bucket" we had brought with us and she secured it to her board with four colorful clips. Back when Gabrielle was teaching herself how to paint names, she had come up with the idea of drawing red lines on the Plexiglas backboard that held the paper, then when the paper was clipped to the boards, she could just make out the red lines that shown through and she could space her letters and know where the middle was to keep all her names even.

In theory a good idea. In reality, crap. The paper Gabrielle used was more of a card weight and once the paper was secured to the board, you couldn't see any lines through the paper at all.

"Do mind if we watch?"

"I'm a bit backed up. Want to take a lap and come back?"

"No, we're happy to wait. Never saw this kind of art before…"

"Great," Gabrielle said, eyeing me in panic.

As Gabrielle painted, the boys asked a few questions about where she'd learned her art. I did all the answering, so Gabrielle wouldn't have to multi task in this high-strung environment. About halfway through PEANUT, I turned and looked behind us. There was a crowd. A large crowd of people watching, many families with children. Most had never seen this type of artwork before, and it was freezing people in their tracks. The fascination was that Gabrielle put multiple different colors on each brush, so for example, if she wanted to paint a rainbow, you would dip different parts of the leather brush in the ROY G BIV, and with one stroke, she had a rainbow.

It was magical to watch.

I looked back into the crowd. Standing off to the side was a broad-shouldered man, with a smile wider than his shoulders. It was the director of the Ocean Key Resort again.

Gabrielle finished the name PEANUT, then she rolled it in a colorful mailing tube. She did the same thing with KEY WEST. The boys thanked Gabrielle and headed off down Duval in the direction of the 801 Bar.

We ended up staying until midnight. I did crowd control and Gabrielle painted a whole lot of names for kids, one more dog's name and even A-ROD SUCKS. The customer had a Boston accent.

Gabrielle's new little business was a gigantic success and we'd brought in a whopping one-hundred and fifty dollars.

We were over the moon.

And we were going to survive high season in Key West.

CHAPTER THIRTY EIGHT

Gabrielle, Popcorn Joe and I have woken up with serious hangovers.

Yes, you've heard right, and *wow what a big surprise* you're thinking, aren't you? But, no, contrary to popular belief and conventional wisdom, we did not drag Popcorn Joe out last night and celebrate Gabrielle's good fortune with vats of grog.

We have *book* hangovers.

Have you ever had a book hangover? You have, haven't you? You know what I'm talking about. That awful, gnawing feeling that overcomes you and occupies your very being after you've just put down a good book and now have to return to the real world ... but the real world feels all discombobulated and incomplete ... because you're still *living in the book world.*

There's no immediate anecdote. Sure, you can thumb through the book again, revisiting your favorite passages, but you will still feel a lost soul. Your only hope (to keep from going through book withdrawal) is to pick up another book by the offending author. Dive right in. Don't even think about going to sleep. But that's often when you realize that your neighborhood book store is not open in the middle of the night. Cue the sound of screams ... screams that even the Harpies would be proud to call their own. And do you know why I bring up the subject of horrific, unrelenting screams? YOU WILL HAVE TO WAIT UNTIL THE MORNING. When the book store opens. You will be standing there before the crack of nine, when the owner walks up, key in hand, and you will be imploring her/him to "Hurry!" You need your fix. Then you will rush to the section of the book store where you spend so much time: CRIME (for crime pays), and if you're lucky, you will find the next book in the series. You will look behind you to ensure that no literary low-life enters your space and plucks the book from your clutches, and you will sniff it and hold it close to your chest (as a gambler holds a full house) with shaky hands and you will meet eyes with the owner, and you know that she knows, but she doesn't say anything, because she's been there before, as well. Being compassionate, she will make the exchange quickly, professionally, discreetly, and allow you to slip from the book store, post haste, or should that be hell-bent? As you scarper down the street, dressed still in your jammies (the ones with the manatee on the front), you will be salivating and your bowels will long for evacuation. Your eyes are now dilated and everything around you will appear bright. You cast furtive glances at no one, but avoid eye contact with everyone and before you know it, you are back in the safety, comfort and seclusion of your home and then, only then, does your heart stop racing, your forehead no longer break out in a cold sweat, and the dog approach. You climb back into bed, or tuck up under the blanket on the front couch and you read the back jacket, you lovingly caress the front cover and run a finger over the embossed title, then with an orgasmic inhalation of breath which makes you almost giddy, you open the front cover and begin to slake your addiction with one of the true, great, natural highs on the planet: *reading*.

I took a sip of my espresso and looked over at Gabrielle. Gabrielle got her book hangover from reading James W. Hall's *Mean High Tide*.

Popcorn Joe got his book hangover on account of just finishing Tim Dorsey's *Florida Roadkill*.

And I'm suffering mightily on account of Tom Corcoran's *Air Dance Iguana*.

So now, instead of doing anything resembling work, we are sitting out on the back deck of the Pineapple Apartments, seriously wired on Cuban coffee and discussing the three tomes. Gabrielle tells us that *Mean High Tide* rips our hero Thorn from his world of mangrove islands and open waters and plunges him into a nightmare of violence and deception. Someone near and dear to Thorn is offed and he must find the killer. Gabrielle's face is flushed as she recounts just enough to hook us, but not to give too much away.

I ask Popcorn Joe what *Flamingo Roadkill* is about, and Joe says "Everything! It takes place in Tampa, the Florida Keys and the Dry Tortugas, and it has con men, a con woman, gratuitous violence, pigeon-eating maniacs--"

"Did you say pidgin talking?"

"NO! PIGEON-EATING! And it's got cocaine trafficking and traffic jams and biker gangs and hot-tub accidents ..."

"Did you say hot-tub accidents?"

Popcorn Joe gives us one of his bemused looks. "Yes."

"What kind?"

"The worst kind ... and it's got satanic heavy metal bands, frozen crocodiles, the World Series and the Space Shuttle!"

"So, did you like it?"

"It's a blast."

"The Space Shuttle?"

"NO! THE BOOK!"

"It was my turn, so I said: "My name is Jon. I'm a bookaholic."

"What did you say you read?"

"*Air Dance Iguana.*"

"Good?"

"A killer read. Tom Corcoran is a wordsmith. The book is about photographer Alex Rutledge who has rented his house in Key West to a friend, so he can house-sit elsewhere, chill, have peace and quiet and kayak whenever he wants. But the night before he heads off, in the middle of the night, the phone rings and his world gets turned upside down, big time. Anyway, I don't want to spoil it, but there's a series of murders, your usual bodies hanging off davits, that sort of thing, and all fingers are pointing to the hero's brother. There's tons of local color and the twists and turns that Corcoran is famous for."

We sat there in a stupor of sorts, then I handed *Air Dance Iguana* to Popcorn Joe, he handed *Flamingo Roadkill* to Gabrielle and Gabrielle handed *Mean High Tide* to me.

We fondled the titles that would be soon keeping us up late at night again. Then had a peek at the blurb on the back jackets.

Gabrielle's color returned to her face.

Popcorn Joe's hands stopped twitching.

And I stopped making that movement that cats do with their mouths when they're looking at a bird that's just out of reach.

Or Henley, the live-aboard.

Then Gabrielle pointed to a different book sitting on the table near Popcorn Joe. A book with a colorful cover.

"What's that?"

"*Dance of the Reptiles* by Carl Hiaasen.

"Have you read it?"

"Just the back jacket. It's a collection of his wildest and wackiest stories."

"Good?"

"Hilarious."

CHAPTER THIRTY NINE

It's spring now.

The island is alive with the scent of a new beginning. And old clichés. We can smell frangipani and wild orchids, star jasmine and, in the evenings, night blooming cactus. There is nothing better than strolling about the Old Town in the spring, letting your olfactory senses be assaulted with the glorious tropical fragrances.

And the weather is changing. The cold fronts are not marching through on such a regular basis and the other day, the high was 78 degrees and the low was only 72. It is a remarkable climate.

Our biggest decisions are should we wear shorts with flip flops or shorts with sandals when we go to the Key West Songwriters' Festival.

Big decision.

With it being Daylight Savings Time now, it's still light until after seven. I've only just managed to get back on the pier selling sunset photographs. I try to set up on the Ocean Key Resort side, while Don and Shirley set up down by Will Soto, the tightrope walker. Every once in a while, someone walks up to my display holding a matted or framed sunset photo that they've just purchased from Don and Shirley. They see my work, and they whisper among themselves "Should've waited and got one of these."

Don and Shirley say much the same thing happens to them.

I help Gabrielle get set up at the Ocean Key Resort, then I go to Mallory and draw my key out of the bucket, get my pitch and wait for my first sale. As you know, we're only allowed to be there for two hours after sunset, but most vendors are gone by that time.

Only the escape artist, still struggling in his chains, remains.

With no crowd.

And no one who cares.

I pack up all my sunset photos and then cut through the undercover parking lot to meet up with Gabrielle. Then we stay at the Ocean Key Resort until business dies and the tourists' interests turn to scoring _____. You fill in the blank.

Earlier today, Gabrielle had a woman come up to her and order a name. The woman said that she was just going to "go for one drink and would be right back." That was seven hours ago.

"What did she look like?" I asked.

"She was dressed to the nines. Way OTT for Key West."

"Perhaps she got lucky."

"Perhaps." "Did she pay upfront?"

"Yes."

Gabrielle had learned early to ask for the payment upfront, or at least a deposit. Many folk visiting Key West end up falling off the edge of the earth right then and there, never to resurface. Such was the case with a fellow from Brazil. He had ordered a particularly long name, a Brazilian name. With a surplus of vowels. We think it had something to do with having flagitious sex with animals, but then, we weren't so sure, only knowing nine words of Brazilian Portuguese. The name was a nightmare to paint. Gabrielle had to start over once after misjudging the spacing, and again after a passing dove strafed her easel with bird poop, on the eighth letter of the painting. Third time around, Gabrielle got the name right and didn't fall fowl, I mean foul, of the local fauna.

But our Brazilian friend, with the unhealthy interest in animals, never returned. Is it possible he got lucky? It is possible he got_____. You fill in the blank.

And Gabrielle hadn't taken payment upfront.

CHAPTER FORTY

The Key West Songwriters' Festival is here!
We decided on the flip flops!

The Key West Songwriters' Festival is the largest festival of its kind in the world and we are really excited to go listen to Chris Rehm. There are 150 songwriters from all over the world and this is a tremendous honor for Key West Chris to be in the lineup. I should point out that since 1997, BMI has been a charter sponsor of the festival and has helped it grow into both a tourist attraction and favorite of island locals as it brings scores of appreciative tourists to the island.

It is a win-win for everyone.

This is how it all works: the festival lasts five days and five nights. There are 30 venues, staged at Key West's most popular watering holes and hot spots. Visitors love it because they get to rub shoulders and meet the artists. It's a chance to be introduced to the faces, voices and stories behind all the great songs.

There's even an event-capping street concert, which adds an enticing Mardi Gras atmosphere to the proceedings. To give you an example of the songwriters present, might I just take you aside for a moment and recount this little story that Key West Chris told me: "A few years back, I was attending an event at Blue Heaven and there was an attractive young blonde playing the piano. I was standing there enjoying the music, and I overheard the woman next to me say to the woman next to her 'Oh look! She's playing a Taylor Swift song!' to which I gave her a nudge and said with a wink: 'Actually, that *is* Taylor Swift up there.'"

Key West Chris was playing at Southernmost on the Beach, at the other end of Duval from Rick's and Sloppy's. Accompanying Chris, was Misty Loggins. They did a song that Chris wrote especially for her. The song is called "Island Blue," and it's already enjoyed bucket loads of radio airtime from Hawaii, across the Pacific to California, across the Continental United States, hopping the Atlantic Ocean to Great Britain and even down to the European continent.

If you are the type of person who not only likes to listen to music, but would like to get to know the people behind it, those who write it, then dust off your flip flops and hump on down to Key West next spring and grab a front row seat at the Key West Songwriters' festival. It's five says and five nights of FREE ENTERTAINMENT.

And, best of all, you will make some new friends!

* * *

Did you know there is a key called … "Dildo Key?"

Neither did we.

We were talking to Key West Chris after the Key West Songwriters' festival was history for another year and he was telling us that he had been poring (or in his case perhaps *pouring*) over some Coast Guard sounding charts (depth charts) late one lonely night with Cajun and Tooloulou nestled up next to him. Chris is fascinated by the topography of the Florida Keys and is a bit of a historian, so he couldn't believe his eyes. He blinked. Blinked again. Picked up the glass jar of Mango Moonshine he was drinking, regarded it for a worryingly long moment, then switched to a bottle of Prestige beer (from Haiti). Then he studied the chart again. No, it wasn't the moonshine, and his eyes weren't playing tricks. There it was alright, Dildo Key, protruding proudly, off in Florida Bay two-thirds of the way to Flamingo from Islamorada, by the way the osprey flies.

Chris, of course, was immediately inspired and decided right then and there that this needed to be documented. Much historical fact has been passed down in sagas and verse, so he wrote a song to educate and entertain. Coincidentally, it's entitled DILDO KEY. Below are bits and pieces of the lyrics (don't want to spoil it by giving you the entire song).

See if you can pick up on the sexual innuendo:

A HAND FULL OF MILES SOUTH/SOUTHEAST OF OLD FLAMINGO …
MOTOR MY WAY INTO FLORIDA BAY THAT'S WHERE I'M GONNA GO

DROP THE ANCHOR, ROCK THE WAVES,
CAST A LINE,
ENJOY THE DAY
YOU KNOW GOIN' FISHIN' TO MY FAVORITE SPOT,
BETTER KNOWN AS
DILDO KEY
WAAAAHT DID HE SAY??? THAT'S RIGHT
BETTER KNOWN AS DILDO KEY
MAN IN THE BOAT IS READY FOR A DAY OUT ON
DILDO KEY
EAGER BEAVER CAN'T WAIT, MAY NOT COME
BACK FOR THE REST OF THE DAY
GOT A MAGIC WAND, IT'LL MAKE 'EM COME
SURE BEATS HELL OUTTA BAG OF CHUM
EVERYTHING'S SHAKIN' AT MY FAVORITE SPOT,
DOWN, WAY DOWN ON
DILDO KEY

You can well imagine that the minute I heard about this, I felt obliged to report it to you. It seems that Dildo Key got its name, not from its shape, which is sort of like a piece of toast with a splodge of jam off to the left side, rather from the patently phallic Dildo cacti, which are native to the leafy little uninhabited islet.

I wanted to know more about Dildo Key, so when we got home, I Googled "Dildo Key" and by mistake ended up on a kinky site which actually offered *real* sexual adjuncts for sale, one being a *wireless* dildo. Of course, as I was wondering if I could access the Internet on a wireless dildo and check to see if I had any "likes" on Facebook, I realized Gabrielle was looking over my shoulder. Try to explain that to your better half, the part about being addicted to "likes" on Facebook, I mean.

Dildo Key can be a great conversation opener, wouldn't you agree?

THE QUESTION: "Did you know there is a key called Dildo Key?"

THE RESPONSE: "WTF?"

And then you take it from there, you've just entered into robust intercourse.

To settle my nerves after cruising what is essentially a porn site, I had myself a stiff one (I'm talking about the drink), and began wondering about Florida Bay. I knew the average depth was only about three feet, but that's about all I knew. Then I came across this from the Florida Bay Education Project, so I wrote it down for you: "Florida Bay is a shallow inner-shelf lagoon located at the southern end of the south Florida watershed. It is an area where fresh water from the Everglades mixes with the salty waters from the Gulf of Mexico to form an estuary that is surrounded by mangroves forests and encompasses over 200 mangrove islands. The nearly 1,000 square miles of interconnected basins, grassy mud banks, and mangrove islands are nesting, nursery, and/or feeding grounds for a host of marine animals: the American crocodile, the West Indian manatee, the loggerhead turtle, bottlenose dolphins, a variety of bird species and many game fish. Parts of the bay are also the nursery grounds for the economically valuable pink shrimp and Caribbean spiny lobster. Florida Bay is also important economically, supporting a 59-million dollar shrimp fishery and 22-million dollar stone crab fishery."

Wow. I was hooked, so to speak, and I now wanted more. I wanted to know how the Florida Keys came about, and to know that, I had to address the grander issue, sooo...

How did Florida get to be Florida in the first place?

The following is a *simplified* explanation:

There once was a super-continent called "Pangaea" (sometimes spelled "Pangea"). Pangaea was comprised of most of the Earth's landmasses and covered almost one-third of the Earth's surface. It was surrounded by a "global ocean" called Panthalassa. Pangaea consisted of two lesser -- albeit highly impressive, nevertheless -- super-continents: Gondwana (Gondwanaland) and Laurasia, with Laurasia being the more northerly of the two. Basically, Laurasia was made up of present day North America, Europe and Asia. Gondwana consisted of present day South America, Africa, India, Antarctica and Australia.

As geo forces did their thing over a period of millions of years, Pangaea began to split, rift and shift, and Gondwana separated from Laurasia. Without splitting, ah, hairs (mammoth hairs?), meaning what's a few million years between friends,

205

during this time Florida was forming along what would one day become the coast of northwest Africa. This formation occurred through a combination of really spectacular volcanic activity and the gentle and slow deposit of marine sediment.

And then Africa went its own way.

South America went its way.

(Remember, this is the short version.)

And lonely Florida was left behind wailing: "Anyone? Anyone?" just like the incomprehensively boring teacher in *Ferris Buehler's Day Off.* "Anyone? Anyone?"

When no one listened, Florida displayed just a bit of independence and clamped on with North America.

And thank Christ, say I, or the drive down to Key West would take even longer.

Florida was flat, with little geographical relief, as it is now, so as the oceans rose, it slowly slipped beneath the sea (problems even back then with beachfront property) and became part of North America's continental shelf. Over time, more coral, shellfish and fish skeletons began piling up and this formed a layer of limestone hundreds of feet thick.

At some point during all this, the Appalachian Mountains began to erode. The erosion created sand. Much of the sand was comprised of quartz crystals and the quartz was washed down the great rivers into the Atlantic Ocean and the Gulf of Mexico. Swirling ocean currents and crashing waves then deposited the sand over the limestone layer of what was to become Florida.

And the fine-sand beaches of Florida were not far behind.

More coral, shellfish and fish skeletons piled up and a reef formed along the edge of the submerged Florida plateau, stretching south and west from present day Miami all the way down to what is now the Dry Tortugas.

About 70,000 years ago, when the Wisconsin glaciation kicked off, it sucked waters from the Atlantic Ocean, lowering the sea levels and exposing the coral reef. Now come with me and jump forward to 15,000 years ago and you will see that the sea level had dropped to 300 to 350 feet below today's level. The exposed reefs slowly eroded and began collapsing in on themselves forming islands (keys).

For those of you who haven't figured it out all on your own, this has all taken quite a long time (even longer than me just explaining it), so you might just want to rethink walking all over the reef with your big fat feet, or taking bits and pieces as souvenirs, or dumping your plastic, non-biodegradable shit out there.

CHAPTER FORTY ONE

There is a four-foot long iguana in a palm tree.

At least it's not a Burmese python.

Gabrielle and I have been invited to spend the night at our friends Tina and Patty's. They live on Geiger Key. I mentioned that little tidbit as we sped by on our Greyhound Bus Tour To Hell, do you remember or were you busy booking your ticket for next year's Songwriters' Festival?

Patty and Tina bought a cottage together and have been fixing it up.

I woke up at about 7 a.m. and looked out the back sliding-glass door. Right out in the "backyard" is a canal. Across the canal is a thirty-foot tall palm tree with a four-foot long iguana. I've decided to name him "Iggy."

Iggy has crawled out on one of the palm fronds and is endeavoring to catch the early morning sun. Iguanas, like snakes, are cold-blooded and they are useless until they get a dose of sunshine to get them going.

I'm much the same.

Especially after last night, when Tina and Patty treated us to dinner at the Geiger Key Marina Tiki Bar.

Here's what happened: Tina drove down to Key West in the "Pig." The Pig is a 1987, vomit-green Shitmobile. The Pig might be a rust-bucket, but we were impressed that Tina had *wheels*, (bald or not), and of course we were looking forward to our mini holiday -- with the specter of Immigration no longer looming over our quivering heads.

Patty and Tina live on Mars, the *road* not the planet. Many of the names of the streets on Geiger Key are celestial: Mars Lane, Venus Lane, Star Lane, Sun Lane.

Tina and Patty showed us around "Patty and Tina's Castle." They had just put down a ton of white pea rock out front, built a new front gate and fence, laid down flagstone for a walkway and built a clever lattice structure where they could store their paddleboards and keep them off the ground.

All that work and they only cut into their main water supply twice!

After the tour, we all jumped in the Pig and drove the three minutes over to the Geiger Key Marina. The temperature had dipped to below sixty and we were all wearing sweaters and long pants. Kind of looks neat when you are tanned a deep brown. Don't get to do that in the Great White North, unless you ski, and then you are only tan from the turtle neck up.

For those of you who have been to this restaurant/bar/marina/RV park, you know that it is somewhat of a well-kept secret. And it is "ON THE BACKSIDE OF PARADISE" as a sign proudly (and rightly) states.

It was Saturday evening and two guys were playing the guitar and keyboards and singing up on stage: "Take me back to the islands ..."

There's a bar, bordered by picnic tables and you are outdoors, but undercover. Another sign happily states: "IF YOUR (sic) DRINKING TO FORGET, PLEASE PAY IN ADVANCE."

The Atlantic is just right there about three feet away. It is an exceedingly romantic, laid back and cool venue. With this atmosphere, you could only be in the Florida Keys.

In old Key West.

Gabrielle and I looked around, there were more dogs in here than patrons.

Patty pointed and yelled "Skip!" It was her brother and his wife Teresa. Skip, we soon learned, lives just a few doors away from the "Castle."

"Cold weather'll bring out the scorpions," Skip says good naturedly, as he approaches. "That and a good rain." Skip knows about these things. He's been around. And he's a damn good fisherman. Lives for it. Has seventy different fishing rods. Almost as many rods as Patty has pairs of socks.

Patty doesn't have a sock drawer, she has a sock chest-of-drawers.

Gabrielle ordered a Cabernet Sauvignon, Patty a diet coke,

Tina a Michelob Ultra, and I ordered a regular Michelob. They didn't have the Michelob Ultra, or the regular Michelob, so Tina settled for a Corona (without the lime) and I settled for a Bud (without the taste of the Michelob). I threw my Bud down, as is my thirsty wont, then started on Gabrielle's Cabernet, so I had to order another one for her after being punched in the shoulder, twice.

With Patty and Tina, and Skip and Teresa, it was all very far-flung and agreeable, drinking, and with the Trop Rock music playing in the background.

We ordered dinner. Gabrielle and I had the blackened grouper (to die for) and Tina and Patty had the famous fish sandwich.

Late in the evening, Skip and Teresa exited, stage right

We listened to the band some more, then when they took a break and it got quiet, Tina held up her glass. "I would like to make a toast."

We all held up our glasses.

"To Patty and me, we're getting married!"

We toasted. And we were thrilled for the two of them. How many people really ever get a chance to find their soul mate?

It's the next morning now, and I'm watching Iggy the iguana, and I think he's watching me. Gabrielle sneaks up behind me and just brushes the gnarled hair on my bare leg with a kitchen broom, and I jump sky high.

Tina and Patty are standing there as well, in the PJs, looking cute and adorable. Tina in red, Patty in blue (same as the trim on their paddleboards). They are laughing and I laugh, too, until Patty says: "Skip drove to work the other morning and counted 80 of them."

"Eighty of what?"

"Iguanas ..."

"There are eighty iguanas like Iggy running around Geiger Key!"

"No, many are bigger."

"Bigger!"

"Wait until you see the Gran-Poo-Pa. He's really big. He crawls out on the same palm frond up there to catch the sun and on cloudy days he falls off."

210

"What?"

"He doesn't get hurt, just waits to warm up and then climbs back on up," Patty says.

"Sometimes they all come out of the tree and just sun themselves right there across the canal," Tina says.

"What about those people who live in the trailers to the right and left of the palm tree?"

"The guy to the right doesn't seem to mind. He plays his music really loud, but we don't mind. He's got good taste."

"And to the left?"

"There's an old bat who lives over there. She comes outside in her rollers and sings opera. The iguanas don't seem to mind."

"The singing or the rollers."

"The singing, although now that I've said that, when she's wearing the rollers, they stay up in the tree."

A friend of Tina and Patty has come over. Her name is Sharon. She lives just around the corner in a different part of the trailer park. She's short and blond. And she used to drive an 18-wheeler. Got that image? She loved driving the 18-wheeler because "I was up so high."

Sharon's from the Northern Neck peninsula of Virginia and she speaks with a Tangier Island accent. She discovered the Florida Keys when she used to deliver bait to Islamorada in her "reefer." I said delivering *bait*, not *reefer*. Why bait needs to be delivered to the "Sport Fishing Capital of the World" we haven't quite figured out yet.

Sharon is a hoot.

Sharon takes her leave and we settle down in the living room, chatting with Tina and Patty. We have one eye on them and one on the iguanas. Gabrielle suddenly lets out an opened-mouth silent scream and points. Crawling out from under the "rocking" couch where Tina and Patty are sitting is a nice big black fat scorpion.

Being the only man there, and having had experience with the nosy little buggers, I jump into a black-belt karate position and implore Patty to "Do something!"

Patty is the hunter/gatherer around the castle and she quickly shows the arachnid little bastard the back door -- which leads out to the canal and 80 iguanas across the way.

Scorpions in the living room and iguanas in the palm trees. Living in Key West is like living in the Discovery Channel.

And we've decided to find it all charming.

CHAPTER FORTY TWO

From the trailer park to Truman Annex.

The very next day, Popcorn Joe introduces us to Dennis and Mindy. They own a glorious conch house (read: mansion) in Truman Annex, and a cute Volkswagen Beetle. The Beetle is green. Most green cars aren't so very attractive (think the Pig), but this one is. It's sort of a Key lime pie green and that seems just perfect for Key West.

Dennis and Mindy: They, too, are a hoot.

And they are an attractive couple: Dennis tall and blond. Could have been an Austrian ski instructor. Mindy gorgeous with a smile that would melt the ice in your gin and tonic. The type of gal an Austrian ski instructor would chase all over the mountain.

It's 70 degrees and we are sitting out by the pool, in between the main house and the pool house. When we'd first arrived, we were seriously impressed by the grandeur of the Victorian home. That's when Popcorn Joe told us we were looking at just the pool house.

Gabrielle and I live in an attic with a hatch in the tin roof. They live in a château. They should be all full of themselves and snobby, but they are just the opposite. They are down to earth and grounded. These are good folk. They laugh in all the right places. These are people that you want to hang out with.

I've met folk of wealth before and the first thing they do is tell you how wonderful they are and how many toys they have. Mindy and Dennis just want to offer you a drink and pass the Wheat Thins.

Did I mention that these are good folk?

Something is rustling the palm trees by the swimming pool. Iguana, I'm thinking when out from near the base of one of the trees comes a husky/malamute mix. A rescue dog, oh so happy to have a couple of humans to look after. Poor thing must have arthritis as she limps a bit. I'm hoping the dog will come over to Gabrielle and me, and Mindy -- who must be clairvoyant -- says: "Give Britney a minute, you'll know when she's ready."

Five minutes later, we are lost in conversation and laughter and Britney has snuck up on me and nuzzled my hand with her nose in that way that good dogs do when they want you to pet them.

So I'm petting.

And Britney is all smiles.

Just like Mindy and Dennis.

CHAPTER FORTY THREE

Cowboy Bill's has inexplicably locked its door. Rumor has it that it will open again in a week or two, but nobody seems to know why it's suddenly closed down.

Gabrielle and I rush over to Aronovitz Lane and find Mrs. Grace sitting out on her front porch.

Mr. Leroy is asleep on her lap.

"He's been laid off," Mrs. Grace tells us.

"What's going on over there?"

"Nobody knows. Rumors are swirling ..."

"Perhaps Mr. Leroy should retire?"

"Think he already has."

Gabrielle lifts Mr. Leroy onto her lap. "If I can make enough money doing my Tropical Lettering, we can move out of the attic. Sam next door to the Pineapple Apartments has two rental units. We could move in there and bring Mr. Leroy home."

"But this lane is his home," I say.

"Not for long," Gabrielle says. "Look across at Villa Alberto."

I looked across the lane at our old home. There was a small sign out front, the sort of sign realtors stick out there.

It read: SOLD.

CHAPTER FORTY FOUR

As spring turned to summer and the heat settled over the island, a transformation was taking place: Cowboy Bills was back open and all the old cottages and barracks (including Villa Alberto) in Aronovitz Lane were torn down and new cottages were built. The Pig Man was gone, as was our old neighbor "Snake" and the Bahamian gentleman two doors over with just the one leg.

Where did these good and colorful people go? Key West is expensive. When you live in the ghetto and the ghetto is gentrified, there are not a lot of places left to go.

And we moved, as well.

Just as we'd hoped, a unit at Sam Hochman's at 704 Caroline, right next to the Pineapple Apartments, became available. It was a tiny, fully furnished one-bedroom, and it was a thousand dollars a month, lot of money for a shoe box. The bedroom had a small A/C unit in the window. I think the A/C unit was rated at only about 3 BTUs, but it somehow kept the tiny apartment cool enough when needed. It helped that the house was an old conch house and was built about three feet off the ground so that air could sweep underneath it and help with the cooling process.

We kept our jobs at the Pineapple Apartments and every morning we had a ten-foot commute. Mr. Leroy came to live with us and he seemed content in his retirement. He spent a lot of time sleeping on the porch out front, when it wasn't being commandeered by a local transient waiting for the Caroline Street Market to open so he could procure beer. When it got too hot in the height of the summer, Mr. Leroy demanded to be let in and then he dozed in the middle of our bed.

Sam was a true Key West character. He had long, white hair which he always kept in a ponytail and he always wore long trousers, but never a shirt. Chicken legs, perhaps? He spent an inordinate amount of time sweeping the sidewalk in front of the house, so he could flirt with every female who walked by.

Sam would tell us stories about him and his good friend Shel Silverstein (before he passed away) going off to Thailand to, ah, how can I say this sensitively? I can't, so I'll just whisper it: GET LAID. Sam was always very graphic with his descriptions and you know the expression "too much information!"? Sam could've invented it. One day, after he and Shel returned from Thailand, he educated us on the proclivities of the young girls of Thailand and their fondness for "beads."

This is not to be confused with Fantasy Fest and everyone's fondness for "Beads! Beads!"

* * *

A month after moving into Sam's, it rained for 72 hours straight. Perhaps it was just me, but it sure seemed as if we were getting more rain this summer than last. At high tide, Duval looked more like the Grand Canal in Venice, than the Duval we came to know and love. Stores had sandbags guarding their front entrances, and folk on paddleboards could be seen plying the Duval waters. It wasn't unusual to see a gaggle of kayaks tied up to Two Friends, Rick's or Pepe's. There wasn't a lot to do in Key West other than sit on a barstool and talk about the weather.

About the time the rains stopped and folk started venturing further afield, we were awoken by screaming and then sirens.

The sirens stopped right out front of our house and we watched in horror as paramedics rushed upstairs and brought our landlord Sam down on a gurney. The next day he was back out in front, shirtless, still wearing long trousers, sweeping the sidewalk.

Gabrielle and I went outside. "Sam, what the hell?"

"I was at the Red Garter and picked up one of the lap dancers. We came home and went upstairs, smoked a joint and then were fucking. Suddenly I couldn't breathe. I'm going over to the post office. Wanna come with?"

We walked with Sam but he clearly wasn't the same individual. He had always been vibrant, cheeky and spunky. Now he had become a beaten man.

"I've got emphysema," he told us. "Got to give up my vices. Life is not going to be fun anymore."

CHAPTER FORTY FIVE

As I write this chapter, I'm sad to report that we've just learned that Jerry, or Geraldo as we called him, the Wizard of Key West, has moved on to green, albeit, less colorful pastures ...

The Wizard of Key West.

Sam.

Shel.

Feather.

Captain Tony.

Freddie Cabanas.

Shark Man.

Bowling Ball Frank.

Different characters from different ends of the spectrum.

The colorful spectrum that is Bone Island.

Key West will never quite be the same.

* * *

Speaking of never being quite the same, as we speak, I'm online reading *The Blue Paper (Key West the Newspaper)*. Arnaud and Naja Giraud have written an in-depth article about that logistic catastrophe (read: fiasco) that is the "boulevard enhancement" construction taking place on North Roosevelt Blvd. I'm going to just scribble down the URL here for you (www.thebluepaper.com), so you can go online and check this out if you don't already know about it. And while you're there, check out the entire site. There's much to be gleaned about the serious stuff that's going on in and around Key West.

Naja and Arnaud are the publishers of *The Blue Paper* and are dogged, crafty investigative reporters in their own right. It is not widely known, but a chunk of paradise remains paradise to this day on account of their grit and determination: The local couple cherished the memories of their two children growing up and playing on Christmas Tree Island with kids from other live-aboard families who were anchored just offshore. The Girards began digging in archives in Washington, D.C., and cross referencing with online databases, trying to find a way to keep the island undeveloped when greed in the form of development was peeking over the horizon instead of the famous and much loved sunset.

And Eureka!

Or perhaps I should shout Wisteria!

They unearthed documents that showed the *purported* owners (the Bernsteins of Stock Island fame) could not own the island as they openly claimed, as the Navy had not given up title to it until 1982. When it finally transferred title, it did so to the U.S. Department of the Interior, not the state of Florida.

That's the CliffsNotes' version of what was an extremely lengthy and protracted endeavor.

And Christmas Tree Island remains undeveloped, thanks to Arnaud and Naja Giraud.

And while I have you here, might I just mention to check out David Lybrand's column in *The Blue Paper*.

David will open your eyes.

Wide.

3 March, 2014, BREAKING NEWS from *The Blue Paper*: An unexpected development in the Wisteria Island ownership saga: A "For Sale" sign appeared today on Wisteria Island's (Christmas Tree Island) beach.

7 March, 2014, BREAKING NEWS from *The Blue Paper* again: Naja Girard of *The Blue Paper* reports:

A HOAX

Turns out the mysterious "For Sale" sign that appeared last week on the beach of Wisteria Island was a hoax. *The Blue Paper* spoke with Bob Cardenas, General Manager of Sunset Key Development Corporation. "We had thrown a pile of old signs away in a dumpster. When we heard about the sign we went out and took it down immediately. We had absolutely nothing to do with it. Someone must have taken it out of our dumpster and put it there as a joke."

CHAPTER FORTY SIX

We popped into the gift shop at Margaritaville.

If you haven't ever been, I suggest you put on your flip flops and slap on down there. This is not your usual gift shop. The staff is friendly and knowledgeable. It boasts a wonderful selection of Jimmy Buffett CDs and DVDs, a selection of books about Key West, all sizes and shapes of Parrot Head paraphernalia and a bunch of fun items that you just won't find back home. Or anywhere else on the island.

"Do you need any help?"

Gabrielle and I turned. An attractive blonde named Amy had materialized.

"We're looking for a book entitled *PAPA*," Gabrielle said.

"Right over here."

Amy led us to the book section and plucked a copy off the shelf.

"It's written by James McLendon," Amy said. "It documents Hemingway and his literary friends in Key West. It's loaded with great photos, as well."

Amy guided us to the cash register and a smiley woman by the name of Janet who took our money and put the book in a nifty bag. Was everyone in this store so friendly? So often you go into an establishment in Key West and are met with just a bit of "I LIVE HERE AND YOU DON'T" attitude. But not in the Margaritaville gift shop. This must be a great place to work.

It's certainly a great place to shop.

We exited the shop, stage right, and walked right into the bar at Margaritaville.

"You're going to tell me that 'IT MUST BE FIVE O'CLOCK SOMEWHERE,' aren't you?"

"We don't have to have anything to drink ..."

"Have you ever walked into a bar in your life and NOT had something to drink?"

"What about that time in up in the mountains near Boone, North Carolina? Didn't drink then."

"Did indeed. You drank some evil hooch out of a glass jar."

"I thought it came from a local stream ..."

"It did. It was bootlegged moonshine that could peal paint off a double-wide."

"What about that time we were in Kitzbühel, Austria, skiing with Chip and Tom, I didn't drink anything then."

"Are you referring to when we were in Big Ben?"

"Yes, that time."

"You *drank*, you just didn't *pay*."

"Did we do a runner?"

"Not by design. You went upstairs to the Gents and then just walked back down the stairs and out the front door."

"How about that time in Gibraltar?"

"With John and Ian and Will?"

"Yes, that time."

"When we walked across the border between Gibraltar and Spain and had dinner in that scary border town called La Linea?"

"*Si.*"

That dark, moody bodega, down that dark, dangerous street?"

"*Si.*"

"When I went to the Ladies and you all said you would wait for me just outside, but when I came out you had all gone off to try to find some place selling Pringles and I was left there standing all alone on a dark, dangerous street, in a scruffy, violent border town?"

"Ah ..."

"Just answer the question."

"What *was* the question?"

Gabrielle looked at me and laughed. "The question was: What do you want to drink?"

"It has to be margaritas, doesn't it?"

A young thing with a Liverpool, Texas, accent came by and took our order. While we waited for our margies to arrive, I paged through *PAPA*.

"Hey, look at this, Gabrielle," I said, pointing at a section in the book.

Gabrielle took the book from me, read, then looked up.

"Key West in the 30s when Hemingway and his mob were running rampant. Oh, to be a fly on the wall ..."

We put down *PAPA* and picked up menus.

"Feeling peckish?"

"Constantly."

Gabrielle noted an item in the menu.

"A Cheeseburger Paradise?"

"Everyone has to try it at least once."

"But that's what tourons do ..."

"EVERYONE HAS TO TRY IT AT LEAST ONCE!"

"Can't we at least just get it to go?"

"Just order. Here she comes."

Our lovely server appeared right on cue.

"We would like two Cheeseburgers in Paradise," I said.

"We're all out."

Gabrielle and I shot the server a look, then she burst into laughter. "Joking! How would you like those?"

"Well side of medium," I said.

She shot us a flirty smile. "Done."

Well, for those of you who are too snobbish to go into Margaritaville and order a Cheeseburger in Paradise, because GOD FORBID that somehow doesn't seem cool, then lose your haughty ways and get your sunburned behind over there and chow down. You won't be disappointed.

FYI: JB opened the gift shop on Duval in January of 1985 and just before Christmas in 1987 opened the café next door. On stage, during the opening, Jimmy told an enthusiastic audience: "When I started out playing bars in this town, all I wanted was enough money to buy a boat I could sail away on if success faded. The other alternative was to buy my own bar so I could hire myself and just keep singing. Welcome to Margaritaville!"

So while you're in there gnawing on your Cheeseburger in Paradise, think about that and chew on this about JB. Parrot Heads will know these tidbits, but those PH fledglings who haven't flown the nest yet, may not, so please bear with me:

1) Jimmy Buffett is one of just seven authors to ever have a

number one book on both the *New York Times* Fiction and Non-Fiction Best Sellers list. The other authors were John Steinbeck, Mitch Albom, William Styron, Irving Wallace, Dr. Seuss and, yes, none other than Ernest Hemingway. Something in the Key West air?

2) Jimmy was born on Christmas Day (1946), in Pascagoula, Mississippi.

3) His father worked in and around ships and his grandfather was the captain of a ship: *"The son of the son of a sailor."*

4) In 2006, he hooked up with Anheuser-Busch to create his own brewski, "Land Shark Lager."

5) In the Ladakh region of northernmost India, a road-building operation called Project Himank is responsible for maintaining transport lines through some of the most difficult terrain on earth. Company employees have marked their roads with large, bright yellow signs featuring slogans and quotes from notable people, including Jimmy Buffett: "Without geography, you're nowhere."

6) He and Bono almost got killed in Jamaica. On January 16, 1996, Jimmy Buffett's Grumman HU-16 Albatross seaplane, named the *Hemisphere Dancer*, was shot at by Jamaican police as he taxied in the translucent waters off Negril, on Jamaica's north-west coast. Negril is a small beach town, population 3,000 or so, with beaches that are routinely in the Top Ten Best Beaches in the world. As JB brought his Grumman closer to shore, with designs on kicking back and spending some quality time there, the police opened fire. They had received an anonymous tip that a plane loaded with drugs would be landing that day. Onboard the plane was Chris Blackwell from Island Records and U2's Bono and his family. When the police started firing, Bono, his wife Ali, and their children dived for cover fearing they were about to be killed. Bono was so upset by the scary incident, he and his family got the hell out of Jamaica and flew straight to Miami, where of course it's much safer. Bono described the incident in the *Belfast Telegraph*: "These boys were shooting all over the place. I felt as if we were in the middle of a James Bond movie, only this was real. It was absolutely terrifying and I honestly thought we were all going to die. Thank God we

were safe and sound. My only concern was for their safety. It was very scary, let me tell you. You can't believe the relief I felt when I saw the kids were okay."

The *Hemisphere Dancer* escaped relatively unscathed except for a few bullet holes.

And no drugs were found.

As many of you know, Buffett penned a tune about the incident: "Jamaica Mistaica," which appeared on the 1996 album *Banana Wind*. Here is a sampling of lyrics:

It was a beautiful day
The kind you'd want to toast
We were treetop flyin'
Movin' west along the coast
Then we landed in the water
Just about my favorite thrill
When some assholes started firing
As we taxied to Negril

7) In *High Times*, JB has been quoted: "I don't get stoned before shows, but afterwards, I get real high." And his favorite is "Good Colombian, when you can get it." He has also been quoted in the same magazine: "My vices these days consist of boat drinks, beer, wine and the occasional hot fudge sundae."

8) Urban myth regarding his LOST SHAKER OF SALT and you can tell me if you think either of these is plausible:

#1 JB bet some strangers he'd met in a hole-in-the-wall down in the Keys that he could drink an entire bottle of tequila – and he won the bet. This happened, the sole reason being, he had a salt shaker filled with cocaine. He slipped away from the table to use the head. While he was in the can, the waitress cleared the table and put the salt shaker away with the others in the restaurant. When he came back, he freaked out and began to search for his lost shaker of salt. Some person who gets that salt will blame the woman waitress, but Jimmy knows it's all his fault.

#2 Jimmy B was in a bar and had some blow on him. He heard there was going to be a raid. He dumped out a salt shaker and poured his coke into it. He left it on a table and calmly walked away. When the raid was over, JB returned for his salt shaker. The waitress had cleared the tables and he couldn't find it anywhere. Hence, the "lost shaker of salt."

****NOTE:** What do you think? Plausible or not? How did he know there was going to be a raid? When a raid is in progress can you "calmly walk away?" Would you put cocaine in a salt shaker? No, really, would you? If you *did* put it in a salt shaker and the salt shaker was placed among a bunch of others, would you perhaps look for it? How many salt shakers does a small eatery in the Keys have? If you have any other theories, please email them to me and I will put them in my next book.

9) Here's another one that Parrot Heads know: The lyrics on the final album version of "Margaritaville" are different than the original version. The 1973 version featured an additional verse before the verse that begins "I blew out my flip-flop ..." That verse was removed reportedly to make "Margaritaville" more radio-airplay friendly. The lost verse went like this:

Old men in tank tops
Cruisin' the gift shops
Checkin' out Chiquitas down by the shore
They dream about weight loss
Wish they could be their own boss
Those three-day vacations can be (or become) such a bore

10) The radio edit version of "Margaritaville" was released on 45 rpm records in the U.S., Italy, Germany and Spain with the song "Miss You So Badly" as the B-side of the 45.

11) In 2005, JB lost his cell phone in a Delray Beach restaurant. A busboy (who was soon to be an unemployed busboy) found the cell phone and instead of doing the right thing and returning it, thought it would make a nifty souvenir. When the crook/busboy refused to return the cell phone after repeated attempts from Buffett's camp (and even Buffett's wife), things really went in the toilet for the busboy. Seems there were some fairly important people in Jimmy's phonebook, like George Clooney, Michael Douglas, George Strait, Al Gore, Harrison Ford and Bill Gates. A week went by and the busboy still refused to return the cell phone. Silly shit. That's when a Secret Service Agent turned up at his house: former President Bill Clinton's private number was also on the list.

12) Did you know that author Tom Corcoran co-wrote "Fins" and "Cuban Crime of Passion?"

13) Buffett managed one of Captain Tony's unsuccessful

mayoral bids, and immortalized him with his song "Last Mango in Paris" about the tales of Tarracino. Here's how the song starts, plus the first chorus:

> **I went down to Captain Tony's**
> **To get out of the heat**
> **I heard a voice call out to me**
> **"Son, come have a seat"**
> **I had to search my memories**
> **As I looked into those eyes**
> **Our lives change like the weather**
> **But a legend never dies**
> **He said, "I ate the last mango in Paris**
> **Took the last plane out of Saigon**
> **I took the first fast boat to China**
> **And Jimmy, there's still so much to be done"**

14) Here's my favorite: JB was ejected from his courtside seat under the basket at a New York Knicks/Miami Heat game on the 4th of February, 2001, for cursing at one of the referees when the game was tied at 91. "It was a bad call. It still is a rotten call!" JB said at the time. "John Starks clobbered Tim Hardaway. It was a close game. I just said 'You stupid, motherfucker, that is the worst call I ever heard.' People yell all the time but he turned at me. Normally, referees do not make eye contact. So while he did not come over to me, he told the local security guard. By then the crowd was getting into it. Pat Riley was on the bench, asking 'They are kicking you out of the game?' Alonzo was like: 'Sit down. You stay there. I told the security guard. This is probably not a good idea.' Then they came to me and said they would give the Heat a technical foul. So I said, okay, I'll go."

Buffett was escorted by a bevy of cops to the tunnel known as "the Vomitorium," used by players to get to the locker rooms.

The ref, Joe Forte, was unimpressed with the verbal assault and didn't know who Jimmy Buffett was and that Jimmy often sang the national anthem at playoff games.

"He was there with his son," said Heat coach Pat Riley about Buffett. Riley had a front-row seat for the confrontation. "I don't think it was that bad. I mean, come on, a few words."

Riley later approached the ref and said to him "Do you

226

mean to tell me you've never been a Parrot Head in your life?" The ref hadn't had a clue who Jimmy Buffett was.

Coach Riley went on to say that the ref "thought I was insulting him. He wanted to give me a technical for calling him a Parrot Head. So that tells you where our officials are coming from."

The thing that upset Buffett the most about the entire event was that some news outlets reported that he was "at the game with his grandson."

The Knicks won the game in overtime, 103-100 (as of this writing, Joe Forte is now in his 19th year refereeing in the NBA, at the age of 70, and I'm willing to bet he now knows what a Parrot Head is).

So there you go, a bit of JB stuff you may or may not have known. Either way, order that Cheeseburger in Paradise the next time you are in KW, and be sure to wash it down with a blender full of margaritas.

CHAPTER FORTY SEVEN

We are back down at the Ocean Key Resort.

Gabrielle is painting her Tropical Lettering for a family from the U.K. I'm watching some guy feed freshwater from a hose to a manatee.

Manatees are thirty creatures. This one has been sucking away for fifteen minutes and it doesn't look like it will end anytime soon. Much like me last night at Margaritaville.

Would you be interested to learn that manatees are really West Indian manatees and they are Florida's state marine mammal? A lofty position and well-deserved, say I.

Who could be more representative?

Who is more adorable?

Would you be further interested to know that the manatee's closest relatives are the elephant and some curious creature called a "hyrax," which is a small, gopher-sized mammal.

If you take out your notepad now, or your iPad, I will now tell you that manatees evolved from a wading, plant-eating animal. The manatee that we sometime see in Key West -- and have grown to love -- has a bunch of cool relatives like the West African manatee, the Amazonian manatee, the Dugong (his tail is fluked like a whale's), and what is known as "Steller's sea cow," which was sadly hunted to extinction in 1768.

The average adult manatee is about ten feet long and weighs between 800 and 1,200 pounds, before dinner. Manatees eat 10 – 15% of their body weight, daily. You do the math. That's a lot when you're on a leafy green diet.

Manatees have really great vision, so know that while you're looking down at them, smiling, they're noticing. Not unlike most of us, they are not so very keen on cold water. The water in Key West in the summer can rise over 85 degrees (in Florida Bay, it can rise even higher) and almost feels as if you were stepping into a bath. Manatees like this. They don't usually venture into water that drops below 68 degrees Fahrenheit.

Have you ever ridden around the Old Town on your bike and seen one of those manatee mail boxes? You know the kind I mean, the ones where a three-foot high replica of a manatee is holding your mail box with its front flippers. Well, in the wild, those flippers can do even more than that. You, see, they steer with those front flippers and when in shallow water, sometimes even "walk" along the bottom, remember they evolved from wading animals.

Like you and me, manatees like to travel. You come to Key West from San Francisco, or Alexandria, or Galveston, or the Jersey Shore, or New York, or Pennsylvania or Michigan or even Punta Gorda. Well, guess what? Manatees can do that, as well. Only they migrate "up," perhaps not to Michigan, but they do go as far as Galveston, New Orleans, the Carolinas and even Cape Cod. They do so in the warm summer months, so it is unlikely you will ever pass one on the way. They travel at only four to five miles an hour, but can rocket at 20 miles an hour if they feel the need. Much like me when I hear the dinner bell -- or "Last Call!" at the Bull. I might sit on my numb behind for much of the evening, but when I hear that Last Call bell, the race is on. Having said that, I try to preempt Last Call. No good to stand at the bar behind sweaty bodies three deep, waiting to be served when it cuts into quality drinking time.

But this is not about me and my, ah, issues, this is about manatees. A manatee will need to come up for air every three to five minutes. Just like when you were a teenager and you went on a date to the drive-in. If a manatee is using up a lot of energy: swimming at 20 miles per hour, for example, they need to breath every 30 seconds. At rest, they can hang out on the bottom for 20 minutes before needing to surface.

Like me -- perhaps like you -- manatees like to rest, feed often, and drink. Even though they love to find some friendly human who will dangle a hose in the water to give them a nice drink of water, it is not advised.

Like you and me, manatees are social creatures and make friends easily. They would receive many "Likes" on Facebook if they could ever get a good signal.

One manatee was known to have "adopted" a ranger up in the St. Johns River area. The ranger took care of the manatee for a few years. One day the ranger drove back home after a long day's work and the manatee was there waiting for him in the canal in his backyard "Hi! It's me! Wassup?"

Manatee babies are called calves and when they are born they can weigh in the neighborhood of 60-70 pounds and are three-to-four feet long. That's a big boy! The logistics of it all for the mother doesn't *bear* thinking about. Mom manatees' gestation period is about a year, so that means lots of cookie-dough-ice-cream-flavored sea grass, I guess. Manatees can squeal under water to show excitement or even fear, so a lot of that must go on in that year. Only one calf is born every two to five years. Perhaps that's stating the obvious what with them being REALLY BIG at birth. Mom manatees nurse their young for one to two years and during this period, the calf remains extremely dependent on its mother.

Manatees have no natural enemies, other than irresponsible boat owners, fish hooks, monofilament line and litter.

They can live 60 years or more.

In short: manatees are cool.

As of this past January, there were only 4,834 manatees in the entire United States. The Marine Mammal Protection Act of 1972, and the Endangered Species Act of 1973, make it illegal to harass, hunt, capture, or kill any marine mammal.

Pass it on after you read this report from the Associated Press: "A St. Petersburg, Fla., woman was arrested on a misdemeanor warrant Saturday after being photographed two months ago riding a manatee. Florida's Manatee Sanctuary Act protects the endangered sea mammal and says in part, 'It is unlawful for any person at any time, by any means, or in any manner intentionally or negligently to annoy, molest, harass, or disturb or attempt to molest, harass, or disturb any manatee.'

"Ana Gloria Garcia Gutierrez, 53, was taken into custody without incident at a Sears department store where she works, according to the Pinellas County Sheriff's Office.

"The incident first came to the public's attention when Sheriff Bob Gualtieri held a news conference on Oct. 2 and asked for help in identifying the woman photographed riding the manatee at nearby Fort De Soto Park in late September.

"Gutierrez has admitted touching the endangered sea mammal, the sheriff's office said. She told deputies that she was new to the area at the time and didn't know it was illegal to touch a manatee."

**AUTHOR'S INCENSED NOTE: WTF! Was she new to common sense? The manatee was not hurt. Freaked out, fearing for its life and most likely pissed of, for sure. The maximum penalty is a $500 fine and six months in jail. Gutierrez was released on $1,500 bail."

Stupid shit.

**ADDENDUM: Gabrielle just tapped me on my shoulder and told me that I shouldn't use the term "stupid shit." She said I should use something more literary. Okay, so I won't use "stupid shit" anymore.

Fuck-head.

* * *

The manatee drinking from the hose has finally quenched his thirst and has moved down the dock so he can look cute and adorable for all the folk holding sway on the Sunset Pier. I watch him swim in a waddling fashion of sorts, then return to watch Gabrielle paint. About now Popcorn Joe magically appears.

"Giuseppe! Sixty three!"

"Sixty three!"

"What are you doing here?"

"Came to check out Gabrielle's location."

"Who's watching the popcorn business?"

"Becky. She's entertaining a family from Glasgow, Scotland."

"Can she understand them?"

"Not a word, but they're really nice. And funny."

We watch Gabrielle paint for about half an hour, endeavoring to lure tourists, then Popcorn Joe says "Pssst! Jon!" and motions with his head. I turn and see an impressive figure dressed in all white, sporting a straw hat and Navigators, while holding a cigar in one hand and what looks to be a mojito in the other. I hold both palms up to Popcorn Joe.

Popcorn Joe doesn't say anything to me, but he does say: "Evening, Your Honor!"

"*Your Honor?*" Gabrielle whispers.

"Do you know who that is?" Popcorn Joe whispers back.

"No."

"That Sammie Mays, the Official Honorary Mayor of Key West."

"For real?"

"Yeah, AKA Mayor Gonzo Mays."

Well, dear Reader, enquiring minds want to know, so I just better tell you how Sammie Mays got to be the Official Honorary Mayor of Key West, and how the "Gonzo" tag was earned.

We all know that Key West is a "sunny place for shady people," so it helps if you have a colorful past. Even better if that past is delightfully checkered, you see, Sammie Mays did something that no one ever dared.

Let me set the offending stage: In 1963, the United States Penitentiary Marion, in Marion, Illinois, was opened to replace a certain maximum security federal prison you just may have heard of: Alcatraz, the freakin' Rock. USP Marion was originally constructed to hold 500 of the most dangerous, evil sumbitches, mostly pissed-off transfers from Alcatraz, who would miss the view but not the cold and damp.

On October 22, 1983, two of Marion's correction officers Merle E. Clutts and Robert L. Hoffman were stabbed to death, both at the hands of members of the Aryan Brotherhood, a white-supremacist prison gang (and organized crime syndicate) once aligned with Charles Manson. Despite being known as *the most secure federal prison in the system*, two inmates were able to summarily murder their accompanying guards as they were being escorted through the prison confines.

As a result of the murders, USP Marion went into *permanent lockdown* for the next 23 years, yes, you heard right, TWENTY THREE YEARS, and the entire prison complex was effectively transformed into a "super-maximum" security prison -- a SuperMax.

Inmates were placed in strict solitary confinement (to ensure sensory deprivation to "alter human behavior") 23 hours a day. For exercise, there was only a small, windowless room with a chin-up bar. There were no group activities, no work, no educational opportunities, no eating together, no sports, no religious services, and no attempts at rehabilitation. There were no "contact visits," prisoners were kept behind bulletproof Plexiglas windows. Phone calls and visitation privileges were strictly limited. Books and magazines were often denied and pens were restricted. TV and radios were prohibited for the hardcore offenders. If you earned the privilege of a TV, it had no controls and the only station you could receive was the prison's own mind-numbing channel which offered "institutional programing" and religious programs. Prisoners' personal privacy was all but nonexistent.

Guards monitored the inmates' movements via video cameras. Communication between prisoners and Control Booth officers was through speakers and microphones. An officer at a Control Center monitored cells and corridors and controlled all doors electronically. Cells had no windows.

Lights were controlled by guards who could leave them on night and day, if they so wished. Showers were limited to three per week for not more than ten minutes (you try that).

The prisoners were confined to a concrete world, with lidless stainless-steel toilets, where they would never see a blade of grass, feel the earth, see trees, birds, blue sky, a cloud, a thunderstorm, a rainbow, or any part of the natural world.

Rumors were rampant that there were "cockfights" as they called them, where two inmates who hated each other's guts (and were likely to attack each other) were placed in the same suffocating small cell, about the size of your bathroom. And, no, I'm not saying your bathroom is small or suffocating … but it sure could use a coat of fresh paint (and the cat box emptied).

This was Marion. It had been built for prisoners who had been deemed either too dangerous, too high-profile, or too great a national security risk, for even a maximum-security prison: 99% of the prisoners were determined to be highly assaultive or an escape-risk, 25% had been involved in prison murders or attempted murders elsewhere, 48% in escape or attempted escape and more than 70% had a history of assaultive behavior while in prison (If you do the math, that adds up to 242%, but you understand what I'm getting at.)

Are you getting the picture here? The prison had become a

fortress under a microscope, arguably the most inescapable and impenetrable on the planet. The Warden controlled all movement within the prison grounds with a twitchy iron fist and he was damn well determined that there would be no more hiccups (after the killings of his guards) on his watch.

Flashback to the 1960s, America was in love with its athletes: Muhammad Ali, Jack Nicklaus, Arthur Ashe, Willie Mays, Wilt Chamberlain, Johnny Unitas.

Jump forward to the 70s, it was Dorothy Hamill, Bruce Jenner, Hank Aaron, Mark Spitz and Terry Bradshaw. Jack Nicklaus and Arthur Ashe were still wildly popular.

In the 1980s, it was Mary Lou Retton, Michael Jordan, Bo Jackson, Magic Johnson and Joe Montana.

Okay, think about all those for a moment (and, yes, yes, yes, I omitted some worthy athletes).

Did you think about them?

Now add Pete Rose into the mix, only remember, Charlie Hustle was wildly popular over ALL THREE of those decades. He was supremely popular because of his unbridled desire, his dogged will and his unconditional love of the game. Then the man spit on Mom, apple pie and the great American pastime and became persona non grata and a pariah without remorse.

Peter Edward Rose, born April 14, 1941, could do it all, and by the end of his career had pretty much done it all: He was Rookie of the Year in 1963. As a switch hitter, Rose was the all-time Major League leader in hits with 4,256, games played 3,562, and at-bats with 14,053. He won three World Series rings, three batting titles, one MVP, two Gold Gloves and made 17 All-Star appearances at *five* different positions. No one had ever done that previously. He finished as an active player with a lifetime batting average of 303.

Pete Rose went on to be player-manager for the Cincinnati Reds from 1984 to 1986 and recorded a record of 412-373.

The man was Mr. Baseball, a living legend, an icon, idolized, a role model for any little boy or girl who ever picked up a baseball mitt or blown his or her allowance on baseball cards.

But all this wasn't enough for him.

And it was the beginning of the end: a sad ending for a hero.

Rumors flew that, as the manager of the Cincinnati Reds, Rose was betting against his own team and laying down as much as $10,000 a day. This allegation was tough to pin on him, but on April 20, 1990, Rose pleaded guilty to two charges of filing false income tax returns (fiscal shades of Al Capone?) due to failure to declare income he'd received from selling autographs and memorabilia, and from horse-race winnings. On July 19, 1990, Rose was sentenced to five months in yes, you guessed it, the United States Penitentiary Marion. Rose wasn't mafia, and he wasn't one of America's hardened criminals, but he was a major celebrity, and he had to be incarcerated where no one could get to him. If no one could break out of SuperMax Marion, no one was sure as hell going to break in.

Rose wasn't placed in solitary confinement like the violent "worst of the worst of the worst" prisoners, but nevertheless within the same outer walls, same razor wire, same CCTV security, same fences, and same don't-fuck-with-me attitude of the Doberman Warden and pit-bull guards.

When news of Peter Rose's incarceration hit the headlines, every newspaper in America wanted the story, but more importantly, they wanted the *photo*.

A picture may be worth a thousand words, but in this case it was worth $100,000!

And the Warden knew this, and being the hard-assed son-of-a-bitch he was, he spewed these words: "As long as Pete Rose is in my prison, there will be no photographs or interviews -- not today, not tomorrow. Not ever!" Indeed, a reporter from *People* had just been arrested for posing as a visitor.

At about the same time, as all this was unfolding in Illinois, 605 miles to the south, down in the Navy shipbuilding town of Pascagoula, Mississippi, some degenerate bottom-feeder was breaking into a saloon called Sammie's Key West Bar & Grill and stealing everything he could get his hands on. And Sammie will tell you: "They stole not just liquor, money, and beer: they stole the pool table, barstools, cash register and even the air conditioning unit! Ya know, I've always heard that a bad artist borrows and a good artist steals. I wonder what they named their new bar?"

Sammie Mays needed big bucks to rebuild and needed those

big bucks fast. This hell-raising, bacchanalian honky-tonk was the only bar in the county with resort status, thus could stay open 24/7, so the place would get wall-to-wall bodies, and they could party hearty for as long as they damn well pleased, with no one ringing a bell and shouting "Last call!" in their ear as the clock ticked loudly and annoyingly toward 2 a.m.

A dry watering hole makes for an unhappy-and-tetchy restive county.

AUTHOR'S CHEEKY NOTE: Jimmy Buffett's one-legged uncle, Billy Buffett, had once been a regular at this venue and he had struck a deal with management back then for underage Jimmy to sweep cigarette butts, and mop spilled swill and slop from the bar-room floor in exchange for stage time. In exchange, JB's one-legged, crazy Uncle Bill got to imbibe for free.

Do you remember the last lines from Buffett's "Pascagoula Run?"

> **Bring that young man over here**
> **We gonna buy that boy a beer**
> **And that ain't all we want to do**
> **And bring your crazy uncle too**

Desperate to get the bar reopened, a thunderbolt struck in the form of a life-saving, fund-raising idea: Sammie was a seasoned writer, kick-ass freelance reporter and fearless as hell, so the game plan was going to try to do what no one else in the entire country was able to do. No one from NBC or CBS or ABC or CNN or ESPN or the New York *Times*, or the *Washington Post*, or *People* Magazine: Sammie was going to break INTO the SuperMax penitentiary in Marion, Illinois, the nation's toughest, most impenetrable prison and secure an interview AND photo of fallen bad-boy Pete Rose.

I don't know what *you're* thinking about right about now, but I'm thinking what that S.O.B. hard-ass Warden had spewed: "As long as Pete Rose is in my prison, there will be no photographs or interviews -- not today, not tomorrow. Not ever!"

This was a Warden who ate his young -- and had newspaper reporters for a high-protein dessert.

Soon a plan was hatched with the notorious tabloid *National*

Enquirer. Sammie was a weekend entertainer in the Key West Bar & Grill, so the idea was to penetrate the SuperMax under cloak *of putting on a free concert for the inmates.* And you thought only Johnny Cash did that. That alone took big *cajones*, something the future Mayor had drawers full of. Remember, if Sammie Mays could get the story and that all important photo, the *National Enquirer* was prepared to pay $100,000.

One-hundred grand back in 1990. Think about it.

Let me ask you a question: Would you have the blazing guts to call up the snarling Warden of the nation's toughest penitentiary and convince him to allow you to put on a free concert? Was it going to be for the murderers and rapists and terrorists who were just as happy to spit their HIV-laced saliva at you or throw their feces in your direction or stab you, than clap and sing along? No, not the Level I offenders, just a happy, snarling gathering of Level III offenders: the conmen and career criminals and loan sharks and extortionists and a few with tattoos all over their bodies, including the face and ears.

Would you have the guts to organize it all and *smuggle* two 35mm cameras in the speakers of the band equipment? Remember, these were not nifty, miniature smartphones, rather noisy-to-snap, noisy-to-wind 35mm cameras. Then, could you keep it together and pass through *two* body-and-equipment searches? Would you then have the freakin' guts to chat with and charm the endomorphic guards and bribe one of the gun-packing, taser-wielding beasts to take you into a part of the prison where you weren't allowed to be?

Sammie Mays did.

And Sammie interviewed Pete Rose.

And took his photo.

A photo that would be referred to as "Pete in the Pokey" and would win Best Photo of the Year for *Sports Illustrated* magazine in 1990.

By the by: Pete Rose was wildly impressed once he'd realized that Sammie penetrated the SuperMax prison to see him: "How the hell'd you get a camera in here? Y'all got balls! What a great ruse. Here take my photo. I'm giving you a ticket to ride. You're gonna be rich on this one. Man, y'all Mississippians are hell!"

Ain't it the truth.

Then Pete Rose took off the Cincinnati Reds baseball cap he was wearing and put it on smiling Sammie's head. But Sammie was in a quandary: thrilled to have the Pete Rose souvenir (that alone worth a small fortune), but now it would have to be *smuggled out* of the penitentiary, as well as the two 35mm cameras! Can't exactly stroll out with a Cincinnati Reds baseball cap on your head as you blow a kiss to the beaming Warden, can you?

Interview over.

Photo taken.

Cameras concealed.

Baseball hat enshrouded.

And Sammie Mays still had to do a 90-minute concert!

Could YOU go back to work for an hour and a half with $100,000 dancing in your brain and thoughts of being arrested? Would you be edgy? Just a bit jittery? Climbing the flippin' walls?

If Sammie Mays had been caught, it would have meant five years in the slammer.

This threat real and present, yet still as cool as the backside of the pillow, Sammie hung around for the 90 minutes, playing to 230 stomping, clapping inmates, including Pete Rose in the back row who was smiling and giving the thumbs up. Can you imagine the unmitigated stress? All it took was the guard who had been bribed to open his mouth and boast to a fellow guard, or a disenchanted prisoner who had seen Sammie in there photographing Mr. Baseball, inmate number 01832-061, and more than just shit would have hit the proverbial fan.

Once the concert was over, and back now outside, Sammie jumped into what had just become a *getaway* car and sped off, rocked with adrenaline for pulling off the impossible. I don't know how Sammie kept her wheels under the posted speed limit.

About now things went south for the now *gonzo* reporter. Sammie pulled into a gas station for a much-needed pit stop and probably a bottle of Cuervo and a few faux Cuban cigars for the journey home. Refreshed, reinvigorated, Sammie stepped back outside.

And the car was gone!

238

Stolen, along with negatives worth $100,000!

A stolen-car victim can be a pissed-off creature, but a gonzo journalist *ripped* off is the mother of all venomous beings and a car thief's worst nightmare.

The car was quickly recovered, with negatives still intact, and urban myth has it the thief was not able to sit down for quite a long time.

And Sammie Mays had the story and photo of the decade.

Holy shit, say I!

So what else do you need on your résumé for you to be proclaimed the Official Honorary Mayor of Key West? Well, it helps that you understand a bit about what a major hurricane can do. Sammie was holed up in Pass Christian, Mississippi, ground zero, when hurricane Camille hit with a ferocity never before seen. Recorded wind speeds of 190 miles per hour decimated Pass Christian. Wind gusts were estimated to have approached 200 mph, before it destroyed ALL the wind-measuring devices along the coast. Camille was one of the strongest hurricanes/tropical cyclones to make landfall ever recorded on earth.

Then there was another tropical disturbance you just may have heard of: Hurricane Katrina. Katrina's powerful right-front quadrant passed over the Mississippi coast, spawning 11 tornadoes, and sending a storm surge of 28 feet rushing 12 miles inland with seawater flooding parts of Interstate 10 under two feet of water.

This tells me, if a hurricane is ever bearing down on Key West, Mayor Gonzo Mays is not going to be in the first car evacuating north, rather hunkering down, leading from experience and throwing the best damn hurricane party Key West has ever seen!

That's the kind of person I want on my side when trouble erupts in the form of enraged Mother Nature.

But what else does it take to be the Official Honorary Mayor of Key West? How about sneaking onto a New Orleans movie set and interviewing Paul Newman, while walking down Bourbon Street. Most movie stars would have been infuriated by the in-your-face aggressive tactics, but then most reporters aren't the ilk of Sammie Mays.

239

It also important to have been spawned of good stock: "I was strong-headed. My nickname as a child was 'mule,'" says Mays, "I came from a background of saloon owners, politicians and the Dixie mafia from New Orleans."

Now if this isn't the right kind of pedigree, then I don't know what is.

So how did MGM, Mayor Gonzo Mays, end up in Key West? Perhaps it began when the Warden at the United States Penitentiary Marion was relieved of his duties on account of the Pete Rose fiasco and he spewed this vitriol on his way out the door: "Where Sammie Mays is going, there won't be any place to spend that money."

Motivation.

Then, the morning after the photo became the "shot that was seen around the world," Sammie pulled into a Denny's for a quick bite of breakfast and from a row of newspaper vending machines, bold black headlines screamed, "Pete Rose In Prison/National Enquirer World Exclusive!"

Sammie was livid, the yellow-press tabloid had also used a *personal photo and private information* to sell papers! Plus, about now, Sammie pissed off the editor of the *National Enquirer* and began receiving death threats.

More motivation to head south. Way south!

Concerned about freedom and safety, Sammie went underground and there's no better place than Key West for that! Ask half the locals sitting in the bars along Duval on any given day.

When the smoke finally cleared, Sammie's British tabloid peers had begun referring to their new hotshot celebrity reporter as The Gonz.

And it stuck.

As Mayor Gonzo Mays now humbly says: "I'm not trying to be Hunter S. Thompson or even Captain Tony ... I'm just interested in giving out as many political favors as humanly possible and accepting all bribes no matter how insignificant."

All mayors should be that honest!

I should add, that as hard-assed as MGM might come off, there's a soft and cuddly side as well: Sammie pens children's books.

Check out *PIRATE NIGHT BEFORE CHRISTMAS.*

"Shiver me timbers and a yo ho, ho, ho! There's a little something you might not know about Ol' Saint Nick. So move over Red Beard, Black Beard, and Blue Beard, there's a pirate known as Ol' White Beard and when it comes to getting pirates their holiday loot n' booty, he sails the seven seas with an endangered team of fantastic beluga white whales that are a thundering sight upon ocean waves."

Sammie Mays, Mayor Gonzo Mays, MGM, is like no one you'll ever encounter.

And only three degrees of separation from Kevin Bacon.

CHAPTER FORTY EIGHT

Popcorn Joe has gone back over to Mallory to relieve Becky of looking after his popcorn cart, then he will sneak up the back streets, past Smokin' Tuna, and head up to the Bull and anchor it there on the sidewalk outside for the remainder of the evening. Popcorn Joe has become somewhat of a celebrity in Key West, and if he's not in his spot, folk start to get twitchy. Not Prudent to do all that drinking if you can't lay your paws on a bulging bag of Pretty Good Popcorn, when you need the salt.

Back at the Ocean Key Resort, I take delight in the balmy night air and watch the glass bottom boat returning, then something highly unusual catches my eye: Gabrielle has a customer! And this brings me great joy. Perhaps not as much joy as it brings Gabrielle. The customer is elegantly dressed. Lots of bling. Gucci purse. An off-white, silk pantsuit, with a plunging top. Her breasts, which would be clearly visible from orbit, are threatening to decamp (or perhaps they already have and they're endeavoring to get back in). Dressed like this, she should be at a big-city bash in the Great White North, rather than on a pier in Key West where she might frighten the cute manatees. She's sipping some vile concoction from a Styrofoam cup.

And she's sozzled.

Drunk to the gills.

Pissed as a newt.

Palatic.

Three Fieldcrest sheets to the wind.

And her eyes are dilated like the Great Cave of Elephanta.

I decide to listen in.

"Could you paint a name for me?"

Gabrielle hands over the clipboard. "I paint the name in capitals," Gabrielle informs the woman.

"Whatever floats your boat," she slurs.

The woman endeavors to write down the name, but is fighting a losing battle with the ethanol.

"Pen's not working ..."

Always the epitome of tact, Gabrielle gently points out that Miss Inappropriately Dressed is holding the pen upside down.

"Now I'm on top of it," she says, and begins to write. But she doesn't just write down a name, she begins writing screeds. She's writing a novel and having more success than I usually do. When she's finished, she hands the clipboard back to Gabrielle.

Gabrielle studies what the woman has just written. I sneak a peek and can see that it's written in a childish hand. The hand of a child who'd been knocking back the plonk since the Bellini brunch.

Gabrielle reads the scrawl back to the woman: "Do you think I'm sexy, do you want my body, uh huh ..."

The woman seems pleased.

Gabrielle explains. "That's 31 letters. I don't charge for 'uh, huh' after six p.m. on weekends. At three dollars per letter that comes to $93 ..." Gabrielle looks to the woman for succor.

"Money's not an issue," Miss ID says.

Gabrielle's eyes meet mine and her eyes say *money may not be an issue. But alcohol is.*

Gabrielle turns her attention back to the woman. "All those words won't fit on one sheet of paper. Or two. Or three. As you can see, each letter I paint is six inches tall. How about if I just paint *I LOVE YOU?*"

"No. No. No. No," Miss ID says. "That's not my intent. Can you just paint DO YOU THINK I'M SEXY?'

Gabrielle counts the letters. "That's 16 letters, not counting the spaces. I can only get a max 12 spaces on a sheet."

Miss ID is temporarily disappointed, but not deterred. "How about just THINK I'M SEXY?"

Gabrielle looks my way, then says to her new best friend: "Because today's Friday, there's no charge for apostrophes or question marks, either."

The woman laughs.

Gabrielle carries on. "But that's still fourteen spaces and no can do."

Miss ID takes a sip and goes into deep thought. When she

comes out of her trance, she has a smile on her face, albeit slightly askew: "Just paint AVAILABLE!"

"There's no charge for exclamation points on Fridays, and that's nine letters, so we're good to go. Let me just get payment up front. Paper or plastic?"

The paper or plastic remark sails over Miss ID's head like a jet-propelled Frisbee. She hands Gabrielle a C-note.

Gabrielle makes change. "Do you want to watch while I paint … or do you want to take a lap?"

"I'll take a lap, there's something I've got to do."

Miss ID saunters off, not so steady as she goes, and Gabrielle whispers to me. "Crikey, she was cranked. Not just the booze, either. She's on a two-way highway leading to the city center, going uptown and downtown at the same time. Follow her!"

I am always up for urban adventure, and this whacked-out creature doesn't know I exist, so I set off after her. She sashays past the entrance to the Ocean Key Resort, and adjusts her thong as she crosses Front Street. She's turning heads as she goes, what with the decamping boobs (and the thong subluxation).

Sitting on the corner of Front Street and Duval is a homegrown transient, the fellow I've told you about in the past. You know, the one with the hairy knees and the lost-at-sea beard? He watches her go, then turns to me as I follow in the woman's slipstream.

"What the fuck?" he says.

"Totally agree," I say.

At the part of Duval where you can look through the car park over there at the Hog's Breath Saloon, Miss ID hesitates to listen to the Copper Sky band for a moment and synapses start to spark. Clearly, she's looking for something and not having any luck. What is she looking for? A discreet place to do some blow? Someone to blow? It's unclear to me, so I move closer. When she suddenly spins around in my direction, to be inconspicuous, I blend in with all the tourists on Duval and look in the window of a T-shirt shop.

Our Miss ID, moves resolutely off, clearly displaying hell-bent intent for reasons unknown.

My cell phone rings. It's Gabrielle.

"What's she doing?"

"I think she's trolling."

"Where are you?"

"Passing the Hog's Breath."

"Did she go in?"

"She had a good, hard look, but we had a refusal. She doesn't seem the type that would wear the T-shirt—"

"Gotta go. Got a customer."

"I'll keep you posted."

CLICK.

CLICK.

The punters sitting on the stools at Rick's, have stopped talking and are watching Miss ID as she struts by. She has even caught the attention of Al Subarsky, who's on his break after having just finished a set. Al, who has seen it all, gives me an incredulous look.

"Can't talk. I'll text you. I'm on assignment," I say, and continue the pursuit.

Sure, a lot of folk who come to Key West have money, lots of it, but most have the wherewithal to keep it under wraps. You can flaunt your wealth back up in the Great White North, but folk down here will get tired of it really fast if you flash the bling and toot your horn.

I said toot your "horn."

Wait! She's stopped and is talking to a tall, tanned, blond fellow. If this guy is not a skipper on a charter boat out of Key West, then he should quit whatever the heck it is he does and become one. I'm sure sparks and body fluids are going to fly between the two of them, but they don't, rather the charter boat skipper points across the street in the direction of Sloppy's.

She takes off, giving a come-hither sway with her hips, to no one in particular.

I continue to stalk.

When we get even with Sloppy Joe's, Miss ID crosses over Duval and nearly gets flattened by a pink taxi. The cabbie, who had been cruising Duval just dying for an opportunity like this, honks a bit too long and with a bit too much brio to show someone that he's not to be fucked with, but Miss ID is in her own desensitized world and doesn't even give him the finger.

About now, I see Dani Hoy lying in the gutter in front of Sloppy's. I know she likes the odd beverage, but I'm thinking WHOA, this is so out of character. If she were going to be lying in the gutter anywhere, it would be in front of Captain Tony's or Smokin' Tuna or the Cork & Stogie. Someone from the Naples Parrot Heads hands her a beer and she looks up at me with that infectious smile of hers. "I'll tell you about it later. Got to get to 801 Bourbon for the late show!"

Dani scrambles up and limps off with her Parrot Head contingency and I turn my attention back to Miss Inappropriately Dressed.

Now, get ready for this, she has finally found what she's looking for: She walks up near the entrance to the gift shop at Sloppy's, stops and looks up at the webcam. Then she smiles at the webcam and flashes a breast!

Then she covers up and stands in the front door for a moment. I hear these disconcerting words of winter coming from the band up on stage: 'This is what you tourists want ... you want this bullshit!"

And they play an iconic tropical ballad.

Miss ID wraps both her arms around herself and sort of hugs herself, and I truly believe she's thinking about having sex right then and there. This is all getting somewhere between really bizarre and downright creepy. Key West attracts all kinds, but Miss ID seems bent on carving out her own niche. Is she planning to have sex at Sloppy Joe's? It's happened, you know. What worries me, is I think she's not going to include anyone else.

Suddenly, she stops the self-fondling and a 25-watt light bulb flickers on and she hurries back down Duval in the direction of the glass-bottom boat -- and Gabrielle!

I flip open my cell phone and punch speed dial.

"Speak."

"She's on her way! She's in the preliminary stages of orgasm! Did you finish her painting?"

"Just doing the last letter."

"Hurry!"

"What's she up to?"

246

"I just figured it out. Walking on Duval is foreplay for her."

"Crikey …"

"Wait!"

"Now what?"

"She's just stopped at the little booth and purchased a cigar!"

"Hope she's planning to smoke it!"

I ring off, and close the gap on Miss ID, as she crosses back over Duval (like the great fire). The night has suddenly gone steamy (or perhaps that's just me), and I make haste.

Gabrielle has Miss ID's painting up on the easel, so she will see it right off.

"I love it!" she purrs. "How much do I owe you?"

"You paid already."

Miss ID looks confused, then uptown clicks in and she says: "I did, didn't I?"

Miss ID pulls out her Android and thumbs it. Fondles it, actually. "Do you ship?" she says to Gabrielle. "Don't want to get it wet."

According to the Weather Channel, there is no chance of precipitation for the next five days, so I'm not sure where Miss ID is going with this.

"Yes, I'll roll it up in a secure mailing tube and post it tomorrow morning."

"Can you wait a week? I want to see the look on his face when he opens the tube. We work in the same department."

I'm hoping she'll say *which department*, because I'm just dying to know, but I know it's not going to happen. I would outright ask her, but I don't want to appear nosy.

"Where do you work?" Gabrielle asks, to my great joy.

"I work for the guv'mint," she says.

Gabrielle hands the woman the clipboard. "Write down the address where you want it shipped."

The woman writes down the address and Gabrielle looks at it: "You work *there*?"

"Second term already."

Then Miss ID goes into deep, protracted thought. "Changed my mind, I'll take it with me."

Gabrielle looks over at me. The boat's leaving the harbor,

but this woman's not onboard.

Gabrielle turns her back to the woman and unclips the painting from the board on her easel. I reach down and pull a red mailing tube out of the storage. When we turn to hand the painting to Miss ID, she's gone.

She's already heading back up Duval!

Gabrielle thrusts the painting in my hands. "Go!"

I take off after Miss ID, but lose her in the Duval throngs.

By the time I reach the transient with the hairy knees and lost-at-sea beard, he's already on to me.

"She went that way!" And he points up Duval.

I catch a glimpse of Miss ID moving quickly through the crowd well up ahead. She seems on a mission now. Foreplay over? Screeching toward climax? She's making tracks and fast.

Miss ID doesn't turn right towards the Hog's Breath and she ignores the charter boat skipper at Rick's and when she's even with Sloppy Joe's, she doesn't cross over to flash the twin.

I'm chasing after her, holding the bright red mailing tube in my right hand. I look like a relay runner who's trying to pass the baton.

I chase her all the way up to the Bull & Whistle and now I've got Gabrielle on the phone and I'm doing a play-by-play.

"Where's she going?" Gabrielle asks.

"She's heading up Duval, she's about to pass Caroline … Wait! I've lost her!"

Someone catches my eye. It's Popcorn Joe. I describe the woman to Popcorn Joe and ask if he's seen her.

"I did. She looked like a lioness in the hunt."

I hear in my ear Gabrielle ask: "Is that Popcorn Joe's voice?"

"Yes."

I ask Popcorn Joe where she went.

"That way!"

"Which way?"

"Up there!"

I look up and I see Miss ID climbing the back stairs of the Bull!" I relate this to Gabrielle.

"Keep talking!"

"She's passed on the Whistle and she's climbing higher."

"She's climbing higher!"

"She's going all the way to the top.

"She's going to the Garden of Eden. Follow her!"

"I can't go up there, it's a clothing optional bar!"

"So you have the option …"

"I'm not going up there without you, we barely made it out of there unfettered the last time!"

"Unfettered?"

"You know what I mean …"

"You have to go, consider it good customer service, if that doesn't work for you, then consider it research!"

"Research?"

"You know what I mean …"

"Okay, I'll go, but I'm not liking it. What if I'm propositioned?"

"Not going to happen …"

"Huh?"

"Call me once you get up there."

CLICK.

CLICK.

I turn back to Popcorn Joe and he says: "You're not going up there, are you?"

"Wanna come?"

"No way, Becky would kill me if she found out."

"She doesn't have to know."

"But I'd know. And I always look guilty, even if I haven't done anything wrong. Go and report back."

"Okay, I'm going. If you hear a scream, it will be me."

I climb the back stairs and reach the level of the Whistle Bar. The Whistle is heaving and everyone is hanging off the wrap-around, Havana-influenced balcony. I climb higher and then the stairway turns. In front of me is a large sign. It's large because it has a lot to say. It tells you all the things you are NOT ALLOWED TO DO in the Garden of Eden Rooftop Bar. Two things stand out in my memory: NO CAMERAS … and NO SEX!

Hmmm, I haven't learned much in life, but one thing I have learned is that signs are always posted *after* a serious offense or offending incident has occurred: NO PARKING! … STAND

CLOSER TO THE URINAL! … NO SEX!

I reach the top of the stairs and there's a long line, like that one when everyone was on the roof of the US Embassy trying to get on the last chopper out of Saigon. I study the males and females in the line. All have hard-body physiques and look as if they'd just stepped out from that new glossy swingers' magazine *HUNG AND BUXUM.*

I look for Miss Inappropriately Dressed. She isn't in the queue. Where did she go? Did she bribe someone to get in? She certainly didn't come back down the steps and penetrate the Whistle Bar, as I had been on her heels. She would have had to pass me on the steps. What was going on?

I wait.

The queue doesn't move.

Music pours out from the Garden of Eden. Techno music by the sound of it.

I'm thinking of using the long line as an excuse not to have to go in. Gabrielle will understand.

I have tried my best.

My cell phone rings. "Hi."

"Where are you?"

"On the steps just below the entrance to the Garden of Eden. There's a queue. I can't get in."

"Where is she?"

"Disappeared."

"What are the people doing in the queue?"

"Smoking."

"Du-uhhh!"

"Duh, what?"

"I don't know how to break the news to you, but we call those people *smokers.* They are getting their fix of nicotine. There is no queue. Go!"

Oh, crap, Gabrielle is right. Everyone standing there is having a fag. I say "Excuse me" to the aficionados of evil toxins and am suddenly standing at the entrance to the clothing optional bar. A young woman, who looks a lot like Jennifer Lawrence, but is able to walk without falling down, is working the door. Where's the woman built like a refrigerator, with the floss, from last year? Perhaps she has the night off? Perhaps she has given up *show* business. Perhaps she has gone back up north?

Jennifer gives me the once over. One good thing about the Garden of Eden, you don't have to worry about a dress code. Jennifer smiles. I smile and slip on in.

The music is pounding. The floor shaking. The place heaving. Louie, the DJ, has the rooftop rocking. Wall-to-wall bodies dancing, drinking and sweating. No one up here perspires or glows. It's the industrial-strength, leaded, full-blown sweat, or nothing at all.

Over in a dark corner, two older guys are shaking their junk, eyes on a topless young *thang* tending bar. What with it being an open-air rooftop bar, there isn't a hint of cannabis, there's an overwhelming reek of it. Of course this must be coming from another establishment on Duval.

I scoot over to the right, just inside the front door and lean against the wall. I need my eyes to adjust to the subdued lighting. When they do adjust, this is what I see: I see two topless women, young and robust, hanging around Yankee Jack who must have the night off from playing down in the Bull. I see a gaggle of shirtless well-muscled young men dressed as firemen complete with the suspenders and puss-in-boots galoshes in a corner drinking and probably discussing what not to wear when they shoot the full-color calendar to raise money for charity ... or the new station.

But I can't see Miss Inappropriately Dressed.

I feel seriously out of place and embarrassed. Then across the dance floor someone catches my attention. It's someone I know! It's salvation in the form of Reverend Gweko. He must be up here endeavoring to get sinners to repent. And there's safety in numbers, right? Right? So I slip through all the hot, pulsating, gyrating, dripping bodies and take up a position next to the good Reverend. But he, too, looks perhaps not out of place, and not embarrassed, as nothing fazes Reverend Gweko, but he seems just gently rocked, as if he's been lightly stunned by an ineffective taser. He's listening to some rabbiting old dobber prattle on about "the Footsie being up." And this didn't compute. How could talk of the U.K. stock exchange make Gweko feel uncomfortable? If ever there was a man of the world, then Gweko is it. He's been around the block, and I don't mean that in a neighborhood sort of way. I hang around, trying to catch the Reverend's eye, but he's focused intently on the aging businessman. I didn't know that Gweko took such an interest in the stocks, and I'm not about to interrupt, so I just hold my ground. And that's when I hear it. It's a sound that I will never forget, the sound swimmers make when they're snorkeling and have sucked in water and need to come up for air.

And that's when I realize why Reverend Gweko is keeping his eyes straight ahead on the aging businessman. Mr. Businessman has been carrying on a perfectly normal conversation, with his shorts around his ankles.

Some chicken head on her knees is creating more suction than a bagless upright Dyson.

I decide to bolt, when something over by the bar catches my eye: It's Miss Inappropriately Dressed. And she's changed clothes. She's not wearing the same slutty outfit. Perhaps this is why I hadn't spotted her earlier? Now she's dressed like a sailor, a sailor with the jaunty white sailor's hat (complete with decorative tally) and tar flap, but blue bikini bottoms instead of the bellbottoms, and a blue plunging top with bare midriff instead of the traditional Navy-issue top. What happened to her original inappropriate attire? Perhaps it's over with all the other gear that folk have stripped off and stuck in paper bags around the side of the room. I glance over at the young *thang,* the topless bartender, and see a fair amount of bras and panties hanging back there, as well. Is this the equivalent of the coat-check room?

I know I should bolt and run for my life, but I'm here on assignment (and to report back to you), so duty-bound, I'm holding my ground. With both hands.

Hold on a minute! As I fight my way over to Miss Inappropriately Dressed. Who's that she's talking to? It's not Yankee Jack, I can tell you that, it's more like Buccaneer Bill. Let's slip a bit closer. Can you tell who it is? Neither can I. Let's slip yet. Well, shit on me, do you recognize him? It's Mr. Charter Boat Captain! Our Charter Boat Captain shifts and adjusts himself and by the looks of it is really glad to see Miss Inappropriately Dressed again.

We sidle up close, and as you now know, it's not easy to sidle amongst a rooftop can of sardines, and this is what we hear: We hear the obligatory "Hey, sailor!" from Mr. Charter Boat Captain.

Then, Miss Inappropriately Dressed: "How 'bout you buy me an adult drink?"

"Name your poison ..."

"Hennessey."

Hennessey, I'm thinking, *not a drink of sailors* ... but then I'm not here to judge, only report. Actually, now that I think of it, the few sailors I know will drink just about anything this side of cheap perfume.

Mr. Charter Boat Captain, *always* the gentleman, and *always* gallant, and *always* just a bit gag-me-with-a-spoon, says: "Right this way, my princess."

I'm not sure why he offers immediate direction, as the place is clogged like Imelda Marcos' shoe closet after a fire sale at Macy's of PoonTang and nobody can breathe, let alone shuffle.

Mr. Charter Boat Captain places his tanned hand on her behind and draws her close to the bar. He whispers something in her ear. I can't hear what he says, but I don't think he's talking mackerel ... although having said that, I'm pretty sure they're talking fish. Her drink arrives and she sips it. He raises his glass of beer in a toast of presumably swift foreplay and anal penetration and I notice that his hand is blue. Why is his hand blue?

Being gallant and perhaps romantic, Mr. Charter Boat Captain takes Miss ID by the hand and leads her out onto the dance floor, which is pretty much the entire rooftop, and says these words: "Let's get that pretty little behind of yours shaking."

"Flattery will get you everywhere."

"Everywhere is where I plan to go."

It's a slow dance and they grind into each other as if they were drilling for oil. When the slow dance is over, the DJ plays something more wildly upbeat and our two heroes shake and shimmy and let it all hang out, which in our Charter Boat Captain's case, is quite a bit, indeed.

As Miss ID dances, her movements become more frenetic

and orgasmic, something is really switching this bosom, I mean boson, on. Is it the coxswain?

Mr. Charter Boat Captain beckons her closer and I see that his other hand has suddenly turned blue as well.

Many of the patrons have stopped whatever it was that they were doing, to become voyeurs, which is why they came up here in the first place.

And I inch closer to see what all the fuss is and, of course, because I'm there to make a delivery.

And then I get it.

Miss Inappropriately Dressed's new outfit, the one where the skimpy sailor's suit is so tight it looks as if it's painted on – IS PAINTED ON!

The reason I couldn't find her when I strolled in is, she was over there in the corner, giving herself to Titio, the body-paint artist.

And it was a damn proper job, might I say.

FYI: The body painters at the Garden of Eden Bar, Key West, FL, not quite the USA, are among the best in the world. If you've ever taken your clothes off in public and feel just a titch hesitant. Allow one of the body painters to use you as a canvas. It will be a thrill of the kind you've never quite experienced. Off course I'm not speaking from experience, as even I have standards.

But, it's what I hear.

I step in front of Miss Inappropriately Dressed and get a funny look from her when I hold up the tube containing her painting, and say: "Available!"

Then, I hear something which resembles an orgasmic moan above the Garden of Eden din.

Has Mr. Businessman made a delivery of his own?

CHAPTER FORTY NINE

Popcorn Joe told us about a story off *The Coconut Telegraph* this morning.

"One of Glunz Ocean Beach Hotel & Resort's owners, Judi, was walking on the beach this morning cleaning up the junk that washed onto shore and finds a bottle with a message in it.

"There was also some sand and 2 one dollar bills in it. Once we got it opened and read the notes we found out that it is in fact not sand. It is the ashes of this woman's husband of 70 years named Gordon!

"She wrote that he loved to travel so she sent him traveling in a bottle with a note and money for someone to call home and tell her where he landed.

"He started at Big Pine Key in March of 2012 and then went to Islamorada where someone found him. They added a note and sent him traveling again and he landed on our beach in Key Colony.

"Judi called the wife in Tennessee who was excited to know of Gordon's travels. Judi added her note, we put him in a rum bottle (you know added a little fun to Gordon's trip) with the three notes. We added another dollar in case Gordon travels far and a long distance call is needed.

"We will be having a memorial service or celebration of his life on our beach later today before sending him on his way again."

**AUTHOR'S QUERY TO YOU: I like this. What do you think? Shouldn't Gordon have a Facebook page or a regular column in the *Miami Herald* Travel Section?

CHAPTER FIFTY

If you live here, you know it.

If you visit a lot, you know it.

But some of you don't know it, and I feel you might just want to know it.

It's not where to buy a used car on the island.

Or a cheap meal.

Or a package store that will slip you a quick fix out the back door.

Or where to buy the latest flesh-eating zombie drug, Krokodil.

Or lesbian sex.

Or whips and crops.

Or authentic Cohibas or Partagas Presidentes.

Or where to get that pulsing, titillating deep-heat Travolta massage.

Or the Ché Guevara coin.

Nope, none of the above.

Rather, it's Fort Zachary Taylor State Park (and you wanted to know about the whips and crops, didn't you?)

Fort Zach is slightly off the beaten track, the *beaten track* being the girls-gone-wild-boys-gone-wild atmosphere that Duval can oft be.

Many visitors to Key West end up at Smathers, playing volleyball, shuffleboard, snorkeling, stepping off the sand that was shipped in and onto an unwelcoming sea bottom of all things sharp and pointy.

Those in the know, may end up hanging out with the locals at Higgs Beach, or South Beach, or even at Dog Beach.

A few in the know, and a few not in the know, end up at old dirt-bag beach at the foot of Simonton.

Those in the know will avoid the small beach at the Pier

House, as it's mostly snowbirds who go there, and the tide will suck your ass all the way to Cuba if you go in the water past your knees at the wrong time of the changing tide. Many used to go there to ogle the topless area, but then have you been there recently and seen some of those who choose to go topless? They would frighten even a body painter who loves to paint dog faces on aging demoiselles.

And, yes, there are a few other patches of sand that those in the know frequent -- and those should remain just for those ...

To get to Fort Zach, slip out of the commercial flow of Duval at Southard and head past the Green Parrot, past the guard gate in Truman Annex. You won't get stopped, but we always stop and talk to the guard. Carry on deeper into leafy Truman Annex, winding your way until you come to Joyce in the Rangers' Tiki Hut.

If you've walked in, or ridden your bike, the entry fee is nominal. If you convey by automobile, I think it's nominal plus a buck fifty more, but we don't know too many people who have a car, (other than Tina and the Pig) so we don't convey in that manner.

I hope you've brought your snorkel because in the water is where we're going. But first, how about a little turn around the Civil War era fort. It's a bit crumbling and falling down, but you can see the original structure and some of the cannons as you walk through. The fort is one of those places that you have to do at least once ... so you then can tell everyone you know that they have to do it at least once.

Did you know that the moat around the fort was not only dug to prevent access, but also to give you an idea how the fort looked in the days of old when it was surrounded by water? Indeed, Fort Zach used to be 1,200 feet offshore from Key West, with a walkway connecting it to the beach.

Fort Zach is a great place to swim, snorkel and paddle about, then be able to return to your towel and find most of what you brought still there. Bums, dirt-bags, transient, lowlifes, your neighbor, call them what you want, but most won't pay the entrance fee for the privilege of stealing your purse with the Tylenol PM, that last Preludin and your Starbucks reward card.

Fort Zach was Shark Man's haunt, (may he rest in peace),

and it's where Gabrielle and I were standing when that Cuban Air Force Major buzzed the beach, before landing at the Naval Air Station on Boca Chica and defecting.

Fort Zach is a great place to lean your bike against one of the many Australian Pines, actually, having said that, I think they frown on that, so use one of the many bike stands and sit in the shade at one of the picnic tables and watch the shrimp boats returning, or the charter boats or even a brand new destroyer like the USS Spruance.

If you go over to the breakwater, you can watch the fisherman casting for mullet and snook and barracuda, or if it's late in the day, you can catch the sunset (without having to wend your way through the carnival atmosphere of Mallory).

When the sea is calm for a few days and the waves have settled down, the water is pleasantly clear and this is where Gabrielle and I go to explore the undersea world in three feet of water.

If you get peckish, there's the small concession stand just there behind us and they even serve various sandwiches, beer and wine. There are also restrooms and showers to get the sand out of the most private part of your Speedos.

If you are brave enough to take your laptop or Tablet or Smartphone with you, there's WIFI. It could be a good place to sit in front of a palm tree and Skype the family back up in the snow.

So hold off the alcohol abuse until this evening and revel in Mother Nature's bosom.

It's a great place to check your emails.

Post a photo on your timeline.

And sleep off the hangover.

CHAPTER FIFTY ONE

It has been raining nonstop again.

We are sitting under the canopy up at Popcorn Joe's sucking on "Gonzo Margarita Bullets," the clever and much-needed brainchild of none other than Mayor Gonzo Mays. "THIS BULLET HAS YOUR NAME ON IT!"

Popcorn Joe tells us that he spotted a fish swimming on Duval Street, down by the glass-bottom boat (and, no, it wasn't a slippery dick); that the water in front of Two Friends is a couple of feet deep, and that paddleboarders are making their way around lower Duval, not pub crawling, rather pub paddling.

Have you noticed there's more flooding on the grassy infield abutting the runway at the airport lately? This area only rarely flooded in the past and would usually dry up in about 48 hours, but now the water sits there for weeks on end, a soggy freshwater pool that beckons mosquitoes and nesting birds which are posing a problem for all the planes trying to take off and land. The birds not the mosquitoes. Propane cannons can be shot off to scare the birds away, but nothing will scare a full moon, extreme high tide or rising ocean levels.

The Key West director of Airports, Peter Horton says: "The runway could be raised, to the tune of $40 million, but if the surrounding roads are not dealt with, it won't matter. There's no point in having an airport if people can't get here."

There was talk of building levees or protective seawalls such as those in New Orleans or in Amsterdam, but the limestone is so porous, the water would just leak in underneath the levees and seawalls and seep up through. As they say: "Put a retaining wall around your house to protect it and you will one day be living in the equivalent of a rice paddy. Eventual inundation in the Conch Republic is a real and not-too-distant problem."

* * *

The humidity is enervating and Gabrielle and I have chosen to hole up at the Bull under one of the large ceiling fans.

I'm reading an article about how Spanish has become the predominant language in Miami, supplanting English. If you are from Latin America or the Canary Islands or the Spanish peninsula and you pay a visit or relocate, you will feel very at home on the streets, without having to speak one single word of English. In neighborhood stores, shopkeepers serve their clients in Spanish. Colleges and universities offer programs for Spanish speakers. In cafés, boutiques, ice cream shops, hotdog stands, car dealerships, supermarkets, shopping malls, dentists, banks, restaurants and Starbucks, Spanish is spoken predominantly. Even at the post office and government offices information is given and assistance is offered in Spanish (think of us up at Immigration). Doctors and nurses speak Spanish with their patients and a large portion of advertising is in Spanish. Daily newspapers, blogs, and radio and television stations cater to the Hispanic public.

Press One For English.

Marque numero dos para español.

According to the U.S. Census (always *up-to-date, accurate* and *reliable*) around about 58.5 percent of Miami-Dade's 2.4 million residents speak Spanish. Half of those say they don't speak English so very well. English-only speakers make up 27.2 percent of Miami-Dade's residents. In 2006, the Census Bureau estimated that the number of English-only speakers in greater Dade was only 18.5 percent. In 2015 it is forecast to be 14 percent. Hispanics now make up about 60 percent.

In the communities of Little Havana and the mainly Cuban city of Hialeah, 94 percent of the residents are Latino.

Andrew Lynch, an expert on linguistics and bilingualism at the University of Miami, said that "the presence of Spanish-speakers first became an issue in Miami-Dade County in the 1960s and '70s with the arrival of Cuban immigrants and intensified in the '80s with immigrants from not just Cuba, but Puerto Rico, Argentina, Venezuela and elsewhere in Latin America."

In most counties of Florida, you can take your driver's test – the written one – in Spanish, you can apply for social security benefits in Spanish (if granted, your benefit will be paid in USD), you can buy a car, secure a mortgage and purchase a gun, all in Spanish.

Front-running presidential candidates clash over everything Immigration while uniformly running radio and TV ads in Spanish.

I am not here to draw conclusions, I am just here to report.

But Gabrielle and I have Spanish on the brain after our experience in Miami with US Immigration.

We looked into Spanish classes at the community college, but decided against it as "going back to school" was just not an option. Then we looked in the Mullet Wrap to see if anyone was offering classes in Spanish. There were none listed, just classes in English. We went back into Aronovitz Lane and asked Mrs. Grace, who was Cuban, if she knew anybody. She was becoming deafer by the day, and told us: "I know lots of people ..."

"But do you know anybody who speaks Spanish?"

"Everybody I know speaks Spanish ..."

"But do you know anybody who speaks Spanish, or ever taught Spanish?"

"Lots of people."

"Could we meet one of them?"

"No."

"Why not?"

"They all live in Havana, except one, she lives in Tenerife, in the north, in Puerto de la Cruz."

Gabrielle and I thanked Mrs. Grace.

Mrs. Grace said we should bring Mr. Leroy by the next time we came by, and then we fled.

Through the menial-job grapevine, we eventually learned of a young Cuban woman with really skinny legs who worked at a guest house. Her name was Sofia, but everyone called her "Phosphorita," her Spanish nickname meaning "matchsticks."

Phosphorita had come to America on a raft at about the same time five-year-old Elián González was suffering his ordeal, both at sea and in Miami's Little Havana. You may recall at 4 a.m., just before Thanksgiving Day, 1999, Elián, his mother, and twelve others left the fishing village of Cárdenas, in the Matanzas province of Cuba, in a small aluminum boat. Two days into the crossing, a horrific storm came up and the engine on the boat died. Waves were ten-to-twelve-feet high and the boat quickly took on water. The Cuban rafters tried to bail out the boat, but had only nylon bags and not buckets. The boat swamped. Elián began to pray: "Guardian angel, sweet companion don't leave my side …" His mother's boyfriend placed Elián in an inner tube.

The rafters held on for most of the day, then one by one slipped away. The storm finally relented and an exhausted Elián fell asleep. When he awoke, his mother was gone. "I think she drowned," he said, "she didn't know how to swim." Ten others drowned that night. Elián and two others survived. Elián was eventually rescued by two fishermen, three miles off Fort Lauderdale, alone, still clinging to his inner tube.

And we all remember how little Elián was taken in by his 21-year-old cousin Marisleysis in Miami's Little Havana until he was unceremoniously ripped from the arms of Donato Dalrymple, one of the fishermen who rescued him, by what some called "Janet Reno's Gestapo."

Whereas Elián González became a pawn in a bad game of political chess, Phosphorita avoided the guns-in-the-face closet nightmare on account of a cousin living on Stock Island, and now Phosphorita is 23, a Latin beauty, and runs a guesthouse in Key West's Old Town.

It was decided that we would meet Phosphorita at her guesthouse, so we rang her and she gave us her address, and this warning: "This will be the last English I will speak with you."

Gabrielle and I climbed on our bikes, pedaled up Peacon Lane, waved at Al Subarsky who was coasting down the lane on his black-and-white TREK bike, then crossed Eaton and cut over to Truman. We found the correct address, climbed off our bikes, chained them to a palm tree and froze.

Gabrielle stared at the front of the guesthouse, then turned to me: "Are you thinking what I'm thinking?"

"This is the guesthouse we stayed at our first night when we arrived from the U.K. over a year ago."

"The clothing-optional guesthouse!"

"The very same. Where the girl at the Check-In desk wore nothing more than subtext."

"And I heard the sound of bongos as she walked."

"Oh, shit."

"Oh, shit."

"Could it be?"

"Unlikely."

"But, *still*, it could be. Don't know if I'm ready for clothing-optional Spanish lessons. I won't be able to focus on the subjunctive…"

"Not to worry. If it's her, we'll recognize her right off when we see her."

"I wasn't looking at her face …"

"Oh, right … the bongos."

Okay, dear Reader, let me ask you a quick question: did you ever see the movie *Crocodile Dundee*? Remember that scene where "Mick" (Paul Hogan) is in his bathtub at The Plaza in New York City and he hears someone in the next room? And he thinks it's "Rosita," the maid? But in reality it's "Sue" (Linda Kozlowski) and she has her skirt hiked up and just a bare leg comes around the door and she purrs in a seductive manner: "Your towels, *señor* Mick?" Remember that, the leg around the door? I'm not talking a pimpled chicken drumstick here, I'm talking a long, slinky, sexy, well-toned appendage around the door? Well, that's what happening to us right now, only it's not *señor* Mick, rather it's "*señor* Jon *y señora* Gabrielle?"

Mortified, petrified, horrified, Gabrielle and I become a still photo and stare at the door.

Finally, it swings completely open and it's Phosphorita!

And she's wearing clothes!

And it's not Bongo-Girl from a year earlier.

And we are greatly relieved.

"*Vamos a la piscina*," Phosphorita said, and then she led us to a table out by the swimming pool.

I held the chair for Phosphorita and she smiled: "*Muy educado*." Then, I held the chair for Gabrielle and Gabrielle hissed: "Teacher's pet!"

"What?" I said in my defense.

"*¿Qué? En español*," Phosphorita commanded.

"*¿Qué?*"

"*Qué.*"

Our lesson lasted one-and-a-half hours and we both had headaches when we were finished. We can't order a beer in Spanish yet, but we know how to say: "Can you tell me where the bus station is?" and "Where can I find the nearest pharmacy?" and "What time does the train leave for Barcelona?"

Naively pleased and wondering why the train didn't leave for Havana, instead of Barcelona, what with Phosphorita being Cuban, we unchained our bikes from the palm tree out front and pedaled straight to the bar down on Mallory Square where we could taste the salt in the air, and we knew there was a bartender who was Cuban. It was a bit early to have drinks, but drinks were what we needed. Either that or morphine. Why is going back to school so hard? Why is knowing *right from left* suddenly so difficult? Why do I now understand definite and indefinite articles in Spanish, but not in English?

We pulled up two barstools and plopped down. The Cuban bartender approached, smiled wearily at us and wiped down the bar. I think he could tell by our expectant faces and lolling tongues that we wanted to try out our Spanish. "*Amigos,*" he said.

"*¿A qué hora sale el tren para Barcelona?*" I said with my best Spanish accent.

The bartender regarded us with sad bloodhound eyes: "Do they dance the Horah in Barcelona?"

"No, no, that's not what I meant. Let me try again, it must be my accent. I repeated: *¿A qué hora sale el tren para Barcelona?*"

"Oh, now I got it: Can you order salad in Barcelona?"

I looked over at Gabrielle and she's just as baffled as I am.

I tried one last time. I cleared my throat. Gabrielle was opening her mouth as a young mother does when she's spoon feeding a baby.

I cleared my throat again. "*¿A—qué—hora—sale—el—tren—para— Barcelona?*"

The Cuban bartender looked at both of us then said, in English: "There is no train to Barcelona today. Everyone is on strike."

"You understood me?"

"Of course I understood you. I understood you the first time. Just playing with your head." The bartender put both hands to his head the way a mind reader or swami would. "Let me guess. On holiday and embracing the Latin ambience of Cayo Hueso?"

"No…"

"Let me guess again: First day of Spanish lessons?"

"*Sí, señor.*"

"You need alcohol?"

"*Sí, señor.*"

"Drinks are on me!"

"Woo hoo!"

Then the Cuban bartender became very serious: "But first, a little Spanish lesson from *me!*"

"On you go," Gabrielle said.

"*Propina grande,*" he said. "Repeat it."

"*Propina grande,*" Gabrielle and I repeated.

"*Perfecto, amigos.*"

"So what do you want to drink?"

"Do you have any Spanish red wine?" Gabrielle asks.

"No, only Australian."

"A red wine for Gabrielle and I'll take a beer," I say.

"*Uno vino tinto y una cerveza.* Repeat."

"*Uno vino tinto,*" Gabrielle said, "*y una cerveza.*"

Then I repeated the request.

"*Bueno,*" our bartender said, then he went to fetch our drinks.

Gabrielle turned to me: "What does *'propina grande'* mean?"

"I don't think it's something rude, but the *'grande'* bit is making me nervous."

Our drinks arrived and we sucked hard at them, two parched travelers from the desert of brain cell depletion conveyed there by language tuition.

We couldn't wait for our next Spanish lesson.

And even more, the brain-soothing drinks afterwards.

CHAPTER FIFTY TWO

Later that night, we were in the middle of addled dreams when we were awoken by a loud scream.

Gabrielle and I shot bolt upright in bed. I jumped up and peered out our bedroom window in the direction of the scream: the Pineapple Apartments.

Another scream.

Loud and terrifying.

I ran to the front door and flung it open. I could see bugs flitting about in the light which governed the Caroline Street Market. Popcorn Joe lived just upstairs.

"Shit! I think the screaming is coming from Popcorn Joe's apartment!"

Gabrielle and I sprang into action and blew outside, in the side gate of the Pineapple Apartments, up the back stairs and out onto the large back deck. I saw a strange man standing in Popcorn Joe's kitchen. He was holding something in his hand.

"He's got a gun!" I hissed at Gabrielle.

Always fearless, Gabrielle peeped in through the kitchen's glass doors.

"That's not a gun, that's a bottle of Michelob."

"What?"

"Michelob Gold by the looks of it."

"Wait! There's Popcorn Joe. He's just wearing his underwear. And there's some woman, she's not wearing much either. Is that Becky?"

"No, Becky's a natural blonde."

"Perhaps that's the husband and he's going to kill Joe. Let's go in. You go first," Gabrielle said.

"No, you go first."

"Why me?"

"You're right. I'll go first."

266

Popcorn Joe's front French doors were open, so in we strolled. Everyone was now in the kitchen — laughing. Joe saw us and introduced us. The couple were young, attractive, very smiley and perhaps just a bit embarrassed.

"You won't believe what happened," Popcorn Joe began. "Remember we were supposed to have a late check-in tonight? The couple weren't going to arrive until after midnight?"

Well, Popcorn Joe finished the story, and we were so aghast, we asked him to tell us all over again …

It was the couple's first time staying at the Pineapple Apartments and Popcorn Joe had told them that they would be staying in 710 up-rear (no comments, please) and that the key would be in the door. When they arrived, they were supposed to go around the back and take the wooden stairway to the second floor. Only problem was, they took the wrong wooden stairway and went up to Popcorn Joe's by mistake. The key wasn't in the door, but the door was open, so they just strolled on in. The man went right to the toilet, and the woman went straight into the bedroom and got undressed. It was a big surprise to her when she crawled in the sack with Popcorn Joe.

CHAPTER FIFTY THREE

Before we knew it, summer was upon us.

Our second summer in Key West.

Our second summer of love bugs.

Acidic love bugs.

Perhaps the summer was starting out hotter than the previous year, or perhaps we'd forgotten how hot it got on Bone Island. The temperature was not the problem, as it gets much hotter "up in America," but it was the humidity. That and the fact the temperature and humidity will be fairly consistent for the next four or five months. It may hit one-hundred degrees in Chicago, one day, but then the wind will shift off Lake Michigan and it will drop down to the sixties or lower the next day. In Key West, what you see today, is what you're going to see until deep into football season.

Having said that, it sure is glorious to walk around in the evening or late at night with just shorts on and be able to sit out at the myriad of open-air restaurants and bars. During the day, you can patronize the odd establishment that has A/C, or simply visit the many *coveted locales* that keep fairly cool, even during the heat of the summer day, such as: under an umbrella at the Sunset Pier, the front porch at the Cork and Stogie, the Afterdeck Bar at Louie's, most places at Kelly's and, of course, out on the balcony of the Whistle, or in one of the open front windows of the Bull.

Please be sure to save a seat for Gabrielle and me.

The summer is the time of the year when you walk down only one side of Duval, or seek refuge in front of establishments that blast the A/C out their open front doors.

The summer is when you see a lot of toes.

Many acceptable.

Most not.

The summer is when you judge the humidity by it being a "1, 2, or 3 T-shirt day."

The average high in Key West in June is 88 degrees Fahrenheit. The average low is 79F. In July it's 89 and 80. August is 90 and 80. September 88 and 79. The ocean can easily reach 87 degrees Fahrenheit by the middle of August. We have had to get out of the water at Ft. Zach just to cool off. As you know, the warm water fuels tropical development, and gives us our hurricane season which lasts from the 1st of June to the 30th of November. In Key West, we don't have any cement urban sprawl to radiate and maintain the heat, but then you do get a moderate drop in the trade winds. For most, the problem is the humidity. The average relative humidity hovers around 70 to 75 for most of the year, dipping into the 60s in January.

FYI: 2005 was the most active Atlantic hurricane season with 28 tropical cyclones (15 became hurricanes) ... and get ready for this: 1914 was the least active hurricane season with only ONE tropical cyclone during that period.

Living in Key West in the summer is glorious because there's less tourism and the pace slows, but you must learn how embrace the heat (if heat's not in your DNA).

Some of the pools at the finer hotels which get a lot of sun are actually cooled. Both the Pier House does this and the Casa Marina does it for their smaller pool.

Imagine: *cooling* the water in the swimming pool.

Gabrielle and I wanted to see if we could embrace the heat again this summer. When we had lived at Villa Alberto, it made sense to sleep out in the hammock most nights. When we had been up in the furnace that was the attic, it was quite a different experience. Our friend, Deirdre, suggested we drink Key lime juice. We purchased bags of Key limes and drank the juice religiously, and I'm not sure if this is widely known or well-founded, but it certainly worked for us. Then when we moved the few doors over to Sam's, we simply realized that life was much more bearable if we didn't venture out too often when the heat index climbed above 100.

* * *

Summer is low season on the pier.

As mentioned, when the temperature goes up, the tourist

numbers go down. The regulars on the pier go back home or to venues up north.

And I had no trouble getting on the pier at Sunset Celebration to sell our Sunset Photographs.

Don and Shirley would usually set up down by Will's Hill, and I would set up down by Popcorn Joe toward the Ocean Key Resort, and just over the wall from where Gabrielle was painting her Tropical Lettering.

I would usually finish selling photos an hour or two after sunset, then I would break down the display and trundle the whole thing over to where Gabrielle was painting and secrete it in the bushes, then I would help Gabrielle take orders, so she could paint and not have to worry about making change, or, if business was slow, I would slip out to the Sunset Pier and commandeer a lonely can of Bud for me and a *vino tinto* in a plastic glass for Gabrielle. When Gabrielle was finished painting for the evening, we would break down Gabrielle's easel, secure it with bungee cords to her trolley, and then we would just sit on the veranda of the Ocean Key Resort and watch the world go by and enjoy the balmy evening, the smell of salt in the air, the wafting of plumeria or night blooming cactus.

We were surviving in Key West. We had jumped off the hamster wheel and it was exhilarating and scary all at the same time. We would never get rich doing this, but we were very happy, indeed.

Most mornings, during this second summer, we had some work to do around the Pineapple Apartments, then as the heat began to build, we would repair to Ft. Zach to snorkel. When the heat settles on the island in the summer like this, the only way to spend the afternoon is underwater ... or at least immersed up to your neck in the water.

You've done this, haven't you, walked into the water at Ft. Zach, or Higg's Beach, or the Pier House or Smathers or dirt-bag beach in the summer and realized you just stepped into a bath.

I don't think we'll ever get used to it.

Or tired of it.

Earlier, I touched on Ft. Zach, but I may have forgotten to mention that a great place to snorkel is by the rocks right there in the middle of the beach. But watch the current! If you step into knee-deep water and the hair is being ripped off your legs (I'm talking about some of the men and many of the women), that's your cue to be cautious. If the tide is ripping from right to left, you will be unceremoniously conveyed out to the far side of the rocks, and if it's the first time happening to you, you will learn a quick lesson in terror, and how not to fight it, rather just let it lead you around to the left side of the rocks where you can make the obligatory whimpering noises on your way back to terra-sandy-firma and over to the facilities to change your Speedos.

The tide hasn't decided to terrorize us quite yet today, and Gabrielle and I are on the far side of the rocks in about six or seven feet of water. We are watching a three-foot barracuda, watching us. The barracuda is dark greenish-blue on the top, with silver sides and chalky-white on the bottom. He's frozen in place—hovering, if you will—having a stand-off of sorts, and that makes him seem all the more menacing.

His eyes appear dead, but we all know better.

Did you know that barracuda have sharp-edged, fang-like teeth of all different sizes? Much like a piranha? I didn't, either, at least not until right this second. The barracuda has just opened his mouth, presumably to display his choppers. It's very effective, I must say, and small barracuda or not, he is still a teethy, flesh-ripping marvel of evolution, so we maintain a respectful distance.

Here's another one for you: Did you know barracuda are attracted to bling, much like many snowbirds? We had a friend who wore his wedding ring while snorkeling and the sun caught the ring just at the right angle and the barracuda thought the shiny flash was his meal ticket. Our friend didn't lose the ring, but he almost lost the finger.

Another friend was following a barracuda out by the reef. Just so you know, many predators don't like being followed. Certainly no more than you would like it if some stranger was following you in *your* neighborhood. These predators think you are there to take their dinner. Or their young. They don't realize that you are there just to snap their photo. Well, our barracuda-following friend swam past the barracuda when the barracuda stopped, presumably because he was now pissed off. Then our barracuda-stalking friend turned and faced the barracuda (think *you* and that stranger in *your* neighborhood). What our barracuda-annoying friend didn't realize was that his face mask was now "facing the sun."

Down here under the water the sun didn't blind him, but when he moved his head just a titch, the sun's rays sure did reflect off his Osprey face mask (sort of like the silvery side of a bait fish) and THWACK!!! The barracuda launched itself lightning fast and crushed the lens of the mask.

Barracudas can hit nearly 30 miles per hour in a short burst.

Our not-using-common-sense friend hasn't given up the lure of the deep, but he now spends his leisure time enjoying the undersea world at the Key West Aquarium.

If I may share one last horror story with you before I turn you loose to enjoy the 85 degree, Tanqueray-clear waters of Ft. Zach, a friend of Popcorn Joe's was spear fishing. He was out near Woman Key, and he came upon a five-foot silver bullet in the form of a barracuda. The barracuda was facing him, but he had removed his wedding ring, so as not to incite or thrill the barracuda. He had also approached the barracuda with the sun at his back, so the sun would not splash off his mask and, well, incite or excite the barracuda. He pulled up close to the barracuda, about six or seven feet away. The barracuda didn't budge. It's not like they are afraid of us, you know. He watched the barracuda watch him and when the barracuda just opened his jaws as they do, he fired his gas-powered spear right straight into the mouth of the barracuda.

And this was his first and last mistake spear fishing.

Spooked and terrified, the injured barracuda shot forward like someone had shot it from a crossbow and the back end of the spear pierced our now startled spear fisherman's stomach.

These were the things I was thinking about as Gabrielle and I watched the three-foot barracuda from a respectful distance. We ensured the sun was at our backs, and we both had one hand behind our backs concealing our wedding rings.

Probably had our fingers crossed, as well.

Jacques Cousteau said it best: "The undersea world is there for our enjoyment, but respect it we must and treasure it all we can, for in a frightening short span of time, it will be no longer and we will all wonder where it went, what happened, and what we could've done to save it and protect it."

Education is the beginning.

And I will just add: Go check how the radiation's doing in that leak from the Japanese nuclear power plant.

Has it reached Hawaii yet?

The west coast of North America?

"... and what we could've done to save it and protect it."

CHAPTER FIFTY FOUR

We have decided to pay a visit to the Key West Aquarium this morning.

We want to find the names of the many fish that approached us yesterday to say "Hi!"

Have you ever been to the aquarium here? It's just there, you know, at the foot of Whitehead Street, right behind Mallory Square and next to the Old Town Trolley stop. You can easily walk to it or bike over on your conch cruiser with the wide tires.

If you haven't as yet been here, let me just mention, don't expect the Shedd Aquarium on Lake Shore Drive in Chicago, or the Steinart Aquarium in San Francisco's Golden Gate Park or even the National Aquarium in the Baltimore city center.

Chomp on this:

Baltimore has a population of 621,000.

San Francisco 826,000.

Chicago 2,715,000.

Key West 25,000.

Do you see where I'm going with this?

No one comes to Key West and says: "Gee, La Concha isn't as tall at the Sears Tower."

The Key West Aquarium is small, but it punches above its weight. It's where you want to come BEFORE you go snorkeling. Key West is one of the few places in the world where you can visit the aquarium in the morning and then go snorkeling in the afternoon and meet the relatives of all the new friends you just made.

Try that off Grant Park in Lake Michigan. Or in the Baltimore inner harbor. Or out in the San Francisco Bay by Alcatraz, or 30 miles off the Golden Gate Bridge in the shark-infested domain (and sometimes patrolling grounds of Killer Whales) that is known at the rodent-dense Farallon Islands.

We were speaking with Genya Yerkes, the Assistant Curator at the Key West Aquarium, and she kindly told us that the aquarium has been around since 1935. It was built as part of President Roosevelt's WPA program (as was the Seven Mile Bridge), during the Depression.

During WWII, the Navy took over the aquarium, filled in all the tanks with concrete blocks and soil, and created a temporary gun range. After the war was over, all the debris was cleared and the City of Key West resumed custody.

Today, with over a 100 species of fish, turtles, sharks and birds, the aquarium features exhibits like Touch Tank, Stingray Bay, Atlantic Shores, Shark Feeding, Jellyfish, and American Alligator.

How about that!

The Touch Tank exhibit, which kids just love, is where you can pick up and say hello to some of your new-found friends. You can also see a living mangrove ecosystem in the Atlantic Shores Exhibit (not to be confused with the old rainbow motel). Did you know that the red mangroves are crucial as a habitat for our native birds, and our first line of defense against land erosion? Here you can see some of the fish that are on the menus and Specials boards in Key West restaurants like: grouper, snapper, and hogfish, then get to meet popular sport fish like tarpon, cobia, permit, jacks, and assorted colorful tropical fish from the reef, such as: angelfish, wrasses, and parrotfish.

You can also get up close and personal with stingrays, sharks, eels, lobster and seahorses.

Have you ever seen a seahorse up close? This alone is well worth the visit. Did you know seahorses are technically fish and they have seriously acute eyesight? That's right, and their eyes can work independently, looking forward and backwards at the same time (just like mine after too much tequila).

Seahorses are, are you ready, predators. They love tiny shrimp and use their snout to suck up food, just like a vacuum cleaner. If a snack is too large for them, they can expand their snout.

Seahorses mate for life. Each morning, the male and the female have a little get-together to reinforce their bond. When they see each other, they change color (which I find rather

275

adorable, as I do that each morning with Gabrielle). This meeting lasts about an hour and can be in the form of a twirling dance of sorts, not unlike the sock dances we used to have in high school. The meeting takes place on the male's turf. After the dance, the female returns to her turf to, presumably, do the laundry, take the kids to school, go grocery shopping, pay bills, go to the gym, pick the kids up, take them to the dentist and then to soccer practice.

Seahorses have a prehensile tail.

Like the manatee, seahorses are cool.

And the aquarium is stroller friendly.

You might want to make a note that your entry ticket is really a Two-day Pass, so come back after you go snorkeling.

Take the tour, we did, it's enlightening, not only about all the fish, but about Key West, itself.

So remember, if you are going to go snorkeling, come here before you go. Your undersea experience will be greatly enriched. Going to Key West without knowing the names of all the great fish that live in the near-shore waters is like going to the Super Bowl and not knowing the names of the players.

**FROM BUZZ FEED: 20 Things That Kill More People Than Sharks Every Year. Sharks get a bad rap for being dangerous predators that are constantly devouring humans, but there is a whole world of things out there that will kill before a shark does.

Here are just a few of those things:

-- OBESITY kills 30,000 people annually

-- LIGHTNING kills 10,000

-- TEXTING 6,000

-- HIPPOS 2,900

-- AIRPLANES 1,200

-- VOLCANOES 845

-- AUTOEROTIC ASPHYXIATION 600 people anally, I mean, annually

-- BLACK FRIDAY 550

-- FALLING OUT OF BED 450

-- BATHTUBS 340

-- DEER 130

-- ICICLES 100 (just in Russia alone)

-- HOTDOGS kill 70 children annually
-- TORNADOES 60
-- JELLYFISH 40
-- DOGS 30
-- ANTS 30
-- HIGH SCHOOL FOOTBALL 20
-- VENDING MACHINES 13
-- ROLLER COASTERS kill 6 people annually
-- SHARKS kill 5 people annually

BITE ME, NOTE: In an average year, toilets injure 43,000 Americans a year. Sharks injure 13.

CHAPTER FIFTY FIVE

Gabrielle is not painting names at the Ocean Key Resort tonight.

So we are going to go down to Mallory and catch Will Soto's act. If you are going to do this, it's obligatory to grab a bag or two from Popcorn Joe. This is not shameless promotion, this is simply tradition.

Will Soto just might be the best entertainer, street theatre, or otherwise, anywhere. See, I could have used the word *arguably*, but there's no need. Will Soto is simply the most fun to watch, with a bag of popcorn in your hand ... or a tropical bevvy smuggled out of your favorite saloon.

I may not be an expert on street theatre, but I most certainly am a connoisseur. I've witnessed performers at Le Show in Paris off behind Notre Dame, and on the streets of Rimini on the Adriatic coast, down in Juan Le Pins on the French Riviera, in Venice, California, and in Venice, Italy, Fisherman's Wharf in San Francisco and Covent Garden in London. There are many other great venues, which of course I have never visited, thus the connoisseur-only moniker, rather than an expert.

We will catch Will Soto's first performance, then go to the top of La Concha and listen to Al Subarsky for sunset (as it's his last week before the venue is turned into a spa), then we will drift over to Captain Tony's where Key West Chris is playing. This is another appealing aspect to Key West, it's so easy to get around town, and there's so much to do. All within walking/staggering distance. In Glasgow, Scotland, we had to take taxis everywhere. Here, we sit in a bar and watch them motor by.

Oh, you won't believe this.

Something else has washed up on the beach.

No, not a head.

No, not a square grouper.

Rather, a sealed tin can of coffee.

What's the big deal, you may well ask?

The big deal is that inside the can is not coffee, rather weed.

What's the big deal you may ask again?

The big deal is the can was shot out of a cannon from a passing speedboat.

And this may only be the tip of the iceberg, if you will excuse the non-tropical reference, or a test-run, if you will.

Recently, in southern Arizona, U.S. Border officers found 33 cans of marijuana in the desert (there was no mention if they were coffee cans or cans of refried beans). Authorities believe the cans were fired over the border from a cannon in Mexico. Similar cans had been discovered near the Colorado River.

Agents found the cans held a combined 85 pounds of marijuana, worth about $42,500 on the street. By comparison, a can of 16oz Rosarita spicy jalapeño refried beans can be purchased at Wal-Mart for just a few dollars.

The smugglers had loaded the cans into a rather large contraption called a *potato gun*. These slick pneumatic-powered cannons are erected on the back of pickup trucks (to ensure swift retreat) and look a lot like those cannons at the circus that fire a daredevil into a net. They are powered by a compressed air source from an old car engine. When fired, contraband weighing up to 30 pounds will carry over 500 yards.

The potato guns have been a great improvement from the previous method: a medieval-style catapult.

Potato guns on the back of cigarette speedboats may not seem realistic for Key West and the Florida Keys, but this next technique may blow the wind up your knickers: Deep within the mangroves of the jungle not so very far from Bogota, Colombian drug dealers are building 30-foot submarines fashioned out of fiberglass. Inside there's enough space for five men and 12 tons of *pure* cocaine. Numerous hatches are installed so that the sub may be scuttled if discovered. Their hulls are painted dark blue, making them nearly impossible to spot, and they are powered by salvaged diesel car engines. They leave little wake and produce an extremely small radar signature.

It's difficult to come by exact figures, but it is estimated that only 10 "narco-submarines" have ever been intercepted, yet an estimated 70% of the cocaine entering America from Colombia is carried across in these homemade submarines.

Drug cartels manufacture upwards of 120 narco-subs per year. It takes anywhere from three months to a year to build one and costs up to $2 million per sub. Two-million bucks might seem a bit stiff, but then when you think that *just one trip* with 12 tons of blow onboard, once cut and sold, will bring in up to $4 million.

The DEA and Colombian Commandos patrol the Bogota jungle daily to prevent the construction of narco-subs, destroying any they discover. But it's difficult to say how hard the commandos are looking. Most narco-submarines are constructed in the bayous of Colombia, and some of these bayous are eight times the size of London and controlled almost entirely by FARC guerrillas.

And finding disposable crew is not a problem in the poorer provinces and jungles of Columbia. The traffickers pay crew members a total of $40,000 per voyage.

Narco-subs generally leave Colombia and make their way to drop off their cargo in Mexico and the Caribbean. But narco-subs have also been seized in Honduras, Guatemala, Costa Rica and even southwest Spain. Some are even rumored to have tried to reach Italy, which means entering the Mediterranean through the closely monitored and exceedingly narrow Strait of Gibraltar, width 7.7 nautical miles.

The next generation of narco-subs, Montoya says, will be piloted remotely like unmanned drone aircraft. And drug traffickers have reportedly already built full-blown submarines, equipped with a periscopes and electric motors, which are able to dive to a depth of 20 meters.

Then, there is the "narco-torpedo." These large torpedo-shaped vessels hold around three kilos of cocaine and are virtually undetectable. The torpedo is attached to the back of a fishing boat, and it runs about 30 meters below the surface of the ocean. If the DEA choose to inspect the fishing boat, the smugglers driving it simply cut the torpedo loose and go back and get it later when it's safe. And they will have no trouble finding it as a remote radio signal is activated on jettison.

But not to despair. There has been some success in the drug

war with Columbia, cocaine producers have been pushed into countries such as Peru and Bolivia. Just cast your mind back to the Irish and Scottish girls being busted in Peru, when they tried to leave with $2.5 million worth of cocaine in their suitcases.

CHAPTER FIFTY SIX

We are sitting with Phosphorita, having our second Spanish lesson.

We hope she will teach us phrases that we can put to use right away, like: "Does your airline arrive at its chosen destination or does it divert without telling the passengers?"

Or ... "Does this hotel have bedbugs like the others in your chain?"

Or ... "Is it too late to get our money back on that two-week cruise around the Caribbean on that particular cruise ship line, the one, you know, where there's never any power to run the elevators or flush the toilets?"

Of course, that last phrase is a bit protracted, and it would take a long time to learn, but just think how often you could put it to use? Pretty much every time you booked a cruise, right?

Anyway, Gabrielle and I sat there with baited breath (not unlike a barracuda), praying that Phosphorita would tease us with something of unprecedented importance.

And she did.

Phosphorita, pursed her lips, then spoke these pearls: "*¿Dónde está el baño?*"

Gabrielle and I gave each other a silent look. Now that I think of it, how else could it be? A look being *silent*. What I'm trying to say, but clearly having trouble, is that Gabrielle and I were decidedly on the same wavelength. *Finally*, we had something that we could put to use.

And then we learned the following phrases: "*Dos cervezas más.*" This is a phrase to be put to use after Spanish class. And ... "*Por favor, una botella de vino tinto.*" This is a phrase to be put to use after Spanish class ... or weekends ... or evenings during the work week. And ... "*¡Puta! Hoy, tengo resaca, hay aspirina?*" This is a phrase that will be put to use after all the above. And, of course, and more importantly, the highly sought after ... *"¡Qué cojones crees que estás haciendo!"* This phrase can be put to use when being asked to vacate the premises of any pub in Key West after you are being awoken from your sleeping position at the end of the bar instead of shifting your sloth-like behind when the bell was rung.

CHAPTER FIFTY SEVEN

David Wolkowsky just walked past us.

He sported his customary Panama hat, sunglasses and curiously another pair of sunny-specs hanging from his neck. Prescription? He was kitted out in a white linen shirt and white linen trousers. Simply elegant and dapper. Gabrielle and I turned and watched him go.

"The man himself," I said.

"Let's follow him," Gabrielle said.

"We can't do that!"

"Hurry, he's getting away!"

We followed David Wolkowsky down Duval from the area of the Pier House. We didn't want to give the impression that we were stalking him as that's what we were doing. He strolled leisurely along, a man in no hurry, and clearly a man who didn't miss anything of interest. A few older locals greeted him, a few others pointed. He cast an impressive figure and carried himself in a curiously contrasting manner that bespoke of wealth and notoriety, but at the same time of *I'm humble and would rather keep a low profile.*

David Wolkowsky's grandfather fled persecution in Lithuania, immigrated to Key West, started out as a peddler and when city officials targeted Jewish peddlers by enacting a license fee of $1000 (nearly $30,000 in today's money), he opened a fine-clothing store on Duval in the late 1880s. In 1919, David was born in Key West, but his family relocated to Miami when he was a child. He attended the University of Pennsylvania, first studied medicine, then architecture, and made a name -- and a fortune -- for himself by restoring buildings in Philadelphia's inner city, including Society Hill and Rittenhouse Square. No easy trick, at the time.

When his father died in 1962, David returned to Key West

to retire, but ended up looking after his late-father's assets: One such asset was a condemned bar on family land on Greene Street, the original Sloppy Joe's, and now Captain Tony's. Other assets included, property on lower Duval and Front Streets including Pirate's Alley and the Original Cigar Factory, the Kress Building (the old dime store), once home to Fast Buck Freddie's, still home to Jimmy Buffett's Margaritaville Café and the Margaritaville Gift Shop. Wolkowsky built a penthouse suite for himself upstairs. There was even a time when the Key West Police rented the floors below the penthouse. "I've never felt more safe than when I lived above the parole board," David Wolkowsky will tell you.

Retirement wasn't in David Wolkowsky's DNA. He was not a man to just sit around and lazily fish or lay claim to the same bar stool every night, he was a man oozing energy and vision and he saw things he not only wanted to do in Key West, but *for* Key West, things that would help Key West become a grander place for all and more than just a rundown island town with no beaches.

In 1963, he acquired a chunk of choice waterfront property near Mallory Square bearing the old Cuban Ferry Dock at the foot of Duval for $106,000. A princely sum in those days. He had designs on building a chic resort. Having said that, there was nothing about Key West in the early 60s that smacked of chic (although the Casa Marina did exude a certain Raffles elegance) and many scoffed at David Wolkowsky. They scoffed until he had the Porter Steamship office jacked up off its foundation, moved 300 feet out into the channel, placed on pilings in 40 feet of water, and renovated into the beckoning form of Tony's Fish Market. Tony's was predominantly a restaurant and cocktail lounge where guests could get shit-faced while watching the shrimp boats slip past on their way in and out of port. Then in 1967, DW constructed a motel around the restaurant and cocktail lounge, which was called the Pier House Resort Motel. Then he added 50 rooms to the existing 50 rooms, and more additions and upgrades over the years, until the venue evolved into the Pier House Resort, and it became a magnet for celebrities. Jimmy Buffett got his first real paying gig in the Pier House's quirky Chart Room Bar, and credits DW with giving him that opportunity.

FYI: Wolkowsky sometimes worked behind the desk, checking in overflow guests from the Howard Johnson's further inland.

Guess who the bartender was back then when Jimmy Buffett played the Chart Room Bar?

Guess again.

It was none other than Tom Corcoran (now a close friend and as you know an oft collaborator with Jimmy Buffett).

Not only was the Pier House Resort a turning point in backwater Key West's transformation from a mosquito-infested, mangrove-covered military outpost to an eclectic and vibrant tourist destination, but so was another Wolkowsky baby: the original Reach Resort at the other end of Simonton. Then, over the decades, DW purchased more than 100 derelict conch houses, two-story wooden structures on stilts, with shady verandas that were built in the 19th century and refurbished them and saved them from decay or demolition.

Back then, most days, if you walked Duval from "ocean to ocean," DW could often be spotted, wearing the customary several pairs of sunglasses on his head and some hanging from his neck, while cruising Duval in either a jaunty golf cart or his sexy 1926 Rolls-Royce.

Even on the island of Key West that embraces its local eccentrics with zeal and fascination, Wolkowsky is legendary.

Legendary BIG TIME.

And then there's his *other* island.

If you stand on the pier at Mallory Square and gaze off past Sunset Key and Christmas Tree Island, way out there toward the setting sun, about eight to nine miles out, depending which channel you take by mistake, lies Ballast Key. David Wolkowsky purchased this scrub-choked rock from the Navy in the late 1970s and built a lighthouse-inspired structure that is now the southernmost private home in the contiguous United States.

Wolkow's Key as it's known is only accessible by a 25-minute boat ride or 10 minutes by helicopter, both of which DW owns. As of this printing, Ballast Key is up for sale: $15.8 million, if you're in the hunt for a slice of idyllic privacy.

FYI: Since Gabrielle and I used to live at Villa Alberto on

Aronovitz Lane, and David Wolkowsky's grandfather was a Lithuanian Jew, and there's a Jewish cemetery in the, ah, well cemetery, it got me thinking about the Jewish history of Key West. Having said that, I did a little digging around for you and this is what I found: One of the first documented Jews to visit Key West, did so in an involuntary albeit thrilling manner. Joe Wolfson, a Romanian Jew, was bound for New Orleans when his ship went down out on the reef in 1884. He was immediately taken with Key West, partly because he was still alive and partly on account of Key West being so patently startlingly beautiful (modifier overload, but Key West earns it). In fact, Joe Wolfson was so enthralled with the island, and once he got up the nerve to travel by sea again, he made the long journey back home to Romania to pack up his family. Upon his return, Joe Wolfson hung out with David Wolkowsky's granddad and the two of them along with Mendell Rippa (from Romania), organized a congregation and held services in private homes. Somewhere about this time, David and Kate Aronovitz arrived on the scene. Do you see where I'm going with this? The Aronovitzs had six children – all boys – and eventually got a street named after them. One son, Abe, went on to become mayor of Miami between 1953 and 1955.

When you're in Key West the next time, go walkabout in the Old Town and see where Jewish names became names of streets: Appelrouth (On January 22, 1912, the first train on Henry Flagler's Overseas Railway chugged from Miami to Key West. Isadore Appelrouth was on that train, coming to settle in Key West) and Aronowitz Lane (Villa Alberto!), Seidenberg Avenue, Ellsberg and Pearlman Courts and Wolfson Street. Then stroll over to Passover Lane by the cemetery, or see if you can spot the faded sign on the S. H. Kress Dime Store building at 500 Duval, or the gingerbread white porch in front of Louis Fine's old conch house at 1125 Duval, which, of course, we all know now as La Te Da. When Louis Fine lived here, he would allow José Marti to make speeches from his elevated front porch.

And while you're out and about, see how many mezuzahs you can count fixed to various establishments, such as the Curry Mansion, where one is affixed to the outside door.

Shalom.

CHAPTER FIFTY EIGHT

Have you ever seen Key West from the water?

Have you been on a sunset cruise?

Or come down to Key West from Fort Myers on the Key West Express?

Or sailed in as Paddy Bettesworth or Gary Cairns might do?

Or as Popcorn Joe did when he first set eyes on the island 28 years ago.

Or rented Jet-skis?

Or taken the ferry out to Sunset Key?

Or drunk too much and have fallen off the pier at Mallory?

It's one thing to cruise the tropical lanes on a moped. Or your bicycle. Or even à pied. It's entirely another adventure to see Key West by boat. I don't mean just hop in a boat and go out a few hundred meters and looked back, I mean to nuzzle the nuances of the island, hugging her sensuous curves, taking your time, taking in the wildlife and the mangroves and the flats and the bights and the bits and the bobs.

So Gabrielle and I humped it over to Simonton, turned right and ended up at the beach. Popcorn Joe was there waiting for us with his 12-foor skiff with the temperamental outboard, a mercurial Mercury.

Giuseppe was doing what boat owners do to outboard motors before setting off on a hearty cruise. Popcorn Joe gave us a smile. "Where's the eats?"

Gabrielle pointed a finger at my backpack.

"Okay, here's the story: I have no idea how long this is going to take, but, I want to show you a few things you've not seen before."

Gabrielle climbed in and Popcorn Joe fired up the old outboard. I gave the bow a good push off the sand to prevent the boat from hitting the neighboring dock. That's when I realized Popcorn Joe and Gabrielle were going boating, but I was still standing on the beach. Why do I keep doing this?

Trying to conceal his amusement, Popcorn Joe thrust the tiller part of the outboard and the boat did a nifty little circle and they picked me up.

I looked at Gabrielle and she, too, was trying to keep from laughing.

We weren't sure how much it would cost to motor walkabout (cruise-about) like this, so we told Popcorn Joe that we would bring the necessary "eats" and that he should keep track of it all and then we would buy him lots of Havana Club or English Harbour rum, which he could keep secreted in his Pretty Good Popcorn cart, only pulling it out to serve to his repeat customers like Ginger, Ken, Chris or Adrienne.

Giuseppe felt this was more than a fair trade.

**AUTHOR'S OH-SO-IMPORTANT NOTE: Ask Popcorn Joe to show you that area just under where he pops his popcorn the next time you are in Key West.

No, really, ask him.

Just don't say it was me who told you.

Soon we were chugging happily along, down the channel, off toward the reef, leaving Cayo Hueso behind. Just like last time, the ineffectual motor on Joe's ramshackle launch juddered and sputtered, but Joe seemed not too bothered by it all.

"We are going to take advantage of the tide. Let's hope the motor keeps going," Popcorn Joe said.

Flooding, ebbing, tides, moons, I didn't understand it all, but what Popcorn Joe said made great sense -- especially the part about: "Let's hope the motor keeps going."

Popcorn Joe aimed for the gap between Christmas Tree Island and Sunset Key. As you know, Sunset Key used to be called Tank Island, but the developers didn't feel it gave the million-dollar homes the correct image. Twelve fuel tanks were originally meant to be stuck deep down in the landfill. I say "deep down" because the tanks were each 80 feet in diameter and 40 feet tall. Allegedly, only two were ever placed, but they were later exhumed never having been filled with fuel.

Allegedly.

You just may want to jot down, that when the two

purported tanks were removed, they were cut into razor-blade-like shards, taken out to the south where you like to fish and unceremoniously *dumped* in 200 feet of pristine, aquamarine water.

And Christmas Tree Island, in reality Wisteria Island, so named because of the US Public Health disinfecting steamship "Wisteria" which caught fire and burned to the waterline while anchored just offshore.

Popcorn Joe jabbed a finger toward Christmas Tree Island. "From late in the 1930s to the early 1940s, the island had a commercial shark processing plant on it. They harvested sharks for their skins and made clothing out of them and sold them all over the world, including China.

"Both islands were created when the navy dredged the harbor at various times, first in the late 1890s, and then later to bring it to a depth of 38 feet to allow diesel submarines to pass silently through."

"Why Christmas Tree Island?"

"Because of all the Christmas trees growing there, although, in reality, they're just Australian Pine, like over at Ft. Zach."

Popcorn Joe guided the boat between Christmas Tree Island and Sunset Key, and we slowly putt, putt, putted off to the west.

The sea was glassy today and once we slipped out of the main channel, the water got shallow and fast, with deep blues metamorphosing into pastel greens. There were fish everywhere and it was like being on the glass-bottom boat without the drunks.

"See way out there where that shrimp boat came from?" Popcorn Joe began. "In 1943, German submarines were torpedoing allied ships so close to Key West, you could see it happening from land. In one year alone, 49 ships were sunk off the coast of Florida, many of them out in the Straits."

"You are a fountain of knowledge," Gabrielle said.

"I read, too," Popcorn Joe said, then he continued on: "Our fly boys used to take off from Naval Air Station Key West in old Curtis biplanes. They flew out there in search of German subs that were dead in the water, resting on the surface to recharge their batteries. The biplanes were only able to carry a single machine gun, but the gunners were armed with, are you ready, hand grenades."

"What?"

"That's right. Small, slow plane, but big problem for the submarines. The biplanes flew low over the water and came out of the sun and the gunners were able to drop the grenades right into the open conning towers. Now *that* is good use of man and available armament!"

We watched as a Delta 737-8000 banked above the emerald waters and descended toward runway 9/27. There would be no grenades being dropped from this aircraft, but later tonight on Duval Street, some of these very passengers would be dropping a depth charge into their pint of Haitian beer.

"Got an idea," Popcorn Joe said. "Want to see something few people have seen?"

"Does this have anything to do with the Garden of Eden Rooftop Bar?"

"Negatore. Other direction."

Gabrielle and I were always up for adventure in any form, but I just had to ask: "Does it involve going out on the flats and getting the boat stuck when the tide goes out?"

"Probably."

Soon the water became so shallow our little boat was just barely skimming over the patches of white sand and grassy expanses. 'Remember being out here last year?" Popcorn Joe said. "These are the flats. It goes on like this for as far as you can see."

About eight miles out, with the water still shallow enough to stand up in, Popcorn Joe nodded toward a group of small islands. "These are the Mule Keys. All part of the Key West National Wildlife Refuge. That's Man Key back there. And over there, that's Woman Key."

"And that tiny island there, just in front?" Gabrielle asked, motioning toward an island covered in sea grapes and grassy palms.

"That's where we're going."

We watched pelicans concertinaing and slicing into the water, as Popcorn Joe guided the boat along the south side of the island, through a shallow channel of sorts and we saw a long wooden pier sticking way out away from the island.

"That's Ballast Key," Popcorn Joe said. "It's named for the flotsam left behind when a Spanish galleon foundered here in 1630. During World War II, the Navy used the island to practice bombing runs."

"There's a house," Gabrielle said. "Someone lives out here?"

"David Wolkowsky," Popcorn Joe said.

Gabrielle and I exchanged looks.

"He used to come out to this island to picnic with friends. He liked it so much out here, he bought the entire island from the Navy in 1974. And that's not the main house you're looking at. That the guesthouse."

"What does he do for fresh water? Somehow I can't see the Florida Keys Aqueduct Authority making it out here?"

"He's got his own desalination plant."

We slipped farther along the island and came upon an expansive conch house with a tin roof, built on stilts. It was built over three levels, had a glass front, a widow's walk and there was a small helicopter parked in the front yard. A white heron was presently examining the chopper, perhaps looking for a tasty gecko or a palmetto bug snack.

"Place is for sale," Popcorn Joe said. "Wolkowsky paid $160,000 for the island, now the entire place is selling for only $15.8 million."

"A steal."

"In many ways, yes, if you want a slice of idyllic privacy. The house has been on the market for a couple of years. When no one buys it and it's been a year, they raise it by another million. It's got something like eight bedrooms and five full baths. Nearly 4000 square feet set on 24 acres. The census had it listed as *One housing unit with a population of one.*"

"The man must like his privacy."

"His father wanted him to be a football player and a boxer. He wanted to be anonymous. But he still knew how to throw a party – a *private* party."

****AUTHOR'S CHEEKY FLY ON THE WALL NOTE:** I did some research for you because I know you're just dying to know who's been here (because I was dying to know who's been here). Feast your eyes on these artists, writers and celebrities: Tennessee Williams, Lillian Hellman, Rudolf Nureyev, Leonard Bernstein, Jimmy Buffett, the Bee Gees, Truman Capote, Prince Michael of Greece, Tony Richardson, Lady Caroline Blackwood (who?), Gloria Estefan, British Prime Minister Edward Heath, Natica Waterbury (huh?), and the occasional Vanderbilt, Rockefeller, Mellon, and Duke.

"I've entertained everyone from garbage collectors …" DW will say, then with a theatrical pause "… down to Vanderbilts."

The island even had a cameo appearance in the Bond movie *Licence to Kill*, and the island and Mr. Wolkowsky made the pages of the novel as well. "David, it's James, James Bond … I've broken into your island. I hope you don't mind," reads a passage in the book.

Popcorn Joe hauled out a pair of binoculars and handed them to Gabrielle. "What do you see?"

"I see a slabbering Rottweiler baring his teeth at me."

"Oh, that's just Camila. She guards the property. See the large room up in the middle. That's the master suite. You can see the sunrise AND the sunset from it."

Gabrielle gave me a look, then turned to Popcorn Joe. "Have you been in the house, Giuseppe?"

"No."

"You have, haven't you?"

"No, I swear."

"Then how do you know all this?"

"I read."

"Yes, you keep saying that."

"Okay, then I've seen photos."

"Don't believe you …"

Well, dear Reader, since you've gotten this far with me and we've been through so much together, I want you to see the photos, as well. Here's what I found on a German real estate website:

http://immobilien.diepresse.com/home/international/1423109/

CHAPTER FIFTY NINE

As Popcorn Joe guided his skiff back home, in between Christmas Tree Island and Sunset Key, we gazed in awe at the island of Key West and I remember it gave us goose bumps.

This is where we now lived. Where we called home. We had given up a fair amount to live here: We had given up jobs that brought both of us no joy whatsoever. We had given up a miserable life-sucking rush-hour commute. We had given up going to work in the dark and coming home in the dark. Now, we didn't own a car, have mortgage payments or car payments.

And we didn't have credit cards.

Popcorn Joe had taken us out to Ballast Key and we would certainly never live on a private island, but what we did have was all that lay before us: Cayo Hueso, Bone Island, Key West (not quite the USA), the funky, quirky, eclectic place we now called home.

All because we jumped off the hamster wheel and had a go at a dream.

"It's great to look at from the water, isn't it?" Popcorn Joe mused.

We watched the island turn golden with the sun slipping low in the western sky. We saw the crafts folk arriving at Mallory Square in preparation for Sunset Celebration. We watched a charter boat returning from the reef.

I thought about how life is short and time flies by so quickly, then, as if reading my mind, Popcorn Joes watched a frigate bird circle lazily overhead and said: 'Life's short."

"Life's short, indeed."

"You only live once" Popcorn Joe added.

* * *

As this book goes to the publishers, this came to mind:

294

Michael Jackson's heart stopped working 5 years ago.

Captain Tony recounted his last story 6 years ago.

Saddam Hussein was left twitching from the end of a rope 8 years ago.

The tsunami at Banda Aceh was 10 years ago.

Michael Jordan retired (for the last time) 11 years ago.

The horror of 9/11 was 13 years ago.

The Concorde went down in flames 14 years ago.

Shel Silverstein jotted down his last note 15 years ago.

The Oakland Raiders were in Oakland, then LA, then back in Oakland. They've been back in Oakland for 19 years.

Pan Am, once America's flag carrier, has been defunct for 23 years.

Chernobyl was 28 years ago.

The movie *E.T.* was released 32 years ago.

Bob Marley died 33 years ago.

Elvis died 37 years ago.

Jimmy Buffett recorded "Margaritaville" 37 years ago.

ROCKY hit the screens 38 years ago.

The movie *JAWS* made a toothy splash 39 years ago.

Patty Hearst joined the Symbionese Liberation Army 40 years ago.

Mark Harmon of *NCIS* was the starting quarterback at UCLA 41 years ago.

The Munich Olympics massacre was 42 years ago.

The Beatles broke up 44 years ago.

* * *

I'm not trying to make you feel old, but …

TEMPUS FUGIT

And you only live once.

For those of you who weren't looking over my shoulder when I was writing **KEY WEST: Tequila, a Pinch of Salt, and a Quirky Slice of America**, might I just say that Gabrielle and I had been living in Glasgow, Scotland, and we came to Key West for a one-week holiday ... and never went back home. This created major conflict with family until they realized they had a free place to stay in the Florida Keys. It also caused serious conflict with our bosses, but our jobs back home were crap and our bosses were prats, so that presented less of a problem.

Only problem now, here at the end of the world -- in paradise -- Gabrielle is living in the U.S. illegally and has overstayed her visa by six months.

And now our year is almost up and, desperately sad, we are preparing to head back to Glasgow.

A FEW WEIRD FLORIDA LAWS TO MULL OVER:

-- It is illegal to sell your children.

-- If an elephant is left tied to a parking meter, the parking fee has to be paid just as it would for a vehicle. *Perhaps it's to cover the cost of cleaning up the pile of steaming shit left behind?*

-- Men may not be seen publicly in any kind of strapless gown. *Presumably this law is relaxed in Key West at Fantasy Fest (and the rest of the year, for that matter).*

-- It is illegal to sing in a public place while attired in a swimsuit.

-- Having sexual relations with a porcupine is illegal. *(Did this really need to be passed into law?)*

-- In Pensacola, citizens may not be caught downtown without at least 10 dollars on their person. *(Is this to move the transients on? Or provide a steady income for muggers?)*

-- In Tampa, women may not expose their breasts while performing "topless dancing." *(WTF?)*

-- Lap dances must be given at least six feet away from a patron. Also, in Tampa.

-- In Broward County, it is illegal for female hotdog stand vendors to wear G-strings.

-- In Miami, it is against the law for a dance hall to have dirty windows.

-- It is illegal to release more than ten balloons into the air per hour. Having said that, it is also illegal to pass gas in a public place after 6pm on Thursdays.

-- In Daytona Beach, it is illegal to molest trash cans. *(There is no law regarding trailer trash.)*

-- Jupiter: A 1959 ordinance considers stubborn children to be vagrants.

-- Sarasota: It is illegal to catch crabs. *Knowing this, I will feel much more comfortable suggesting Sarasota as a destination for all my randy friends.*

-- Tampa Bay: Rats are forbidden from leaving docked ships. *Don't want them to end up getting involved with the Kelley sisters and sully their reputation (I'm talking about the rodents' reputation).*

-- It is Florida law to give prostitutes, if caught, a five-year ban, spending money and a ticket out of town.

-- You may not kiss your wife's breasts.

-- It is an offense to shower naked.

-- It is illegal to NOT tell your neighbor his house is on fire. *(Having said that, I think it's okay to kiss your neighbor's breasts.)*

-- Oral sex is illegal. **Hard to believe, indeed, some of our friends are finding this difficult to swallow.

A COUPLE OF WEIRD KEY WEST LAWS:

-- Chickens are considered a "protected species."

-- Turtle racing is illegal within the city limits. *(Apparently, Turtle Kraals has slipped through the cracks on this one.)*

-- It is illegal to fish while driving across a bridge.

-- It is forbidden to spit on a church floor. *(That goes for the men, as well.)*

-- In Key West, it's illegal to be stupid. No, it's not, but it SHOULD BE LAW!

* * *

KEY WEST INTERESTING FACTS, WHICH WE JUST CAN'T LIVE WITHOUT:

-- Key West is bordered by the third largest coral *barrier* reef system in the world (221 miles from Key Biscayne to the Dry Tortugas). Top of the list, as you have already surmised, is the Great Barrier Reef. The Belize Barrier Reef is the second largest barrier reef. The Great Barrier Reef is 40 miles wide in some places. That's wide.

-- The sun sets in Key West only once per day.

-- Key West is connected to the mainland by 42 bridges, many of them in a good state of repair.

-- The sand which makes up Key West beaches was shipped in on barges from the Caribbean. Some of the crime was shipped in, as well.

-- Key West is closer to Hemmingway's old haunt (the other Sloppy Joe's in Havana) than to the nearest Wal-Mart (which is 126.5 miles away).

-- On account of the myriad of endangered species, the entire island of Key West is a bird sanctuary.

-- Even though Key West is about as far south as you can go, it was Yankee territory during the Civil War.

-- *CrissCross*, the movie starring Goldie Hawn, remember it? It was shot at our beloved Eden House. Filming took five months. The woman upon whom the film was based had been living at the Eden House with her son, Chris, in the 70s. Author Scott Summers wrote the short story *CrissCross* while staying at the Eden House in early 1976. Pictures and memorabilia from the movie can be found throughout the hotel. That, and super friendly staff!

-- Remember *The Rose Tattoo* starring Burt Lancaster? The premier of the movie was held at the Hotel Astor in New York City on December 2, 1955. Before the film, there was the play. The story was set on the Gulf Coast between Mobile and New Orleans, but when it came time to shoot the movie, Tennessee Williams convinced Paramount Studios to film in Cayo Hueso. Tennessee Williams had the Italian actress Anna Magnani in mind for the play and he wanted her to do it on Broadway in 1951, but her English was dreadful and she rightly refused. By the time it came to make the movie, Magnani had become proficient in English. Good thing for all involved, as she won the Academy Award for Best Actress.
And now we have the Rose Tattoo bar at 618 Duval.

-- Tennessee Williams came to Key West for the first time at the age of thirty. That was in 1941. He lived at La Concha where he wrote his first draft of *A Streetcar Named Desire*. Eventually, he purchased a rundown Bahamian cottage over on 1431 Duncan Street, where he built a compound with guest cottage, swimming pool, and a writing studio he coined the "Mad House." This compound is not open to the public, but you might just want to cruise by on the bike you just rented from the Bike Shop Key West and have a discreet look. For those of you in the hunt for a bargain and a bit of cinematic history, the house at 1421, as of this writing, is for sale. Urban legend has that *The Rose Tattoo* was filmed here. Asking price: $885,000.

-- Males make up 55.4 % of the population in Key West.

-- *License to Kill* was filmed at the Garrison Bight Marina, St. Mary's Star of the Sea Church (where Tennessee Williams was baptized), and the Hemingway House.

-- During the filming and "destroying" of the Seven Mile Bridge in *True Lies*, the actors stayed at the Pier House. Long commute, but how nice to come home to the Chart Room Bar!

-- Highway #1 is 2,328 miles long and runs from Fort Kent, Maine, to just past the Courthouse Deli (where they make the best toasted Cuban cheese bread).

-- Key West has more bars per capita than any other place in the country. *Yay!*

-- Key West has more churches per capita than any other place in the country. *Remember not to spit on the floors.*

NEW AND JAUNTY GLOSSARY:

bahookie – Scottish slang for one's derriere.

Benidorm – British destination for package holidaymakers, tacky and cheap in the British section, romantic, picturesque and cheaper in the Spanish section.

bevvy (bevy) – term commonly used in the north of England and Scotland. An adult beverage, usually beer or lager. "I'm going doon the boozer tonight and sink a few bevvies."

bits and bobs – perennial U.K.-ism for bits and pieces.

blighter(s) – An annoying person. Possibly related to "blight," the plant disease that ruined the potato crop in Ireland (as a "blighter" tends to ruin things in which he's involved). A milder invective than "bastard."

bloke – a guy. Not used vocatively. "Hi, guys!" is okay … "Hi, blokes!" is not.

bog – the shitter.

bugger – as a noun: a prick, a dickhead. As a verb: Technically means to sodomize, but most people use the word in a variety of situations, often without knowing the true meaning. Considered, just this side of "fuck" in politeness (as long as you are not in the presence of anyone old enough to remember the actual meaning, then you will get your ears boxed or swung about by the testicles). A few colloquial uses: "He's a right bugger!" "Bugger it!"

bumfuck – an idiot, your noisy neighbor, that guy at the pub who never shuts up … or buys you a drink. A town in Egypt.

chocka (chockablock) U.K. – filled to the gills, filled to capacity, sardine-city.

Dawn French – perennial Brit comedienne, known in the States as the vicar Geraldine Granger in The *Vicar of Dibley*.

deccies (dekkies) – Christmas decorations.

do a runner – make a decision to enjoy a Captain Cabin's meal and then not pay for the dining experience. On a blind date, one can also be on the receiving end. I speak from experience:(

dobber – (U.K) a fat northern male, a penis. Used in greater Glasgow instead of saying "Ya cock!" "Ya dick!"

dosh – contemporary slang for money, loot, dough, bread.

doughball – soft invective coined by my wife (the hard equivalent would be: complete and utter f**king idiot).

("*El sabor que no se detiene*" – "The flavor that doesn't hold back."

fancy-dress party – dressing up in a costume, as we do for Halloween, Fantasy Fest, or if we're going to be on the radio with The Soundman From Hell.

Footsie – the FTSE 100 Index is the share index of the 100 companies listed on the London Stock Exchange.

"Get a leg up …" – score with a member of the opposite sex, or simply gain an advantage.

gobsmacked – totally taken aback or surprised.

great crack – a jolly good time. Possibly dates back as far as Old

English or the older Scots dialect and is still used today in Ireland and by the Ulster Scots in the provinces of Northern Ireland, and in Scottish English. Employed and bastardized by Geordies, as well as Mackems, in North East England. It represents serious fun, lighthearted mischief and can be augmented with excessive drinking and the playing of loud music.

hen party – a bachelorette party. The chance to get dressed up in matching wigs and wear your bra and panties on the outside of your clothes (if you are the bride to be). Diversion may involve binge drinking and sex with complete strangers (a normal night out?).

Hogmanay – New Year's Eve, Scottish style.

kitted out – dressed in, or decked out in.

kludgie – the toilet, in old Scots.

knocking back the plonk – knocking back your drink, rhyming slang for cheap white wine. Bottle of *blanc* (white) = plonk.

loo – chiefly British, the toilet. Possibly derived from the cry of "gardy loo!" (from the French *regardez l'eau!* "watch out for the water!"), which was shouted by medieval servants as they emptied chamber pots out of upstairs windows into the street below. A second theory is that the word stems from a polite use of the French term *le lieu* ("the place") as a euphemism. To many of us it is *the* place. A third theory refers to the brand name "Waterloo," which appeared clearly displayed on the iron cisterns in many British outhouses during the early 20th century. Various other colorful theories also circulate, one of them involves references to doors numbered "00".

M6 – north/south enervating U.K. motorway … the birthplace of road rage, and the bosom of frustration if you have to pass anywhere near Birmingham.

303

margies – margaritas.

mozzie (sometimes spelled mossie) – (Australian and now U.K. slang) an annoying little blighter in the form of a mosquito. Will only bite when you are really enjoying yourself and don't want to go home.

nicked – arrested.

ohne oben – (German) topless.

palaver – fuss/bother.

peely-wally white – the color of a tourist from the U.K. when she/he first arrives in Key West. An unappealing bluish-white. A sick, pale and generally ill-looking complexion.

piker – an idle, lazy sloth.

pissheads – although a derogatory epithet, my people, the type of folk I hang out with at the Bull.

Playa de las Americas – British destination in the south of Tenerife (the Canary Islands). Where Brits go when they want to go abroad, so everything will be exactly the same as it was back home except the weather.

polis – Glaswegian slang for "police."

posh – what I am not. What Victoria Beckham thinks she is.

prat – English, primarily used in United Kingdom. The literal meaning is "bottom," aka backside, buttocks, tail end, bum. This lends itself to the slang meaning of "ass," or "clueless person of arrogant stupidity." Also, think "physical comedy," where one takes a *prat*fall and lands on one's ass.

prezzies – Christmas presents.

Raffles – uniquely elegant, colonial hotel in Singapore. The Singapore Sling cocktail was created in its storied bar, the Long Bar. It is said that if you sit in the *lobby* long enough, everyone you know in the world will walk by. If it was me, I would sit in the *bar* and still hope I got to see them.

Scotch eggs – cockney rhyming slangs for "legs."

splodge – any wet, sticky dollop-like mass. The onomatopoeia sound it makes when it hits your kitchen floor. Splat.

sunny specs – U.K. slang for sunglasses.

tosser – English insult. Someone who masturbates. Common usage typically refers to anyone you have a low opinion of. Our landlord. A person who is a jerkoff. A fuckball.

wanker – pejorative term of contempt, a jerkoff. A term for expressing disdain for somebody. While "to wank" means "to masturbate," the term "wanker" is seldom if ever used in British slang to denote "one who wanks."

"Yeehaa!" – what I say when I've just finished writing a book. Thrills Gabrielle, but frightens Mr. Leroy.

**AUTHOR'S FINAL NOTE, AND THEN I'LL LET YOU GO: I received many comments after the publication of the original KEY WEST that the characters which appeared in those pages "certainly couldn't exist." For those who live in Key West, or come often, they know Key West is all this, plus some. Same goes for all the characters in this sequel. ALL are real, not fictional, and only a few names have been changed to protect those with blown-up photos on the wall at the post office.

Also by Jon Breakfield

Non-Fiction:

KEY WEST: *Tequila, a Pinch of Salt and a Quirky Slice of America*

NAKED EUROPE: *In the Hunt for the Real Europe and Romance*

LIVERPOOL ... TEXAS? LONDON ... ARKANSAS? A cheeky short story

Fiction:

DEATH by GLASGOW